liberal studies in political education and for the need of political scientists to draw knowledge from the humanities.

Recently, as the tide of behavioralism in political science has receded, there has been renewed interest in political theory. Gathered together in book form, these essays by William Havard chronicle the progress of political theory during its period of decline and provides a foundation for the current rebuilding of the discipline of political science.

WILLIAM C. HAVARD is professor and chairman of the department of political science at Vanderbilt University. He is the author or editor of several books on American politics, including (with Walter Sullivan) **A Band of Prophets: The Vanderbilt Agrarians After Fifty Years,** published by LSU Press.

The Recovery of Political Theory

The Recovery
of Political Theory

Limits and Possibilities

William C. Havard

Louisiana State University Press
Baton Rouge and London

Copyright © 1984 by Louisiana State University Press
All rights reserved
Manufactured in the United States of America

Designer: Albert Crochet
Typeface: Linotron Aster
Typesetter: Moran Colorgraphic
Printer & Binder: Vail-Ballou Press

LIBRARY OF CONGRESS CATALOGING IN PUBLICATION DATA

Havard, William C.
   The recovery of political theory.

   Includes index.
   1. Political science—Addresses, essays, lectures.
I. Title.
JA38.H38   1984   320'.01'1   83-14933
ISBN 0-8071-1136-8

To Eric Voegelin
praeceptori mihique non parvo auxilio

In a world that sometimes seems to have forgotten more than it has learnt since Athens fell, the spirit of Socrates can live again.

—F. M. Cornford, *Before and After Socrates*

Contents

Acknowledgments

Ten of the essays in this collection were originally published as indicated below, and are reprinted here with the permission of the cited publishers. Chapter I: "The Disenchantment of the Intellectuals," *Politische Ordnung und Menschliche Existenz: A Festschrift Volume Honoring Professor Eric Voegelin* (Munich: C. H. Beck Verlag, 1962), 271–86; Chapter II: "The Method and Results of Political Anthropology in America," *Archiv für Rechts und Sozial Philosophie* (Wiesbaden: Franz Steiner Verlag, August, 1961), 395–415; Chapter III: "The Philosophical Underpinnings of the Contemporary Controversy in American Political Science," *Festschrift für Karl Lowenstein* (Tübingen: J. C. B. Mohr [Paul Siebeck], 1971), 167–90; Chapter V: "A New Rousseau," *Virginia Quarterly Review*, XLV (Summer, 1969), 509–13; Chapter VI: "The Changing Pattern of Voegelin's Conception of History and Consciousness," *Southern Review*, New Ser., VII (Winter, 1971), 49–67; Chapter VII: "Notes on Voegelin's Contributions to Political Theory," *Polity*, X (Fall, 1977), 33–64; Chapter VIII: "Michael Oakeshott," *Der Gebandigte Kapitalismus: Sozialisten und Konservative in Wohlfahrsstaat, Englishches politisches Denken im 20. Jahrhunderts*, ed. Manfred Weber (Munich: Paul List Verlag, 1974), 71–98, 203–204, 218, 227–28; Chapter IX: "The Politics of *I'll Take My Stand*," *Southern Review*, New Ser., XVI (Autumn, 1980), 757–75; Chapter X: "Political Education: Who Gets What, When, How and Why," *Journal of Politics*, XLII (November, 1980), 934–50; Chapter XI: "Policy Sciences, the Humanities, and Political Coherence," in Francis Canavan (ed.), *The Ethical Dimension of Political Life* (Durham, N.C.: Duke University Press, 1983). Chapter IV, "The New Lexicon of Politics," has not been published previously; it was delivered as the Presidential Address to the New England Political Science Association, Newport, R.I., Spring, 1968.

When I consider how many debts of gratitude I have accumulated over the years I am a bit hesitant about trying to discharge them on an individual basis for fear that I might absentmindedly overlook some who should be remembered. Despite the risk, which is greater than usual here because of the eclectic nature of this book and the length of time involved in its making, I would be in total default if I did not express my appreciation directly to some of those colleagues and friends who have improved my understanding of the subject in both critical and constructive ways, encouraged me in the pursuit of scholarship (especially when confidence, energy, and will lagged), and contributed in a variety of ways to the presentation and dissemination of the results of that scholarship.

Throughout the greater part of my career (and in some cases longer) I have had the benefit of advice, encouragement, instruction, and criticism from Eric Voegelin (to whom this collection is dedicated), Robert J. Harris, Robert B. Heilman, Loren P. Beth, Peter J. Fliess, and Lewis P. Simpson. A number of more recent associates who have contributed to my continuing education in political science and political philosophy include Vanderbilt colleagues Avery Leiserson, George J. Graham, Jr., and William H. Race. Ellis Sandoz, Stephen McKnight, Gregor Sebba, and John Hallowell have done more indirectly than they may realize toward pushing this project to completion, and they should be added to this list "from the outside." The names could go on, but I have had occasion to acknowledge others in various earlier connections or hope to be able to do so in appropriate places in the future.

Without singling out the individual participants, I would like to note a collective obligation to those involved in several ventures that have kept the dialectical exchange going. The Vanderbilt Symposium on Gnosticism and Modernity (1978); the Summer Seminars on the applications of political theory to the subfields of political science that were supported by the National Endowment for the Humanities and held at Vanderbilt in 1979 and 1981; the Agrarian Symposium at Vanderbilt in 1980; and the continuing activities of the International Seminar for Philosophy and Political Theory have all brought together working parties made up of scholars whose common interests enable them to act as small intellectual communities dedicated to the *bios theoretikos*.

Thanks are extended to the College of Arts and Sciences of Vanderbilt University and to the Earhart Foundation for financial support that enabled me to take a long-delayed leave of absence to work on this and other projects on a continuing basis rather than on the sporadic schedule to which academicians are usually committed. I am grateful as well to the Graduate School at Vanderbilt for the provision of funds for clerical assistance during the final preparation of the manuscript. In this connection I warmly acknowledge the cheerful and conscientious way in which Betty McKee and Mildred Tyler, Administrative Assistant and Secretary, respectively, in the Department of Political Science, responded to repeated requests for typing and other assistance beyond the call of ordinary duty. And Louise Durham was, as always, thoroughly professional, accurate, and expeditious in her preparation of the final copy of the manuscript, which was virtually flawless in accuracy of transcription as well as in appearance.

My relations with the Louisiana State University Press go back a long way. The Press has given its imprint to a half-dozen books with my name on the title pages, and to a number of other volumes to which I have contributed. I also served for several years as a member of the LSU Press Committee. The period of involvement includes the full terms or part of the terms of four different directors, at least as many associate directors, and a substantial number of editors, designers, and individuals responsible for sales and promotions. I do not recall a single untoward incident throughout the entire period, and I am aware of too many instances of aid and comfort received to begin to try to list them all here. Charles East was director when the possibility of this book was first brought up, and more recently Leslie Phillabaum, Beverly Jarrett, Catherine Barton, and Mickey Bossier gently prodded me into action and responded encouragingly and with dispatch to all of my actions, as did the copy editor, Barbara Phillips, who saved me from many potentially embarrassing lapses in matters of language and substance.

To all of these individuals and groups, and to my family, I extend warm thanks for their generous help and can assure them that such merits as they find in this collection may be attributed in no small part to the courtesies they have shown me by way of advice, constructive criticism, and the sheer pleasure of their company during many hours of conversation. I hope that they will not be severely disappointed over any optimistic expectations they may have about the book.

The Recovery of Political Theory

Introduction

The eleven essays included in this collection were written over a period of some twenty years, roughly between the early 1960s and the present. Only one of them has not been published previously, some have been reprinted, and the circumstances that led to their being written in the first place varied with each of them. In view of the span of time involved, and the occasional nature of most of the pieces, the potential reader might well be disposed to ask why they were considered worth bringing together for publication as a self-contained volume at this point. Indeed, that is a question I have had to answer to my own satisfaction on several occasions in the course of choosing the contents and preparing the manuscript for publication.

Several years ago it was suggested to me (by academic colleagues in collusion with publishers and editors from whose critical advice and work on earlier manuscripts I had benefited) that the LSU Press might have some interest in publishing a small volume composed of papers I had written in the general area of political philosophy. One of the parties to this flattering overture was kind enough to point out that even though political theory had always been central to my professional interests, most of the social scientists and historians who are familiar with my work (and the finite number of those is not something I wish to dwell on) usually know only the books and essays on American—especially southern—politics. Another colleague from the humanities (and an experienced editor) generously offered to review items that might be considered for inclusion with a view to advising about content. The latter being an offer I was not even momentarily inclined to refuse, I promptly bundled a package of about a dozen reprints and unpublished manuscripts into a large manila envelope and sent them, along with some notes, to this volunteer agent, who responded shortly thereafter in an encouraging way. Acting on his advice, the Press indicated that I should get on with the job of assembling, editing, and retyping the essays suggested for inclusion, and also prepare a suitable introduction for the volume.

At that point, however, the project was delayed by two sets of circumstances that proved to be far more time-consuming than I had anticipated. One was a move to my present academic post, a change that coincided with a last-minute extension of a term as editor of the *Journal of Politics*. The shift of the *Journal*'s editorial office to my new location involved a considerable reduction in the resources needed to support that office and a consequent increase in the number and extent of routine chores left for the editor to handle. The other source of diversion was the enthusiastic acceptance of several new commitments under the totally unwarranted assumption that the transition could be made with no loss of momentum. As a result, several years passed before changing directions in my own work and in political science generally (along with renewed pressures from those who had induced the earlier activity) brought me back to this project.

Since academic autobiography is perhaps the dullest of all forms of reminiscence, I shall confine my comments on the personal and professional changes involved to those things that may clarify parts of the text that follows. When I began an academic career more than thirty years ago the conditions under which one taught and did research were as parlous (in different ways) as they are for young, untenured faculty members today. The boom in postwar enrollments brought about largely by returning veterans had gone into a decline that was not to be reversed until American higher education experienced its massive growth in the late 1950s and 1960s. Not only was an aspirant to an academic career fortunate to locate a teaching position at all, but newcomers to the profession were expected to teach virtually across the entire span of courses offered in the discipline and to range vertically from introductory materials through advanced graduate work. Teaching loads were heavy, and support for research was small to nonexistent in most places. The courses in one's main areas of interest (the full effects of narrow specialization and its correlate, course proliferation, awaited the imminent advent of the multiversity) were likely to be preempted by one's senior colleagues, so most of the juniors stood more or less patiently in line (sometimes for many years) before commandeering or inheriting coveted courses of their own.

Not all of these arrangements were bad, to be sure: with the discipline still being regarded as a fairly unified field of study, and with the confinement of specialization less controlling than it later became, one's reading and teaching experience quickly broadened. And if the sense of vocation included a will to engage in scholarship, out of necessity one seized whatever opportunities might be available to engage in research and writing even if the subjects were not the first choices of the promising apprentice. This enforced eclecticism in teaching and research not only restrained for a time the now common pursuit of a scholarly reputation built on the appropriation of a specialty in one of the subfields in the hope one might become known as *the* expert in the area, but also made it less likely that many of us would reduce the theoretical understanding of politics by subsuming the broad range of human experience represented by politics under some narrowly framed assumption about causation or epistemology.

A second inhibiting condition seriously affected what and where I have published over the past thirty years. I refer to the dominance of political science during much of that time by what Heinz Eulau christened "the behavioral persuasion," but is more frequently referred to by others as the behavioral "movement," or the behavioral "revolution." Since several of the following essays dwell at length on the effect of this movement on the contents (or substance) of political science, I will confine my remarks here to what might be described (in one of the commonplace euphemisms now afflicting the language of the social sciences) as the "institutionalization of the profession." Freely translated, this meant the organization of members of the discipline in a bureaucratic way, so that in due course the "ingroup" (latterly the "elite") controlled enough of the admittedly meager rewards available to induce a substantial conformity among the members in their activities as political scientists. Although many political scientists were and are fond of saying that "political science is what political scientists do," for more than twenty years the programs at the larger meetings and the contents of most of the journals sponsored by the various associations indicated that what political scientists were doing could be readily categorized as "behavioral science." Furthermore, the growing resources for funding research in the social sciences were being channeled almost entirely into behaviorally oriented projects.

The pursuit of political philosophy (too often treated as the history of political ideas), once considered the heart of the discipline, was gradually relegated to a secondary position, and was carried on actively in a relatively few university centers and among small groups of friends, many of which included more philosophers, classicists, and intellectual historians than political scientists. Important work was still being done, but the new orthodoxy that came out of "organized" political science did not acknowledge that work in its creed or give it much of a place in the conduct of its ceremonies.

Even though I was teaching and writing in other areas of political science during this period, including some work that was perceived as behavioral, I made efforts to keep up with what was going on in political philosophy, to participate in some of the groups that were keeping the subject alive, and to try to restore it to parity with the other major subfields of the discipline so far as program participation at meetings and publication in the journals were concerned. But given the increasing domination of the profession by behavioralism throughout the 1950s and 1960s and into the 1970s (a hold that was strengthened by the entry into academia of a whole generation of "Doctors of Philosophy" whose "training" was largely confined to the behavioral techniques of the "new" political science), it seemed necessary to look mainly beyond the established associations to find the intellectual collegiality and publication outlets required to carry on scholarly discourse in political philosophy. For this reason, most of the essays comprising this volume were published in places that are somewhat fugitive (or irrelevant?) from the perspective of most political scientists. The outlets include festschrifts, foreign books and journals, and critical (or "little") magazines. All this is by way of saying, of course, that those encouraging friends mentioned earlier were correct in suggesting that the critical and constructive essays and reviews contributed to the effort to keep political philosophy going are not easily accessible in a form that provides general insight into the way I consider those truths about politics open to man's understanding have been, and are being, realized.

From a narrowly subjective viewpoint, the simple desire to make these diffuse writings more accessible might have been sufficient justification for proceeding with plans for publication. But the emergence within the discipline of a new or renewed interest in political philosophy in the 1970s provided even stronger incentives for moving ahead. Again, some of the reasons for this development are discussed in one or two of the essays themselves and need not be rehearsed here, at least beyond noting that the revival seems to have resulted from a combination of disillusionment over behavioralism's limited capacity for fulfilling its theoretical promise and a confrontation with experiences of political reality that Americans in general (with the possible categorical exception of southerners) had not had to face previously. Certainly some of the essays being considered (including one or two still in process at the beginning of the 1980s) were pertinent to both aspects of this development, and it was possible that the collection as a whole might have more theoretical credibility than I had anticipated, even among political scientists.

Although my diffidence with regard to publishing a collection in monographic form was largely overcome by this assessment, I still had to be convinced that the individual pieces, with their wide topical variation, had some unifying principle or perspective that would give the book a substantial (if not complete) coherence. Rereading these and other pieces several times in the process of making choices about what to include and arranging them in what seemed a logical order renewed my confidence in the relative internal consistency of the essays in terms of the fundamental premises from which I had been working and the theoretical conclusions reached, however tentative and foreshortened the exposition of either may be in a particular context. Of course the attempt to read one's own work in a way that applies the analytic skills of an informed and experienced literary critic (and I consider the acquisition of those skills to be an essential part of the preparation for work in political philosophy) is far from an easy task and certainly provides no assurance that more detached critics will see either what the author intended to say or what he later sees himself in his books and essays. The latter is a risk that any author must run, and beyond being as self-critical as possible in the use of language and framing the dialectic, a writer is largely dependent on the "negative capability" (coupled with experience and background knowledge) of the reader for a clear understanding of a text. Given the deterioration of language used to express our sense of what is "common" or "public" in our culture, a condition that reflects Humpty Dumpty's characterization of words as being entirely subjective in their meanings, I plead for indulgence in offering a few broad generalizations about the study of politics that implicitly or explicitly act as regulative ideas throughout these essays.

First, since politics is a generic human activity, a clearly articulated or implied conception of the nature of man underlies every attempt to develop a general theory of politics. The main characteristic of man that distinguishes him from other categorical entities in nature at large is his rational consciousness, and through it he tries to make sense of his existence in relation to the various realms of being with which experience brings him into contact. Not only does he try to penetrate to reality in his search for meaning but he attempts to order his activities to accord with what he conceives to be the limits and possibilities inherent in the nature of man in adaptation to the circumstances in which he finds himself, and thus he seeks to participate in the shaping of the reality of which he is a part.

Second, since politics involves the relations of man with man, and its arrangements are largely open for man to work out in concrete ways, the formal study of politics begins within a historically established structure that has grown out of the experience of living in a specific society generated out of a combination of necessity and convenience. Thus politics is practiced in a traditional way, and the self-interpretation of a political entity's existence in history is discernible in its myths, rituals, and ceremonials, as well as in the ordinary conduct of its members. In this sense a politics of experience has meaning that is adequately expressed and shared by its participants without the need for rational analysis, at least as long as it works in an orderly way. But in times of crisis, when the experience becomes one of disorder or incipient disorder, the demand arises for theoretical analyses that begin with a critical diagnosis of the failure of politics in terms of the loss of human meaning that informed a politics of experience, and the consequent loss of the capacity to make politics work toward the fulfillment of its basic purposes. Of course there is no certainty that this effort at theoretical recovery will bring knowledge that approaches an apprehension of reality, or even if it does, that the corrective or prescriptive aspects of the theory will affect practice.

Finally, the study of politics is itself pursued as a human activity, both for its own sake (out of the desire to grasp as much of the meaning of human experience as possible) and for assessing the contributions that political knowledge might make to the practice of politics. Many of the essays in this book are as much concerned with trying to understand the activity of political scientists in their quest for knowledge as they are with the meaning of the political experience that is the end of the quest. Just as the development of a general theory of politics involves a critical appraisal of the practice of politics and an effort to recover an understanding of the political reality that might inform that practice, so does an inquiry into the activity of political scientists involve a critical examination of the intellectual activity in an attempt to discern what makes it succeed or fail in its purposes. If a prevailing theory of politics proves on examination to fall short of the claims asserted on its behalf, it is incumbent on the critic to suggest ways in which the theoretical effort might be made more effective. Currently the most promising shift appears to be toward a process of recovering knowledge we once possessed and apparently misplaced.

An anticipatory notation on the sequential arrangement of the essays should also prove useful to the reader. The opening paper, "The Disenchantment of the Intellectuals," is both a historical background piece and a critical introduction to the problems of the Western intellectual in post-Enlightenment modernity. The two lengthy pieces that follow critically survey recent and current trends in American political science, or, as the prevailing academic cliché expresses it, examine the "state of the art" in the discipline. Next come two short exemplifications of contemporary problems discussed more abstractly in the preceding papers. Although the specifics involve the misuse of language (too important a subject to be treated in so seemingly light a manner) and a commentator's reliance on romantic emotionalism to counter the "rationalist" ideology of modern scientistic progressivism, the intellectual backdrop reflects some effects of the principal countervailing ideologies that arose in the eighteenth century.

The next three essays offer critical exegeses of aspects of the work of Eric Voegelin and Michael Oakeshott, two among a very small body of important contributors to the recovery of political theory, and the two political philosophers from whom I have learned most about political science's grounding in history and philosophy. Including two papers on Voegelin might appear to be redundant, and they do overlap slightly, but in major focus and extended content they seem to me to be far more complementary than duplicative. While both essays obviously deal with Voegelin's work, the first attempts to provide at least a limited picture of the man behind the work, in the belief that some misunderstanding of his theory results from lack of perception of certain qualities of his mind and character, and the second concentrates almost exclusively on the essential elements of his theory of politics.

The next piece, "The Politics of *I'll Take My Stand*," might also be grouped with the three preceding ones as a part of the recovery of theory, but its central theme may be construed to be the relations of the literary culture to the understanding and practice of politics. In some respects it also serves as a transition to the two concluding essays. They deal briefly with specific problems that cannot be effectively elided in any general theory of politics—the place of classical humanistic (or liberal) education in political education, and the needed restoration of a place for knowledge drawn from the humanities in the developing focus on public policy in the study of politics in American universities.

I conclude this introduction on a somewhat pedestrian note about scholarly housekeeping. Despite the temptation to incorporate substantive changes in the essays based on afterthoughts, more recent literature on the various topics, and perceived need for clarification, the editing of the papers was confined almost entirely to matters of grammar and syntax.

I The Disenchantment of the Intellectuals

In the eighteenth century a new type of intellectual developed into the predominant influence for the shaping of Western political ideas; this type was the secularized cleric who espoused an anthropocentric doctrine in which reason replaced the Christian and classical symbols as the ordering substance for man and society.[1] The independent intellectual was new only in the sense that the type was perfected in the eighteenth century, and the rise to predominance may be attributed less to the intrinsic merits of the philosophe than to the historical crisis which enabled him to assert himself. For the late eighteenth century was a great historical watershed in the development of European civilization in which the forces of modernity released by the Renaissance and the Reformation converged to wash away the remains (largely in the form of institutions) of the older tradition.

Just as the prototypical *event* was the French Revolution, with its declared intention of wiping out the historical error of the past in order that the new forces in history might take charge of the destiny of man and society, so does the French writer (from Voltaire to Condorcet), who presaged and interpreted the Revolution, furnish the prototype for the modern independent Western intellectual. Although the tradition of philosophy, let alone the traditions of civilization, could not be totally effaced in one fell swoop, the attack leveled against the philosophical heritage of the past succeeded to the extent that the features of the eighteenth-century

---

1. The term *cleric* is borrowed from Julien Benda, *La Trahison des Clercs* (Rev. ed.; Paris: Grasset, 1958). *Reason* here connotes "instrumental" reason rather than reason in the classical (noetic) sense of the term. In the effort to cope with the Age of Reason, critics often refer to the phenomenon by which faith in human knowledge (especially "scientific" knowledge and its technological application) became the presumptive basis for the apprehension of reality, and ultimately the transformation of reality by man, as "rationalism."

philosophe remained broadly characteristic of the more influential intellectual movements throughout the nineteenth and early twentieth centuries. Even today, when the cycle of wars and revolutions which began with the French Revolution has brought the Western world to the brink of destruction, the intellectual type produced in the eighteenth century retains many of the original characteristics and much of the prominence achieved during the two preceding centuries. In the face of this trend, however, and in the philosophical confrontation of recent historical events, a certain disenchantment with the main outgrowths of the Enlightenment doctrines has set in among a considerable number of contemporary intellectuals.

Before we consider the nature and consequences of this change in perspective, it is necessary to indicate something of the form and development of the modern intellectual. Although the type varied in detail from the beginning and has subsequently tended toward a complex differentiation, some of the basic features can be singled out. The primary characteristic has already been indicated: the intellectual is a secular cleric who is intent on replacing what he regards as the false symbols of an outworn tradition with an adequate interpretation of reality. The undertaking requires the dissolution of all traditional forms of authority and the substitution for them of new symbols of existence. The attack on spiritual authority ranges from the stipulation that religious belief is a private matter without meaning for pragmatic existence (and therefore has no claim to public representation) to the denunciation of all religious faith as superstition—"the opium of the people" which must be expunged. The attack on traditional forms of political authority, by the same token, extends from a demand that a complete renovation of the constitutional structure be made to the branding of existent authority as an illegitimate usurpation whose power must be abrogated by revolution before legitimate forms of authority can be instituted. A succinct expression of this attitude toward the persisting symbols of religious and political authority is Voltaire's stricture on the necessity of strangling the last king in the entrails of the last priest as a precondition of political liberty.

A second identifying characteristic is an extreme optimism about the capacity of man to achieve his self-salvation within the world through his newfound ability to control nature and history. This attitude has a number of sources, including the rise of modern physical science, the expansionist tendencies of the European communities, and the development of the autonomous rational individual, particularly through the complementary influences of Protestantism and bourgeois capitalism. These conditions were conjoined in a number of ways to produce the various aspects of the new intellectualist temperament: the growth of science and technology not only gave confidence in man's capacity for conscious direction of nature to his own ends but also provided an explanation of man himself in naturalistic terms analogous to the ordered nature that rational understanding had penetrated. This notion effectively complemented the individualistic premise inasmuch as it served to demonstrate the existence of laws of nature by which an ordered balance of apparently random forces was achieved. The eighteenth and nineteenth centuries are replete with examples of writers who aspired to become the Newtons of social science. The analogy—discovered very early by the economists— was brought to perfection in Bentham's ethical doctrine of the natural harmony of interests by which the greatest happiness of the greatest number would be most effectively promoted by each individual's unrelenting pursuit of his own interests. Of course the individual had to understand his real interests, but his rational capacity ensured this possibility, provided the institutional reorganization of society necessary to allow the natural order to prevail was carried out. Man's control of history, in other words, depended precisely on the elimination of traditional institutional restraints on the autonomous rational individual.

This second characteristic eventuated, as a matter of course, in the doctrine of progress. In the eighteenth century the idea of progress lacked both the teleological and the activist implications that were developed by Comte and Marx; it was conceived vaguely as an extension, into the indefinite future, of conditions of rationality and technology that were already the achievements of contemporary life. Thus the naturalism of the eighteenth century was still some way removed from the historical determinism of the nineteenth century with its several unequivocal visions of the perfected end of man and society and its corresponding urgency to speed progress toward that end. Eighteenth-century ideas of progress, however, did share with later progressivist dogmas the idea of effacing the obstructive residues of the past in order to achieve the glorious future, as well as the emphasis on technology as the determinant form of rationality by which man and society were to be perfected. The confidence in the capacity of the pragmatic intellect to solve the problems of existence, and not merely the material ones, is best illustrated by the task set for themselves by the French Encyclopedists of collecting together in one massive work all of the "useful" knowledge that man had amassed through centuries of civilization and the consignment of everything else to the rubbish heap of a worn-out past.

The enchantment of eighteenth-century intellectuals with the new symbols of human existence that they were creating obscured the realities behind the traditions they destroyed, thereby enabling them to speed the process of destruction. No less important was the fact that the institutional products of the tradition had deteriorated so completely that they were not only incapable of evoking a response to their claims to representative legitimacy and of defending themselves but they were almost pathetically adaptable to the scapegoat role that the new clerics fixed upon them, the role of perpetrators of the evils against which rebellion was necessary. The church's public function had been effectively displaced by prior historical developments. The Reformation had split it asunder and the wars of religion had exhausted its energies in internecine struggles which rendered it incapable of resisting secular trends. In the Protestant areas its spiritual function as the mediator of grace was largely displaced by the doctrine of the individual priesthood of the believer; and almost everywhere the Gelasian principle of dual public representation through the separate institutional spheres of church and state had been undermined by the Caesaropapistic unification of the rising national states under the absolute monarchs. The degeneration of the monarchy (especially in France) and the functional debilitation of the other potential elements in the constitution by the second half of the eighteenth century are so obvious as to require no further comment.

Insofar as the tradition of philosophy is concerned, the most important consequence of the intellectual rebellion of the eighteenth and nineteenth centuries was its radical purge of the Christian and classical interpretations of existential experience, interpretations which had furnished the basis for the self-articulation of European civilization. Not only was the complex Christian conception of faith brought under corrosive attack—with its emphasis on the Logos having been made flesh and on personal salvation through grace outside of mundane history—but the classical humanistic interpretation of being (which had been absorbed into the corpus of Christian thought) was simultaneously subjected to the demand for verification by the new positivist order of reality. The Greek philosophical discovery of the noetic virtues in the soul of man, by which reason transcends the self and thereby achieves some grasp of the end of existence and of the highest good toward which all being moves, was jettisoned in the name of the "pure" reason of the sciences of natural phenomena. And with this reductionism went two millennia of a mode of experience that had furnished the crucial humanistic differentiation of the omnipresent primitive (*i.e.*, prephilosophical) awareness of finite self-existence, the corresponding existence of external things (including other self-cognizant existences), and the limitations that beset these forms of existence. The measures of human limits and possibilities (especially the "unseen" measures) have tended to be displaced in the name of the infinite possibility inherent in the mind and will of the man of knowledge. The problem was thus enormously complicated because the modern intellectuals, in effect, insisted on denying the status of legitimacy to these basic questions of existence with which rational thought begins.

The deliberate exclusion from rational discourse of metaphysical questions tends to blot out the fact that, in the absence of a posture of complete skepticism, an interpretation of existence in metaphysical terms is implicit in all theories of man and society. The doctrine of the universal validity of pragmatic reason as the source of understanding and of moral and political order was, as Hume demonstrated, no more open to the objective proofs of natural science than were miracles or, for that matter, than were the metaphysical doctrines of classical philosophy or the theological doctrines of the church fathers. The assumption that the natural

sciences furnished the preeminent model by which knowledge
might be extended to the interpretation of the objective truth of all
existence was itself a metaphysical conclusion. A major difference
between the metaphysics of the rationalist intellectual and the
metaphysics of classical and Christian philosophy was the recognition by the exponents of the latter positions that the nature of
the experience which motivated their speculation was of a different order than that involving the investigation of the external objects of sense perception. The assertion of the dogma of reason
(particularly in the form of scientific reason) thus represented the
seizure of a fragment of reality and the projection of this fragment
as a total reality whose completion would be achieved only in the
indefinite future.

The characteristic optimism of the Enlightenment concerning
the future performed a function that was vitally necessary for the
validation of its form of reality. The new self-confidence served to
obscure certain realities of existence that were fully accounted for
by the rejected interpretation. Important among these were the
awareness of the finiteness of man and the tenuous nature of mundane existence, the ubiquity of good and evil and the necessity of
willing and acting out of limited knowledge in the face of them,
and the certainty that man's aspirations for perfection outrun his
unaided human capacities. The obscuring of these features of the
human condition opened the way for the conception of man which
seemed to overcome these natural limitations. The enlightened intellectual had the ambition of breaking man out of the bonds of existence, hence his interpretation that human nature is infinitely
pliable, that man is largely the product of his institutions, and that
most perceptible evil results from an imperfection of institutions.
(The natural man tends either to be good or to be a morally neutral
entity apart from the experiences that mold him.) The problem of
society therefore is to perfect the institutions and to fit the individual man for a life of practical reason through education. The
limits on what man might achieve by his own effort were thus rendered virtually nonexistent.

The symbols used to develop the new image of man and society
were not themselves new; they were adaptions of concepts that
were part of the civilizational heritage. Like the reality they de-

picted, they were fragments of traditional symbols which were adapted to the requirements at hand. A few of the more important ones will serve for illustrative purposes. The common substance of reason as a differentiating and unifying attribute of humanity was a reduction of the Aristotelian nous and of the later Christian Logos. The desire to break the bonds of existence imposed by the human condition through a creative effort of the individual was a radical secularization and immanentization of the entire question of transcendence and particularly of the Christian doctrine of salvation through grace. The idea of progress (and its later evolution into progressivist philosophies of history) was an intramundane version of Christian eschatology which had its roots in the Gnostic influence. Even the great symbols of liberty and equality, which were rendered literal by their conversion into the absolutes of liberalism, had their basis in classical and Christian experiences of the transcendent essence of personality and the ethical consequences that this recognition entailed.

The very complexity of the symbolic self-interpretation of the civilization, together with its rich speculative tradition, provided continuously for the possibility that the independent intellectual might take the interpretation of man and society into his own hands. This possibility was especially strong in times of crisis when the rational symbols of the society were beset by an influx of ideas alien to the tradition or when the institutions were unable to accommodate pragmatic changes in the life of the society. In the eighteenth century the standards of both the self-interpretative ideas and the institutions had lost their hold; consequently, the self-conscious attempt at the creation of new standards in both areas became dominant.

However, the development of the new type of intellectual who presided over this process had been prefigured by much earlier historical examples. The first clear-cut forerunner of the type was Siger de Brabant in the thirteenth century. The occasion was the reception by the Faculty of Arts of the University of Paris of Aristotelianism through the medium of the Averroist commentaries. The conflict between faith and reason which this deposit of ideas engendered was eventually resolved philosophically by the reconciliation of Saint Thomas Aquinas, and as a practical matter the

early movement was suppressed by force. But it is the characteristics of Siger's attitude as one of the leading disputants that mark
him as a precursor of the development that we are describing, for
it is his position that "the Western non-historic, ethically active
intellect announces its claim to objective validity and its right to
distinguish between social good and social evil without regard to
the values of historical growth." Although it would have been possible to free the intellect from dogmatic restraints in order to pursue natural science without breaking with Christian transcendentalism, the critical attack by Siger was supplemented by the
development of a counterdogmatism of reason.

> It was not sufficient for him that the doctrine of the creation in time
> proved untenable; he had to advance the equally untenable proposition
> that it existed uncreated in an indefinite time. He was not satisfied that
> the Christian historical drama of fall and redemption should lie beyond
> the scope of the speculative intellect; he had to create a new drama of
> the eternally recurrent world cycles. He could not leave the immortal-
> ity of the individual soul alone, but had to substitute for it the idea of a
> collective *intellectus uno in numero*. And he had to replace, finally, the
> transcendental by an intramundane *summum bonum* as the guiding
> principle of ethics. In all: he formulates the principles of an intramun-
> dane system of metaphysics that is to take the place of Christian tran-
> scendentalism.[2]

The parallels with the later (and, in the practical sense, more
successful) type of intellectual are clear, especially the comprehensive nature of the critical attack, followed by the confident assertions of the constituents of the true life of man and society. One
major point of difference was Siger's reversion to the classical idea
of history as an endlessly recurring cycle of growth and decay par-
alleling the course of nature. The modern doctrine of progress differed both from the classical idea of cyclical history, with its origins
in cosmological interpretations of the life of society, and from the

2. Aristotle clearly distinguished between the metaphysical analysis of existence and the analysis of cause and effect in the natural sciences. The distinction
between Aristotle's position that the world existed from infinity rather than having
been created in time and his metaphysical rejection of infinite regress in favor of
the "limit-end" as a property of reason, with the limit realized in the prime mover,
are elaborated in Eric Voegelin, "On Debate and Existence," *Intercollegiate Review*,
III (1967), 143–52. Quotations describing Siger's position are from Eric Voegelin,
"Siger de Brabant," *Philosophy and Phenomenological Research*, IV (June, 1944), 523,
525.

Augustinian formulation in which the true history was sacred history and intramundane history as such had only a supplementary meaning for the fundamental problems of existence.[3]

The modern progressivist version of worldly historical meaning had a further intellectual prefiguration in Joachim of Fiore. While Joachim's gnostic elaboration of history remained technically within the orthodox framework, the realm of the spirit was immanentized through the application of the symbol of the Trinity to a course of history envisaged as having a meaningful end on earth. For this purpose Joachim developed four sets of symbols. The first is the idea of intramundane history as a sequence of three ages; in Joachim's analysis the age of the Father, the Son, and the Spirit represented successively increasing fulfillments of the life of the spirit within the world. The second symbol is that of the leader of the new realm; the third is the prophet of the new age. The final symbol is the brotherhood of autonomous persons in which the Spirit will have completed its descent and transformed men into members of the new realm without the further necessity for the sacramental mediation of grace or for an institution to perform the sacramental function.[4] The recurring symbol of the third realm (with its prophets, leaders, and community of perfected men) in the secularized philosophies of history of the late eighteenth and nineteenth centuries is another adaptation of older categories of the experience of existence by the new age of the future. The straight-line history of Saint Augustine, which had broken radically with the classical concept of history in both its transcendental implications for man and its continuity beyond the range of existential flux, furnished the grand conception behind the modern conceptions of an unbroken progressivist movement of world history.

The precursor of the modern intellectual did not manage to break through the restraining civilizational tradition of ideas and institutions, nor did the first identifiably modern secular political

---

3. On the problem of the classical cyclical and the Christian straight-line histories and their merger in modernity, see Karl Löwith, *Meaning in History* (Chicago: University of Chicago Press, 1949), viii, 19, 192, 201.

4. Eric Voegelin, *The New Science of Politics* (Chicago: University of Chicago Press, 1952), 111–13.

thinkers attempt to create new symbols of reality superior to those disclosed through the civilizational self-interpretation of the earlier philosophical and theological traditions. Both Machiavelli and Hobbes, modernists par excellence, worked out their respective theories of politics as responses to civil crises, the former in the breakdown of order among the Italian city-states and the latter in the face of the civil war of the Puritan revolution. Each revealed a nostalgia for Christian transcendentalism as a source of order for ethics and politics, but lacked the personal capacity for reenacting the experiences of the life of the spirit; and in the presence of the disturbances created by the conflicting claims of representative institutions (both religious and secular) each felt it necessary to eliminate the spiritual element from his proposed reconstruction of political order. The attribution of "realism" to Machiavelli and Hobbes is warranted in the sense that they perceived that the breakdown of traditional regulatory standards of morals and politics does not liberate man for a life of natural reason and self-regulating political order, but returns him to the primitive existential state in which individual life is dominated by the elementary passions and the social state is one of the perpetual war of all against all. Neither Machiavelli nor Hobbes had lost contact with the reality of the evil inherent in existence and the limitations which this aspect of the human condition imposed on any solution to the problem of social order. Both, however, displayed a striking insensitivity to the latent good inherent in the structure of the human soul. Although their respective attempts to resolve the dilemma of pragmatic reality differ in detail, the general approaches were quite similar. The problem as they saw it was to control the effects of unleashed human passions through the imposition of external restraining power. Machiavelli sought a solution in the dominating heroic personality who would take destiny into his own hands, while Hobbes discovered in the fear of death a passion which might quell the "madness" of the unrestrained pursuit of power after power by compelling consent to the submission of control of external action to the Leviathan who would impose peace. As Leo Strauss has rightly pointed out, modern political thought (since Machiavelli) has been concerned more with the achievement of order than with the discovery of its sources and meaning.[5]

Machiavelli and Hobbes, then, constructed their theories of politics from the residue of reality that was left when the civilizational standards for ethics and politics and the institutions in which these standards were reflected had been broken. Their critical realism prevented them from attempting much more than the salvage of something from the wreckage. This very attitude compelled recognition of the fact that there are limits to what the creative energies of man can do in morals and politics. The prudential rules governing the actions of the prince or the sovereign, under which he is counseled to refrain from undue interference with the peaceable pursuits of the individual concerns of his subjects, establish a commonsense limit of authority. For if the oppression of the subject tends to exceed the limits necessary for the preservation of order, the risks of open disorder may be preferred to the perpetuation of the regime. Furthermore, Machiavelli's emphasis on *fortuna* and his affinity with the cyclical interpretation of history parallel Hobbes's pessimism about the possibility of realizing any greater felicity of man and society than a lessening of the natural precariousness and miseries of existence. It was not for Machiavelli or Hobbes to collectivize the reign of passion by producing a new glimpse of Zion's glory within the future of world history, the attainment of which might require the removal of all limits on the amount of human sacrifice to be exacted. Machiavelli and Hobbes did not proclaim a new metaphysical truth so much as they prepared the way for it by removing the old metaphysical interpretation of reality from the order of existence and by creating models for an intensified political activism in the constitution of existential order.

With Locke, by contrast, there begins the process of transforming the fragment of reality to which Machiavelli and Hobbes limited their pessimistic constructions into a shining new metaphysical reality. Locke performed the alchemic feat of turning the Hobbesian evil of the acquisitive passion into a positive basis for

5. Leo Strauss, *What Is Political Philosophy?* (Glencoe, Ill.: The Free Press, 1959), esp. 46–47.

individual and social utility. The achievement required the manipulation of a great many symbols, including the substitution of the permissive doctrine of natural rights for the restraints characteristic of natural law, the development of the conception that social order could be spontaneously created by atomistic egoistic hedonists, and the advancement of the notion that successful revolution almost invariably prepared the way for a new articulation of individual and social good which had been temporarily overshadowed by institutional corruption. The reception of the Lockean doctrines in France was an intellectual event of the highest order of importance in preparing the way for the optimism of the philosophes about the natural goodness of man, the efficacy of institutional destruction, and the possibilities opened by the idea of a naturalistic order.

With the full articulation of the intellectualist position in the eighteenth century there begins that tendency that has apparently still not run its complete course—the tendency toward perpetual rebellion against the existing historical condition, the regular construction of new and widely varying symbols of reality, and the urgent call to translate these symbols into objective reality. The scientifically planned progressivist society of Comte, the biological determinism of social Darwinism, the race idea of national socialism, and the social class symbol as the basis of differentiating personal and social good and evil in the Marxist-Leninist-Stalinist revolutionary concept are representative (but not exhaustive) of the types of misplacement of reality and the ancillary dream of mastering history that are outgrowths of this process. The anxieties of existence have been organized into more and more unrealistic dreamworlds whose promise of realization permits an increasing dehumanization of political means. Julien Benda has well said, "Grâce à eux [the clerics] on peut dire que, pendant deux mille ans, l'humanité faisait le mal mais honorait le bien. Cette contradiction était l'honneur de l'espèce humaine et constituait la fissure par où pouvait se glisser la civilization."[6] One might well extend Benda's own reservations about the more recent tendencies of the clerics and suggest that we are confronted in the twentieth cen-

6. Benda, *La Trahison des Clercs*, 141.

tury with a new contradiction: Today the worst forms of atrocity are committed against whole sectors of mankind in the name of the future good of humanity, and this new order of things constitutes the massive rupture through which barbarianism has threatened once more to obliterate civilization.

From the contradiction between the promise held out by the symbolic self-interpretation of modernity framed by the enlightened intellectuals and the horrors of the past three generations has come the disenchantment affecting so much of contemporary intellectual life. The range of symptoms in the case of individual intellectuals is too broad for accurate categorization within the limits of a single essay, but the general scope may be indicated by representative examples, together with a somewhat more detailed selection from one or two of the more important exemplars of the trend.

As the term *disenchantment* implies, the common identifying characteristic of the process is a radical disillusionment with the possibilities of immanent self-salvation through pragmatic reason, with progressivist historicism (in both its milder liberal individualistic and its more radical mass movement forms), and with the capacity to reconstitute human nature by institutional means. With the disenchantment has come a new confrontation of the problem of existence, most frequently in the form of an acute consciousness of the alienation of the individual, followed by various degrees of awareness of the necessity for spiritual self-transcendence as the basis for the restoration of a moral and political order that comes to terms with the realities of the human condition rather than seeking to surpass its limits.

Specific manifestations of the disenchantment vary from the pessimism of absolute despair in H. G. Wells's *Mind at the End of Its Tether* to the muted optimism about the possibility of reviving the Christian public representation of the life of the spirit as a sociological expedient in Karl Mannheim's *Diagnosis of Our Times*. The intermediate range is very broad, and examples may be drawn from almost any of the several functional categories into which intellectuals proper may be classified. Walter Lippmann, the closest approximation to an original philosophical mind among contemporary popular journalists, is a case in point. Lippmann has run the gamut from left-wing socialism (with scientific leanings toward Freudian psychology as a complete social cathartic), through an extreme Lockean individualism, and into the recent appeal for the revival of a civil theology in the form of a "public philosophy," the last of which is based on a considerable insight into the symbolic ideas that constitute the core of the Western Civilization. Any number of interesting variations on the theme run through the public confessional of a volume such as *The God That Failed*. And much can be made of the alternation between hope and disillusionment in Arthur Koestler's search for sources of spiritual guidance in the "non-materialistic philosophies" of the East.[7]

To turn, however, to a particular manifestation of the phenomenon in somewhat more detail, the late Harold Laski is an interesting representative of a partial, or abortive, disenchantment which led him to a strange (and wavering) new commitment to unreality. Laski passed through several stages in his brilliant academic career, but all of his phases reveal, in some degree, the characteristics of the enlightened intellectual, including confidence in human self-assertion following the repudiation of religious symbolism, a radical reformist inclination, and a propensity to accept the inevitability of progress. While still under the shadow of the early influence of the pluralistic constitutionalism of Maitland, Laski wrote a small volume on communism which is most perceptive in its treatment of the ideas behind the movement as a dangerous secular theology.[8] Although he was already an exponent of the primacy of economics for politics, Laski's affinity with the British legal tradition, his strong sense of individualism, and his unfailing humanitarianism kept him within the pattern of left-

7. The problem of the intellectuals presented here should not be taken to imply that the philosophical questions that were rejected by the epistemology of the Enlightenment and its positivistic outgrowths disappeared completely. In recent years, particularly, there has been not only a revival of interest in the basic questions of human existence but also a great effort at reconstructing the principles of existence and order that were the achievements of classical philosophy and Christian theology. Even though a description of the latter lies outside the scope of this essay, such a description of the efforts relevant to political science would roughly parallel Bochenski's survey of contemporary philosophy with its emphasis on the degree to which each of the various "schools" approximates reality. See I. M. Bochenski, *Contemporary European Philosophy*, trans. Donald Nicholl and Karl Aschenbrenner (Berkely and Los Angeles: University of California Press, 1956).

8. Harold J. Laski, *Communism* (London: Home University Library, 1927).

wing liberal reformism prior to the 1930s. In this earlier period he belonged to a socialist tradition that might be characterized as collectivized Benthamism, a movement which was closer to eighteenth-century enlightened liberalism (and its secularized Protestant ethics) than to the intramundane mass religions of the twentieth century.

The widespread failure of the national economic systems in the 1920s, the ease with which liberal constitutionalism was subverted by the fascist revolutions, and the increasing international tensions seem to have undermined Laski's gentle confidence in peaceful progress. At the same time his interpretation of the economic basis of politics appears to have been fortified, if anything, by these conditions. Laski resolved the several dilemmas that his change in perspective might have produced in a striking *volte-face* when he wrote *Faith, Reason and Civilization* just as the tide was turning in favor of the Allies in World War II. In this extended essay Laski abandoned his critical rationalism in the exuberant discovery of the necessity for a transcendent faith as the basis for individual and political fulfillment. At the same time he found the historical exemplification of the transforming capacity of that faith in Soviet communism. The authoritarian dogmatism and the irrational appeals of communist doctrine and practice to which he had previously objected were transmuted into the positive attributes of a brave new world. The Russian Revolution, in Laski's view, reveals its capability for renewing human values by reviving man's faith in himself and in his great world purpose even in the face of the blackest threats of disaster evoked by the barbarities of national socialism. The situation in which the revolution of principles finds itself is compared to the historical conditions and state of mind in which Christianity made its successful bid to become the religion of the West. But the Russian experience has an advantage over the Christian faith in its advocacy of true human universalism and its emphasis on the kingdom of this world, for "it seeks salvation for the masses by fulfillment in this life, and, thereby, orders anew the actual world we know."[9]

9. Harold J. Laski, *Faith, Reason and Civilization* (New York: Viking Press, 1944), 64 ff., 51, 143.

In a sense Laski reversed the typical process of disenchantment; he found his faith before the problems of existence arising from the failure of the symbols of eighteenth-century rationalism were fully confronted in his thought. He thus allied his liberal optimism, reformist proclivities, and economic interpretation of politics to the particular secularized gnostic theology that seemed to be on his side in pragmatic political affairs. In doing so he suppressed the critical restraints on political activism that were residues of the civilizational tradition in rationalistic liberalism. He fell under the spell of a newer and more embracive enchantment than the one that had previously possessed him. The most depressing aspect of the case was the tendency to see the Nazi and Communist regimes as opposite extremes on the scale of evil and good, and the correlative blindness to the commonality of their totalitarian base.

By contrast, and perhaps the most interesting example of the critical aspects of the disenchantment, is Albert Camus. In *L'Homme Révolté* Camus produced an analysis of the intellectual trend leading to the beginning of disenchantment that has few equals in vigor and cogency. The most striking aspect of the study is its model character as an excercise in intellectually uncommitted criticism, with no fixed philosophical point of departure and no venture into a positive theory of man and society. The book is informed by a sense of the tragic loss of rational orienting standards and is suffused with a warm sympathy for the suffering lot of humanity. Despite this latter quality, Camus consistently refused to be identified with any past or contemporary school of philosophy or with any established theological position. His critical spirit seemed to be supplemented only by a vague faith which had no identifiable object. In consequence, his function was to discern the contradictions in man's condition which led to the revolt he describes and to single out the destructive futility of the ideologies which are the outcome of the revolt in its more recent phases. Camus' study, then, is not really philosophical, but it conducts to the point where philosophy commences by clearly recognizing the inevitability of certain issues in human experience. Camus' attitude of constraint in the face of the conclusions to be drawn from his own analysis is amply demonstrated by the statement that "l'analyse de la révolte conduit au moins au soupçon qu'il y a une nature humaine, comme le pensaient les Grecs, et contrairement aux postulats de la pensée contemporaine. Pourquoi se révolter s'il n'y a, en soi, rien de permanent à préserver?"[10]

Camus characterizes the spirit of thought since the end of the eighteenth century as one of revolt, and within the framework of the philosopher and artist considered as "rebel" he examines the conditions and consequences of the revolt. The metaphysical revolt, which properly speaking appears in coherent fashion only at the close of the eighteenth century, is a revolt against the condition of man itself, paradoxically, in the aspiration for order; it is a protest against death and evil on behalf of a happy unity against the suffering of life and death. The rebellion moves from the absolute negation of Sade (in the name of a frenetic liberty), through the nihilism of Ivan Karamazov (in which the refusal to accept anything less than unconditional grace opens the battle for justice against truth for the first time), and reaches the absolute affirmation in Nietzsche (with the recognition that God has been killed in the soul of man by the submission of God to a moral judgment and that a human affirmation is a necessity which arises from the murder of God). Throughout the metaphysical revolt is the tragic awareness, frequently on the part of the rebel himself, of the contradictions of the position. The nihilist, for example, to whom "tout est permis" is also the man who wishes for the lamb and the lion to lie down together, the victim to embrace the murderer even while murder is condoned. And Nietzsche knows full well that liberty of the spirit is not a comfort, that "si rien n'est vrai, rien n'est permis"—to be free is truly to abolish ends.[11] Nietzsche has also clearly seen the futility of humanism, which is simply Christianity deprived of all effective justification, an attempt to conserve final causes while rejecting the first cause.

The metaphysical revolt debouches into a historical revolt, according to Camus' analysis. One hundred fifty years of metaphysical revolt and nihilism have been accompanied by the attempt on the part of the rebels to tear away historical obstructions and to construct a purely terrestrial order of their choice. The historical

10. Albert Camus, *L'Homme Révolté* (Paris: Gallimard, 1951), 28.
11. *Ibid.*, 95–96.

rebellion begins with the regicides; if God is killed, it is necessary to kill his representative, and thus originates the confusion of justice with equality. The symbols of the new order are themselves religious: the social contract is a catechism with a dogmatic tone and language; the general will is a mystique in which the contradiction between limitless power and divine innocence is presumably reconciled. Beginning with absolute liberty and moving toward an absolute source of political truth, the revolt has as a consequence the fluctuation between Sade and the dictator, between individual terrorism and the terrorism of the state.

These remarks are no more than hints of the sustained logic of Camus' treatment. And his critical analysis leads always to the barrier surrounding the truth of existence, with Camus skirting the wall rather than attempting to breach it. He clearly implies that the crisis that led to disenchantment results from a false analysis of man and that the true analysis (or at least as much of it as has been vouchsafed to us) lies in the symbols rejected by the rebels. The self-sufficient new empire is constructed only at the price of the destruction of human substance, for it presupposes "une négation et une certitude: la certitude de l'infinie plasticité de l'homme et la négation de la nature humaine." And if there is no such thing as human nature "la plasticité de l'homme est, en effêt, infinie. Le realisme politique, à ce degré, n'est qu'un romantisme sans frein, un romantisme de l'efficacité."[12] In its most profound aspect the attempt to create a society on the basis of a purely relativistic morality is an attempt to live without transcendence, which is a characteristic feature of the nineteenth and twentieth centuries. The historical deterioration that follows is beyond doubt: God was killed in the person of his representative in a revolution of principles; the revolution of the twentieth century killed what remained of God in the principles themselves and consecrated historical nihilism. The revolt was thus turned against its own origins; the revolt against death and the god of death in the despair of personal liberty and survival has turned into a strange dream of the liberty of the species and has produced a prodigious collective agony which it calls immortality. Absolute human justice thus re-

12. *Ibid.*, 292.

sults in the suppression of all contradiction by destroying liberty. Camus ends where he began, with a recognition that the choice is between two interpretations of reality. "L'homme révolté est l'homme situé avant ou après le sacré, et appliqué à revendiquer un ordre humain où toutes les responses soient humaines, c'est-à-dire raisonnablement formulées. . . . Il serait possible de montrer ainsi qu'il ne peut y avoir pour un esprit humain que deux univers possibles, celui du sacré (ou, pour parler le langage chrétien, de la grâce) et celui de la révolte." Despite the fact that "le choix restera ouvert entre la grâce et l'histoire, Dieu ou l'épée," Camus leaves serious doubt that the choice really remains open since the death of God.[13] Still less does he indicate that he has been able to make the sacred a reality within himself.

With Camus we have come as far as the disenchanted intellectual proper is capable of taking us. His analysis reaches the limits of the negation of the philosophical and historical disturbances that broke the enchantment of the enlightened, self-sufficient intellectual. The reconstruction of the reality outside the shattered dreamworld in which the enchanted lived while the spell continued is an unending travail left to others.

13. *Ibid.*, 34, 354.

II   The Method and Results of Political Anthropology in America

The subject that engages us is one of enormous complexity. In ordinary—or commonsense—discourse the term *politics* has a deceptively simple referent; in such a context politics ordinarily means the process by which we settle what we might call public issues, *i.e.*, it is a process of resolving conflicts of interest. Under these circumstances, the existence of a public[1] and of institutions through which the process of politics moves is taken as given because man's entire historical experience is in a social setting. (Even Robinson Crusoe, the mythical prototype of isolated man, had at least the material benefits of social existence in the form of salvage from his wrecked ship.) In a society that is not in a state of crisis the habits of the public may be so attuned to the expectation that such conflicts or public issues as arise will be settled within the framework of the existing practice that, for the mass of the public at any rate, politics will hardly be represented to the conscious mind as a fundamental problem of human existence. Politics, in other words, is so intimately related to the whole complex nature and condition of man and is so patently a self-moved activity that the complexity of its theoretical analysis is likely to be in inverse proportion to the apparent simplicity of its preliminary comprehension through common sense.

1. The term *public* as used here has a double implication. Its simple denotation is a collectivity of individuals who make up the public, but this concept includes by assumption the philosophic meaning of the term to denote an object whose properties (whether external or essential) are present in each individual's experience in the same form. Thus a public as a collectivity of individuals would be a corollary of the unarticulated and unexamined premise that the issues with which the public's politics is concerned are in some way common to the members of the collectivity. This point is required because common sense would not commit the error of materialistic psychology in assuming that there are only individual issues (or interests) even in an orderly society.

However, by using the term *political anthropology* as a general designation of what we seek to know about politics we are hardly in danger of oversimplifying. Anthropology is a science that casts its net broadly indeed. It centers its inquiry on man as a whole and seeks to relate specialized findings in archeology, biology, and directly observed human activities (in the form of habits, customs, technologies, and institutions) to one another in order to create a composite in which the relative influence of the parts may be fully discerned. And the historical dimension is an important part of this study inasmuch as archeology seeks to link prehistory to recorded history and insofar as contemporary cultural anthropology seeks to utilize a chronological notion as part of its method of classifying various "cultures" and relating them to one another as "stages" of development. Analogously, then, "political" anthropology would seek to develop the broadest possible conceptions of the whole of man's political experience and to allocate each of the dimensions of that experience to its appropriate function as part of the whole. This is, of course, a major enterprise, but it is nonetheless the scope of the task that American political science has set for itself if one accepts at face value the many references in recent literature on the subject to a "general science" or "systematic theory" of politics.

In the American literature, at least, I know of only one writer, F. S. C. Northrop, who has applied the specific term *political anthropology* approximately as we are using it here. Northrop's adoption of the phrase is worth noting, however, for reasons other than its general congruence with the meaning ascribed to it here, for his point of departure seems to be an anthropological finding made by Clyde Kluckhohn in his research on the culture of the Navaho Indians. Although the Navahos had no written literature, Kluckhohn found that, despite intensive inductive observation, he was unable to provide any adequate explanation of the activities of the tribe until he was able to extract, bit by bit, the meanings that these activities held for the members of the tribe. Once this barrier was penetrated, he discovered that he was confronted "with a unique, logically consistent and very complex philosophy referring not merely to their normative beliefs about how to order their

political relations to one another, but also to natural phenomena."[2] In other words, Kluckhohn was confronted with an epistemological phenomenon indicating that human activities (of which
politics is certainly an essential one) must first be understood in
terms of the meaning ascribed to them by the actors, and that even
so-called primitive man and primitive societies relate their manifold activities to one another (beginning with the interpretation
of simple sense-data or "facts") by means of logical categories that
have a considerable degree of internal consistency.[3] The phenomenon further *suggests* that political societies as such owe their existence to the common participation of the individuals who compose them in these interpretations. In a somewhat broader sense
any political order is the product of its own self-interpretation or
self-articulation, and this interpretation includes not only the direct political symbols and institutions but also the relation of these
components of the political life to the shared meaning of reality as
a whole.

Now this undifferentiated apprehension of the nature of a political community is hardly the unique discovery that Northrop seems
to assume it is; from its inception philosophy recognized it as basic
and therefore concerned itself with the universality of purpose as
the cause of human activity, with the unanalyzable conjunction of
elementary perception and inference, and with the social consequences of these experiences. But the prior recognition of this condition does not detract from its importance as a theoretical insight, and the fact that a philosopher of Northrop's subtlety and
erudition could look upon it as something new and not generally
apprehended is in itself an important indication of the extent to

2. In F. S. C. Northrop's two most recent books, *The Complexity of Legal and Ethical Experience* (Boston: Little, Brown, 1959) and *Philosophical Anthropology and
Practical Politics* (New York: Macmillan, 1960), he makes frequent use of the term
political anthropology, and the core of both books is an attempt to develop the substance and method of a science to which the term could be applied. Northrop's books
are replete with references to Kluckhohn's discovery. See the basic explanations in
The Complexity of Legal and Ethical Experience, 59, and in *Philosophical Anthropology and Practical Politics*, 38–39.
3. To call this internal consistency of beliefs or ascribed meanings "philosophy" as Northrop does is not warranted, however, for philosophy begins as the conscious attempt to apprehend the truth of these largely unexamined opinions.

which certain philosophical propositions once virtually taken for granted have been submerged by other types of analysis. These problems, however, will concern us in detail later; at the moment it is sufficient to be aware of the fact that the notion of political anthropology which so stirred Northrop's imagination does raise theoretically relevant questions about the nature of politics and suggests the initial steps in a method of inquiry appropriate to these questions.

An enormous shift in emphasis and burden may seem to be involved in moving from certain preliminary observations about highly generalized propositions drawn from an anthropological investigation of a primitive society toward even an elementary outline of an American political anthropology. However, there are certain justifications for this procedure which arise from the fact that the choice of areas of political investigation is related to intuitive conceptions of intrinsic value, as well as from the fact that the compulsion to practical political decisions is no insignificant stimulus to inquiry. In this connection it is important to recall that, following a long period of actual or presumptive insular development, the United States recently emerged as one of the two great powers of world politics. As this occurred there was an increasing recognition (which carried with it an element of surprise both in Western Europe and in the United States) that the United States was a prototype—perhaps even a *desirable* prototype—of the highly industrialized, democratically organized, modern national state. This recognition could be attributed in part to an awareness of the length and stability of the American experience with the institutions and practices appropriate to the political form that represented the main trend of Western political development. And when the United States was seen in juxtaposition to the Soviet Union in a worldwide bipolarity of power this intuition about America's embodiment of inchoate Western politicomoral values was greatly heightened. Further, in the face of the necessity for making a clear choice as to which hegemony (American or Russian) a nation-state should tie its fortunes to, the Western world, at least, could have few rational doubts. Indeed, but for the reluctant American assumption of leadership, there would not even have been a choice.

As Arnold Toynbee has remarked, "America . . . is a leader whom we are fortunate to have."[4] A choice made under such conditions, however, can scarcely avoid generating a retrospective urge to examine the qualifications and prospects of American leadership in more depth than is yielded by intuition.

At the same time, America's accession to its present position brought with it an end to the innocence produced by its insularity and by an optimism that saw its overt political and economic success as symbols of indefinite progress. In the confrontation with a world composed of a multiplicity of political entities reflecting a confusing pluralism in their respective self-interpretations of existence, it has become increasingly apparent that neither the symbols that serve America domestically nor the traditions which inform its practical experience can be directly exported. America might fail, not by virtue of the collapse of its own political form and traditions, but by virtue of an inadequate understanding of what these things mean and the conditions for sharing their meaning with other fully articulated political societies.

Yet another factor suggests the plausibility of an American political anthropology, and that is the existence of a fully developed profession of political science in the United States. In terms of the number of people involved in teaching and research in this area, as well as the amount of publication, American political science is unparalleled in other countries. Insofar as the development of a science depends on vigorous application on the part of a generally recognized body of scholars who maintain close and continuing contact with one another, political science in America is particularly well situated. The question whether other conditions pertinent to the pursuit of science may impede the realization of a mature political anthropology in the United States is a question that is immediately related to the general obligation undertaken in this essay. In fact, the indicated approach to an attempt to integrate the several aspects of the problem of a political anthropology is to examine some of the tendencies of American research in politics,

4. Arnold Toynbee, "An Englishman Looks at America's Changing Role in the World" (Mimeo.).

with a full recognition that limitations of space make this a hazardous undertaking.[5]

In attempting this sweeping survey, we shall be handling problems on more than one level of discourse. A description of the current trends in political science research will indicate some of the purposes and methods of the profession; at the same time it will be necessary to extract from the products of this research (which is characterized by a great diversity of regulatory ideas and methods) some of the substantive conclusions that may contribute to the construction of a political anthropology. And finally, a critical analysis will necessarily accompany this exposition—as part of an effort to evaluate the contribution of research products and methods to the questions posed by the sweeping concept entitled political anthropology.

Although even a cursory review of the activities of political scientists in the United States reveals a tremendous diversity in their objects and methods, a careful observer has recently pointed out that "the most consistent and significant trend in American Political Science for more than two generations has been toward 'science,' and this trend is the one most easily distinguished today."[6] To those who identify themselves with this trend the term *science* has a decidedly positivistic meaning; the model for scientific activity is afforded by the physical and biological sciences, and the conceptions and methods that are identified with those sciences are presumed to exhaust the meaning of science. The contemporary denotation of this trend in the general area of social science is, of course, "behavioral science."

Even though there is considerable diversification of objects of study and perhaps even of methodology within behavioral science itself, the attempt to analyze any significant portion of these materials would divert us into an almost inexhaustible field. It is

5. For an overview of the scope, content, and methods of American political science, see *Contemporary Political Science* (Paris: UNESCO, 1950), and Dwight Waldo, *Political Science in the United States of America* (Paris: UNESCO, 1956).

6. For an illustration of this diversity within the covers of a single volume, see Roland Young (ed.), *Approaches to the Study of Politics* (Evanston: Northwestern University Press, 1958). Waldo, *Political Science in the United States*, 20.

therefore necessary to provide a concise and generalized statement of the conceptions that dominate this trend. For that purpose Dwight Waldo's formulation seems adequate. Waldo notes
that "the distinguishing or characteristic features of the behav-
ioural approach are: an attempt to avoid all 'oughts,' care in the
formulation of hypotheses, preoccupation with fashioning analytical 'models,' meticulous attention to 'research design,' use of
quantification where possible, concern for leaving a trail that can
be followed—'replication'—and caution in conclusions drawn from
particular studies together with the expectation of an ever-grow-
ing body of established generalizations."[7] In accordance with our
suggested procedure it will be necessary to examine the implication of this conception of scientific procedure and of the results of
its application for developing a knowledge of what politics is and
how we know about it.

It will immediately be noted that what we are dealing with is a
rather elaborate methodological proposition; indeed current behavioral literature is replete with references to "nonscientific,"
"unscientific," and "traditionalistic" political analysis, by all of
which the authors appear to mean political analysis that is not
based on a methodology rigidly defined in Baconian terms. Now
there are serious implications in this attitude alone, because science does not arise out of methodology; it is rather the other way
around, methodology proceeds from science. That is to say, methodological formulations are attempts to reconstruct the processes
of intelligence through which scientific discoveries are made;
therefore they require that the scientist who presents them be as
adept at analyzing the human activity involved in science as he is
at analyzing the objects about which knowledge is sought. And it
is little more than a truism to say that the physical and biological
scientists themselves are less sure of their capacity in this area than
they were in the more optimistic days when radical empiricism was
in the ascendency. The attempt to conflate epistemology and
methodology thus causes one to lose sight not only of the meaning
of science in terms of the human purpose that generated it as an
activity but also of the notion of the relation between the objects

7. Waldo, *Political Science in the United States,* 21–22.

of knowledge and the knowing intelligence. Even though this abstraction of the object of knowledge from a connection with the knowing subject and the deliberate refusal to reflect on what the intellect is engaged in while carrying on scientific investigation may not be injurious to efforts in physical and biological science, it may very well make a science of man and society meaningless by cutting the scientist off from those experiences from which such a science appropriately begins. Even if the universe is objectively constructed and its uniformities and variations are subject to description and measurement as external "facts," and when so distinguished can be controlled through technology, nothing is yielded thereby for the meaning of existence. It is possible under these circumstances to adopt a posture of complete skepticism about the meaning of existence despite the ubiquity of the evidence that intelligence does not ever really dissociate itself from the problem of existence.[8] More often than not, however, another unexamined premise is present in the behavioralist's attitude; *i.e.*, the assumption that man's behavior is objectively determined after the manner of the physical and biological world.

This latter solution to the modern problem of epistemology (which has been the bane of philosophy since Descartes) leads directly to the first category in Waldo's characterization of behavioralism—the attempt to avoid all "oughts," or, as it is more frequently expressed, the separation of "facts" and "values" and the development of a "value-free" social science. The number of problems raised by this prescription is so great that one hardly knows where to begin in suggesting objections to it, but some of them may be mentioned briefly. In the first place it is hardly possible to conceive of any human activity that is not directed toward an end; and it is equally difficult, once that end is presented to the conscious mind, not to pass judgment on it, that is, not to consider it good or bad or right or wrong. The usual solution of the behavioralists to this problem of moral appraisal is to suggest that all value judgments are to be regarded as individual preferences which must be treated as data but must not be allowed—qua personal prefer-

8. The skeptical solution of Hume is pertinent, of course; complete knowledge of reality is impossible, but in practical life one always acts as though there were perfect conjunction between his ideas and reality.

ences—to influence the scientist in arriving at his conclusions. Value judgments can thus be treated as "facts" in determining behavior, but are meaningless as forms of knowledge because they are individual, arbitrary, and incapable of objective validation. Intellectually this attitude constitutes a denial of the possibility of rational action, except possibly in relation to the means or techniques by which ends are pursued; it thus dissolves the fundamental notion of ethics as a rational science of behavior because it denies that the man confronted with the necessity for acting has the possibility of knowing that one alternative is right (or at least better than the others) and that that choice is rationally obligatory for him as it *should* be for any other man in his situation.

The practical consequences of this doctrine are drastic indeed. By cutting himself off from the investigation of the validity of man's goals and the attempt to order these goals in accordance with rational standards, the scientist places himself in a peculiar position. He cannot even offer a valid reason for his pursuit of science since he does it merely by preference; ergo, his scientific activity is no more to be valued than the activity of any other man, however base we moralists may judge the other man's preference to be. In these terms, if the scientist hopes to find the key to an objectively ordered political system, and he cannot validate his urge to do so in terms of love of truth and the desire to establish a *good* order, he is still faced with the moral dilemma attending the use to which his findings may be put as means. To speak of a "predictive science of politics," as some behavioralists do, is to open the way to the use of these possibilities of prediction for control. The scientist is then up against the problem of whose preferences are to provide the standards for use of his scientific results in application; *i.e.*, who is to manage the social technology in which a "value-free" science eventuates? We have a name for the condition experienced by man and society deprived of all symbols of rationally ordered interpretation of existence; that name is nihilism, and we are not lacking in recent experience with the types of order that may be imposed where such a condition exists.

Perhaps one way that the behavioralists try to take out of the impasse just outlined should be mentioned. This attempted extrication is characteristic, for example, of the work of Harold Lasswell at certain stages of his manifold ventures in model construction and research design. The form taken is an attempt to identify those dominant preferences men have in common in order that we might apply ourselves to securing as broad a distribution as possible of the means for satisfying the desires expressed by these preferences. This attempt to substitute opinion for knowledge in ordering the hierarchy of goods is no solution for reasons already alluded to. Its superficial plausibility arises from the fact that in identifying collective preferences the behavioralists are perhaps fortunate in interviewing men whose characters have been formed in an atmosphere in which moral values have not been totally submerged. In addition, when making their surveys the behavioralists themselves are hardly free from hidden influences that reflect rationally ordered moral values. Leo Strauss has characterized this tendency for "value-free" research to be conditioned by moral considerations by saying that "when social scientists distinguish between democratic and authoritarian habits or types of human beings, what they call 'authoritarian' is in all cases known to me a caricature of everything of which they as good democrats, of a certain kind, disapprove."[9]

Of course, the social science positivist is allowed to participate in public affairs as a citizen, and in this capacity he is free to make the utmost use of his own preferences. This is tantamount to saying that the moral tension (not to speak of practical frustration) arising from the attempt to exclude values as proper objects of investigation by the social sciences is adjusted by a mutually exclusive separation of the social scientific man into his dual capacities as scientist and citizen. In view of this situation it is hardly surprising to find that so many political scientists pursuing a "value-free" science are activists on behalf of all sorts of morally impregnated public issues. Nor is this form of reconciliation of scientific activity and moral propensities without implications for the reconstruction of a moral self-interpretation in the face of its destruction in the interest of a "value-free" science, because the practical applications of the social scientists (who, in their partic-

9. Leo Strauss, *What Is Political Philosophy?* (Glencoe, Ill.: The Free Press, 1959), 21.

ipation in politics, work within an established political tradition) yield far more results than do their scientific pursuits.[10] For if we consider the quantity of writing done by the behavioralists, they have said astonishingly little about the nature of politics that is either new or relevant to a general theory of politics. Much of the writing of this type has been concerned with abstract methodology in the form of suggested techniques for research and the designation of general areas that could be explored by these methods. Most of the substantive work along these lines seems to have been done in an attempt to validate research techniques by applying them to problems that are either so trivial or so obvious that it is a work of supererogation to "prove" them through the use of such elaborate devices. Furthermore, despite the constant stress of the behavioralists on the formulation of general hypotheses, operational research design, and a continually enlarging area of pertinent generalization, the only generalized "theory" that I am able to identify with this productivity is the concept of "group theory," which has been extant (and periodically revived) since A. F. Bentley's formulation in 1908. The conception advanced by Bentley that the interplay of competing interest groups is the only manifestation of political activity that has pertinence and that the science of politics will be built up by analysis of these group activities seems so patently (and at times explicitly) to presuppose a natural political equilibrium (or naturalistic order) analogous to Newton's physical dynamics that Bentley's strictures about the necessity for working out such a science constitute a tautology.[11] Further, I share the view, advanced by other commentators, that this conception is a product of provincialism, and that one would have to take into account certain influential ideas and conditions in the American tradition which make the activities of interest groups possible in

10. I am thinking in this connection of instances such as the late Charles H. Merriam's participation in local, state, and national affairs and of Harold Lasswell's influence in several practical advisory capacities, as well as of other less well known examples.

11. A. F. Bentley, *The Process of Government* (Bloomington: Principia Press, 1908). In this respect it seems to me on the basis of a cursory appraisal that the "group theorists" have done little more than collectivize the radically empirical individualism of Bentham and are operating with an unarticulated assumption about the "natural harmony" of competing interests that Bentham made an explicit part of his naturalistic optimism.

order to provide any understanding of their nature or for understanding why an interest group hypothesis projected in universal terms may be largely irrelevant in political contexts other than the United States.[12]

Those of us who are interested in the political science profession in the United States are fortunate in having access to a recent, very able analysis of the scientistic bent of American political science written by a young English scholar, Bernard Crick. Crick finds that the persistent concern with a positivist science of politics in America may be explained largely in terms of American political history and experience. He interprets this scientism as the product of general American political thought (or self-interpretation) rather than as a potential explanation of politics. Underlying the confidence about a science of politics and growing out of America's successful insular experience with its own political system is a broadly diffused moral attitude that espouses democracy and a liberal progressive optimism. This underlying confidence (designated by Crick as a "psychological unity of belief," without clarity as to what the belief is) enables American political scientists to narrow the conception of political problems to questions of means and to eschew all considerations of the moral implication of political order—indeed there is an implicit fear that any attempt to establish "first principles" constitutes a threat to democracy. To attempt a brief summary of the way in which Crick demonstrates the interplay of these self-interpreting beliefs with the quest for a "value-free" science of politics in the several stages through which this quest has passed would work an injustice on a book characterized by subtlety of analysis and depth of perception. It is sufficient to

12. I have no desire to depreciate the work that has been done in "empirical" political science in the United States, but I would suggest that the most useful research in this area has been done by persons who are not operating under the persisting shadow of Comte. Some of the quantified studies in voting habits, such as those carried out by Samuel Lubell, to take one example, provide excellent materials and insights for a general understanding of American politics. See especially Lubell's *Future of American Politics* (New York: Harper and Brothers, 1952). For a sharp contrast between a shrewd political observer utilizing his common sense and whatever materials seemed pertinent to his inquiry (including his understanding of political types measured in moral dimensions) and the same observer operating under the influence of a behavioralistic scientism, see V. O. Key, Jr., *Southern Politics* (New York: Knopf, 1949), and V. O. Key, Jr., *American State Politics* (New York: Knopf, 1956).

note not only that Crick's treatment demonstrates the conditions that make a positivistically oriented social science possible in the United States but that in doing so he reveals its inadequacy for the task of constructing a theory of politics. It is possible to indulge in a behavioralist scientific dreamworld only in a society whose symbolization of social order is so deeply embedded in the minds of the participants and so fully reflected in the practical institutions that it does not seem to require rational examination. Furthermore Crick recognizes the dangers implicit in the lack of an adequate formulation of the self-interpretation of the society and of theoretical standards by which the self-interpretation can be measured. As long as the practical political issues which arise can be related to the external historical development of the society they can be resolved pragmatically, or at least on the basis of a minimum understanding of the rational principles that sustain the unarticulated tradition, but when the order itself is threatened we need to know much more.[13]

The currently dominant trend in American political science, then, seems to offer little in the way of method or results that would advance us toward a theoretical conception of politics that could merit the application of the term *political anthropology*. Behavioralism is limited (if not positively destructive) because it restricts its conception of the politically relevant to the most superficial manifestations of political experience and because it is socially derivative as a form of knowledge rather than transcending the material it claims to interpret.

Fortunately American political science does not exhaust its efforts in behavioralism. There is a large body of materials in which American political ideas and institutions are analyzed historically, often by political scientists with considerable philosophical insight. Some of these materials reveal the main elements in the American symbolic self-interpretation, demonstrate the function of these symbols in the institutional arrangements, and provide a criticism of the circumstances under which the American society

13. Bernard Crick, *The American Science of Politics: Its Origins and Conditions* (London: Routledge and Kegan Paul, 1959).

fails to fulfill the moral expectations that arise from its self-interpretation. The great historical examples of this type of political analysis are works such as *The Federalist* and Tocqueville's *Democracy in America*. However, it is important to concentrate on examples that are more recent than these classic sources; for this purpose two types of analysis are singled out, one concerning the history of American ideas and the other relating to legal institutions.

Earlier I referred to the underlying moral consensus in American life and suggested its relevance for the creation of a cohesive community in America. This conception has been analyzed in detail by Louis Hartz in his *Liberal Tradition in America*. Hartz ranges over American history from the Revolution to the present in an effort to see what ideas, as expressed by the most influential thinkers as well as in practical decisions, motivate reactions to major issues in American political history, including the Revolution itself, the emergence of democracy in the struggles between the Federalists and the Jeffersonians and later between Jackson and the Whigs, the slavery controversy, the great age of capitalist expansion, the reform movement, the New Deal, and the present involvement in world affairs. As a background to the American experience Hartz continually refers to the correlative development of European political controversies, and he draws on this comparison to indicate the distinctive features of the American experience.[14]

As a result of this diligent application to the history of ideas Hartz concludes that the American experience is heavily influenced, if not virtually controlled, by the absence of feudalism and a wholesale addiction to the liberal ideas of John Locke. The openness of American life, both in terms of a deliberate shunning of the overt symbols of European social inequalities and the abundance of and access to economic goods ("property"), toward which Locke's abstract libertarian pronouncements were so heavily directed, af-

14. Louis Hartz, *The Liberal Tradition in America* (New York: Harcourt, Brace, 1955), is not the only recent interpretation which stresses the almost universal acquiescence of Americans in a "received" or "given" set of moral attitudes which are heavily determinant of the national political life. Compare Daniel Boorstin, *The Genius of American Politics* (Chicago: University of Chicago Press, 1953). On the whole, however, Hartz's work seems to me to be much the best of its type.

forded a unique opportunity for liberalism to take hold in America. More than this, however, it was possible in such an environment for liberalism to afford the basis for a *conservative* tradition. Not only were the great symbols of national unity—the Revolution and the Constitution—framed in an atmosphere in which liberal ideas were very prominent, but it was possible to assimilate American small farmers and laborers to the bourgeois image, thereby creating virtually a permanent electoral majority which unconsciously adheres to a liberal conception of society.

Hartz is able to show how this tenacious, widely disseminated ideational influence affects the specific reactions of the public to political questions, and especially the way in which it serves as a sort of axiological principle in terms of which events are interpreted and effective, majority-supported decisions are made. Particularly interesting in this respect are the tendencies toward democratic majoritarianism and the firm rejection of any concept of class distinction, which worked to such a disadvantage for the Hamiltonian Federalists, even to the point of seeming (though not actually) to threaten another basic attitude—the capitalist mentality. It was not until the Whig successors to Hamilton recognized the necessity for using the democratic symbols to mobilize the majority, in the first ballyhoo campaign of 1840, that the Federalist (Whig-capitalist) conception of national development was able to triumph once again. And the successors to Whigs, the Republicans, were able to solidify the conjunction of the capitalist and the democratic ideas, thereby effectively putting paid to any propensity toward socialism, whose class appeals, economics, and emphasis on government at the expense of society all ran counter to the overwhelmingly dominant living moral self-interpretation. Even in the face of the economic catastrophe of depression, the New Deal reform made its appeals in terms of the dominant symbols and measured its success by the extent to which these symbols were preserved and strengthened.

The solidity of these symbols is demonstrated most fully by the failure of political efforts whose moral basis differs from the living content of the American tradition. The most conspicuous of these failures was the attempt of the South to erect a paternalistic, landed aristocracy based on slavery, with many of its self-interpretative symbols being drawn from Filmer. The attempt was, of course, in direct contradiction to the main content of the liberal ethos, which further consolidated its hold on the American mind as a result of the Civil War. Even in the case of the South, however, the liberal ethos was sufficiently diffused to split the intellectual defenders of the Southern cause in their justifications, if not in their practical intentions. Feudal romanticism vied with the elaborate legalisms of Calhoun that depended on contractual assumptions deriving in no small part from liberalism.[15] Furthermore the South was a *capitalistic* agricultural economy, which in itself constituted an implicit denial of its illiberal proclivities. In these and a number of other ways the South was, and still is, self-defeating (or, in the current jargon, schizophrenic) in its self-interpretation.

What we are confronted with here is a submerged creed that has perhaps found its most concentrated expression in the now trite-sounding phrase the "American Way of Life," an expression which does not seem to have a precise counterpart in any other country. And Hartz is fully aware of the dangers as well as the advantages of such a creed. The great danger is the one perceived by Tocqueville—the tyranny of opinion, especially of an opinion which is not aware of the delicate balance of the various influences out of which the underlying consensus was constructed. As Hartz puts it, "a sense of community based on a sense of uniformity is a deceptive thing. It looks individualistic, and in part it actually is. . . . But in another sense it is profoundly anti-individualistic, because the common standard is its very essence, and deviations from that standard inspire it with an irrational fright."[16]

Thus it is that anything alien to the tradition is strongly suspect, and it is possible to manipulate the majority so that it closes ranks against the alien influence, sometimes to the detriment of its own declared values. This threat is omnipresent, as is demonstrated by some of the early native American movements, by the anticommunist and antisocialist hysteria and relapse into isolationism

15. Among a number of important subsidiary propositions offered by Hartz is that the legalism so characteristic of American politics flourishes where agreement on political principles is accepted; a society in which political conflict is intense would not agree to put the largest issues of public policy "before nine Talmudic judges examining a single text" (Hartz, *The Liberal Tradition in America*, 10).
16. *Ibid.*, 56.

after World War I, and the recent experience with the late Senator McCarthy. There are, on the other hand, built-in correctives since the liberal tradition in its full articulation contains values that are antithetical to irrational mass absolutism. As Hartz says, one may turn Wilsonianism upside down, and ask when has the nation better appreciated the limits of its own cultural pattern as applied to the rest of the world than during the post–World War I crisis. Or one may do the same with McCarthyism and ask when has the meaning of civil liberties been better understood than now. "A dialectical process is at work, evil eliciting the challenge of a conscious good." But even so, "the outcome of the battle between intensified 'Americanism' and the new enlightenment is . . . an open question."[17]

As much as Hartz's interpretation is able to tell us about the substance of American politics and about methods appropriate to its analysis, his thesis needs to be supplemented by criticism and extension. For one thing, he seems to place too much emphasis on the immediate influence of Locke, a defect that might have been remedied if he had examined the source and content of Locke's ideas in more detail. There are a great many internally unreconciled doctrines in Locke: His radically empirical sensationalist psychology is hardly compatible with his rationalistic natural law—natural rights moralism, for example—and his majoritarian proclivity is not easily adjusted to some of the constitutional arrangements that he draws out of the Whig settlement of 1689. I do not mean to suggest that Locke was not immediately and permanently influential in relation to American ideas, but rather to point out that Locke's thought was an eclectic product (and by no means at the highest level) of a differentiated civilizational experience and that the more diversified experience was already at work in America before the reception of Locke.

The overemphasis on Locke and its effects are most clearly revealed in Hartz's lack of attention to American institutions as carriers and sanctifiers of the symbols of American self-interpretation. Locke's effect on American institutions, which were grounded in experience, was less influential than the justifications of these

17. *Ibid.*, 14.

institutions in Lockean terms might imply. If the American moral consensus is, as has been suggested by Hartz and others, so widespread and so deeply seated that it tends to suppress the urge to deeper political thought and yet the concepts basic to that consensus continue to provide the self-interpretation of an orderly, tradition-based society, the institutions must not only reflect that self-interpretation in practice but must also be an important element in its diffusion. In this connection the works of American scholars on institutions, especially in the general area of constitutional law, provide a necessary supplement to studies in political ideas such as that by Hartz. One major reason for this stress is the continuity between American constitutional experience and that of Britain, which in its broader implications was barely touched by the Revolution; in fact the continuity was self-consciously preserved in the transition from constitutional monarchy to constitutional republic.

Limitations of space preclude more than a passing reference to the manner in which students of American constitutional law have identified the sources and established the practical meaning of certain legal notions that bridge the gap between the American self-interpretation and practice. McIlwain's study of Bracton's ideas of the separation of *gubernaculum* and *jurisdictio*, for example, assists us in understanding the American devotion to the Constitution as a general limitation on governmental authority, even when that authority is based on popular sovereignty. The idea of constitutionalism is so habitual a part of American life that it manifests itself in hundreds of ways, is reaffirmed through education and practice in each generation, and thus serves as a continuous symbol of order and authority as well as a check on simple plebiscitarianism. A number of other sources indicate the reliance of American constitutionalism on the natural law tradition of classical antiquity and Christianity, and in so doing suggest the moral reality behind the use of the Constitution as symbol. And there is a vast literature on the American civil liberties tradition, part of which traces the sources and helps toward an understanding of the concrete meaning of the two great abstractions of liberalism—liberty and equality. By removing these notions from the hortatory adaptation of the marketplace and tracing them to their origins in the philosophic conception of personality and then analyzing the way that the courts have attempted to develop their application to specific issues, the constitutional law scholar has shown how they can provide standards for the practical fulfillment of the self-interpretation while avoiding the deterioration of liberty into license or equality into a uniform leveling destructive of all consideration of merit.[18]

This method of historical analysis of political ideas and institutions represents a considerable advancement over the results achieved by the behavioral school. In its most imaginative use it reveals the underlying moral basis which is the ground for the self-articulation of the society; and if the observations of Northrop (cited earlier) are pertinent, this exposure is basic to the idea of political anthropology. Moreover, by giving a more specific content to the undifferentiated symbols of that self-interpretation, the historic-analytic method provides an understanding of the way in which the political tradition works. The latter is especially important to the politician as craftsman because it establishes the limits of the possibilities open to him in making decisions on the issues that confront him; i.e., it offers considerable insight into the practical resolution of the tension between the necessity for change and the desirability of conserving a tradition of order, which is a basic problem of nondemagogic democratic political leadership. Finally, its importance for political education is obvious; a broad understanding of a political tradition is vital to its survival since the fundamentals of that tradition are subject to constant attrition, not only by direct attack on it, but also by neglect or by overemphasis on one aspect of the political life at the expense of others.

For all of its advantages, however, the historic-analytic method has decided limits. While it probes the self-interpretation of the society in an effort to understand the meaning of its symbols, it rarely penetrates to the reality of these symbols; thus the stan-

18. Charles Howard McIlwain, *Constitutionalism: Ancient and Modern* (Revised ed.; Ithaca: Cornell University Press, 1947); Edward S. Corwin, "The 'Higher Law' Background of American Constitutional Law," *Harvard Law Review*, XLII (December, 1928), 149–85, (January, 1929), 365–409; Robert J. Harris, *The Quest for Equality* (Baton Rouge: Louisiana State University Press, 1960).

dards that it discovers and applies critically are confined to the specific political tradition. The perception of the *good* in that tradition remains at the level of intuition, and the practical effort remains at the level of maintaining that tradition intact for the particular society. Although it may raise questions that are fundamental to political order, it rarely approaches the level of generality that could be designated as theory. It is to the credit of many practitioners of the method that they recognize its limits. Hartz, for example, suggests something that goes beyond his own analysis when he points out that Russian development has turned its back on the Western concept of personality while the American development, despite its provincialism, is based on that concept. And he adds that "the hope for a free world surely lies in the power for transcending itself inherent in American liberalism." He ends his book with the question with which it began, "Can a people 'born equal' ever understand peoples elsewhere that have to become so? Can it ever understand itself?" And Crick reminds us that the limitation of politics to its appropriate functions "depends upon a transcendent essence of personality that is not created by ourselves and thus cannot be utterly lost by anything that is done to us or even by anything that we do ourselves."[19]

These statements constitute a recognition of the fact that a political tradition may embody goods that were recognized intuitively but that the validation of these goods depends on a higher level of generality than the tradition alone displays. Expressing this in another way, one might say that the problem of political anthropology culminates in the necessity for the formulation of a philosophical anthropology; the science of politics depends on a science that penetrates to the understanding of the nature of man. An American political anthropology may limit itself to an analysis of the concrete elements of its own tradition in ordinary times, but the present crisis evokes the need for a reconstruction of the experiences of reality out of which the existing order emerged, both for self-understanding and for an understanding of the self-articulation of other societies. At this point the idea of a distinctly

19. Hartz, *The Liberal Tradition in America*, 308–309; Crick, *The American Science of Politics*, 223.

American political anthropology merges into the conception of a general science of politics, and the question is raised whether the grounds for such a science exist.

An affirmative answer can be given to the question just asked, because there is a small core of political scientists (along with classical philosophers, Orientalists, and others) who are concerned with the problem of philosophical anthropology and its meaning for politics. Much of this work takes the form of *reconstruction* of classical and Christian conceptions of philosophical anthropology because the questions relevant to this inquiry—*e.g.*, the ontological questions and the moral questions pertaining to the qualities that characterize a good man and a just political order—have been ruled out by positivistically oriented political scientists such as the behavioralists.

Among the political scientists who have worked on these problems in the United States for approximately the past forty years, Leo Strauss and Eric Voegelin are undoubtedly the most distinguished figures. Although an attempt to delineate even the elemental aspects of the work of these philosophers would require an exposition far beyond the entire length of this essay, some general idea of the work they are engaged in must be offered in order to round out the broad trends of political research and to show how the methods and results of the attempt to gain political knowledge stand in relation to one another.

I have indicated that the very idea of a philosophical anthropology involves a reconstruction of philosophical materials and, beyond that, of the experiences that originally produced a concern with the main problems of a science based on the fullest meaning of the nature of man. The works of both Strauss and Voegelin are characterized by such an attempt, although the results are somewhat different in the two instances.[20]

20. The following comments on Strauss depend largely on his recent volume of essays, *What Is Political Philosophy?*, and especially on the first essay, which furnishes the book's title and which constitutes a useful distillation of the ideas he has developed in the detailed analysis of the political thought of a formidable number of ancients and moderns. Voegelin's major works on the problems indicated here are the first three volumes of his projected five-volume *Order and History*, published by the Louisiana State University Press—*Israel and Revelation* (Vol. I, 1956), *The World of the Polis* (Vol. II, 1957), and *Plato and Aristotle* (Vol. III, 1957)—and his earlier *The New Science of Politics* (Chicago: University of Chicago Press, 1952).

Strauss relies on the classical philosophers, particularly Plato and Aristotle, for furnishing the models for political philosophy, if not indeed the final philosophical truths about politics insofar as they are open to man's knowledge. They are able to do this because they correctly sought to know the nature of things political and the right or good political order, while realizing that one does not understand the realities of politics unless he has some standard of goodness and justice by which to measure them. These moral standards cannot create themselves; they are part of the reality of existence. They are apprehended by philosophical penetration that transcends the merely human (and especially the traditional, which is fraught with opinion rather than knowledge) and reaches to the "natural," *i.e.*, to the true or best things that the cosmic limitations of our human condition will permit us to know and act on.

By contrast, modern political philosophy, beginning with Machiavelli, moves through a great variety of changes, but all of its representatives hold to the common principle of rejecting the classical scheme as unrealistic. Against the classical position of a substantive morality which was a force in the soul of man and which might or might not affect the existent regime, the modernists are more concerned with the actualization of order than with discovering its sources and meaning. The selfish nature of man (displayed by his "behavior"?) must be altered in the direction of social life by institutions that are established with this end in view. Man's nature is assumed to be infinitely malleable, and compulsion is permissible (perhaps necessary) in reshaping it and in bending the factor of chance in historical action.

In his emphasis on the classical philosophers Strauss calls our attention to many important issues in political philosophy, including the distinction between knowledge and opinion in regard to things political, the dependence on knowledge of the human soul (which is the philosophical source of knowledge of the whole man) for ordering human ends in accordance with reason, and the necessity for characterizing a regime in terms of the virtue of the men who compose it. However, there are significant omissions in his treatment. Although he points out (somewhat indirectly) the necessity for transcendence of the strictly human in order to understand the highest potentialities and therefore the true ends of man, he does not (to my knowledge) indicate that he follows Plato in his search into the depths of the soul, as expressed in the Platonic myths, for the experiences of the good. Thus although *virtue* is a singularly important word in Strauss's lexicon, I am unable to discern a sufficient attention to the way in which knowledge of virtue is reached. There is a reason for this, I think, and it is that such a search brings us too close to the experience of the divine as the ground of all being, and it is characteristic of Strauss that he repudiates any connection between theology and political philosophy. And this may well be the reason that his work has consisted so largely of the examination of modern political thinkers: It is less difficult to distinguish the evils which arise from the attempt to construct a political order solely on the basis of a grasp of primitive human drives (the passions) than it is to provide the basis for a good life and a just political order without introducing the problem of theology. It is certainly significant in this connection that Strauss does not indicate that Christian political thought added anything to classical philosophy that was relevant to the ordering of man's political life. This attitude causes Strauss to skirt dangerously close to a moralism which depends simply on approval or disapproval, with authoritative approval resting with the men whose character has been formed by a classical education.

Strauss's handling of the problem of history is closely related to this problem of identifying the sources of good. He is rightly concerned with the modern trend toward the bending of political order toward a historically predetermined end which takes the form of one or another of the intramundane perfectionist ideologies. He refers to this attempt to construct a theory of society on the basis of an immanentist teleological principle as "historicism." But his rejection of historicism results also in a rejection of any idea of a connection between philosophy and historical experience. Now the repudiation of the idea of future or present perfection of life and of political order in this world (in the interest of which idea so many atrocities have been committed) does not indicate that there is no meaning in history. The very regimes that Strauss would have us judge as good and bad on the basis of a classical philosophical anthropology are historical regimes. Further, Strauss's careful studies of modern political thinkers (and his periodization of political thought into the eras dominated respectively by the classicists and the modernists) indicate that there is a philosophical falling away from right principles of order in certain historical epochs, and certainly he must consider that this deterioration of principles has some effect on existential order—otherwise his own philosophic activity would have little meaning.

It is my contention that the strength of Voegelin's contribution lies precisely in those areas Strauss is careful to avoid. Let us take these problems in the order indicated in the foregoing remarks about Strauss. When Voegelin leads us through the maze of Platonic and Aristotelian philosophy he re-creates the sequence of experiences of the philosophers themselves as they were led by the stirrings of the soul through the love of truth to the realization of its transcendent sources. And he is not leery of following the Platonic search as it reaches to the perimeter of theological speculation which is the means of the full transcendence of the human—for what we can know about God is the standard by which man knows himself. Voegelin is not, therefore, precluded from considering what Christianity may yield in the way of a further dimension of man's approach to the knowledge of reality.

These differences become clearer when we begin to comprehend Voegelin's understanding of history, for in his conception a penetration to principles will culminate in a philosophy of history. The analysis of principles, in fact, depends on the exploration of the symbols by which societies interpret themselves as representatives of transcendent, or ultimate, truth or reality, since this is the form taken by the self-articulation which establishes the existence of a political order in history. If we examine the ways in which societies have symbolized this existence—or rather penetrate the ways in which these symbols represent reality—it is possible to order them in relation to one another according to the relative degrees of their grasp of reality. Thus the earliest societies were articulated through compact cosmological symbols, and subsequent interpretations represent most differentiated symbolization, such as was achieved by revelation in Hebraic society, the opening of the soul in Hellenic philosophy, and the soteriological truth of Christianity. Each of these stages in the closer approximation to reality is referred to by Voegelin as a "leap in being." To attempt

to summarize the rich historical detail by which Voegelin establishes this theory and its full implication for a science of politics
would result in an even more elliptical exposition than the necessity for curtailment already compels us to give. The studies must
be read for their meaning to be grasped; it is as much as we can do
at this point to call attention to them.

   One thing does need to be mentioned to indicate the way in which
Voegelin's enlarged understanding of order enables Strauss's objections to modern political thought to be made with more precision. Western civilization is an articulation based on the Christian
anthropology (which incorporates the truths of classical philosophy in a higher generalization about the nature of man and society); therefore the ills of modernity that Strauss identifies may be
theoretically interpreted as secular extensions of the Gnostic heresy—the immanentization of Christian transcendental reality. The
modern mass movements achieve their meaning through the
transfer to their worldly perfectionist ends of the Christian grace,
which has its true meaning only outside of history. Voegelin's adaptation of the Gnostic concept is a tool for understanding the need
for the restoration of the real civilizational standards and especially of those which comprehend the universal spiritual substance of man and the limits of action imposed by the human condition.

The method and results of the work of Strauss and Voegelin, then,
indicate that various conceptions of what political knowledge is
and how it may be achieved may themselves be arranged hierarchically in accordance with the degree to which they approach
reality. Although the researches done by political scientists in all
three of the degrees of penetration that have been suggested here
have the capacity to make some contribution to political knowledge, the claims that they make as to the relevance of that knowledge depend on a proper relation of the various levels of understanding to one another. Thus it is not the findings of a behavioral
political science that disorient theory, for radical empiricism can
yield results that the theorist may use. It is rather the claim to exhaust the knowledge of things political (*i.e.*, the lack of awareness
of behavioralism's limitations) that results in its capacity for cor-

ruption. The examples we have given of the traditionalist historic-analytic school indicate that those who work within its confines are much more aware of its limitations of methods and results than is the behavioralist school in relation to its own activities. The modesty of the historic-analytic claim prevents its craftsmen from indulging in the temptation (amply warned against on the highest level by Strauss and Voegelin) of supposing that the possibilities of man's ultimate knowledge of reality are unlimited and therefore that the possibilities of what may be done through politics are similarly unlimited.

We have no assurance that the voice of the real theorist, the philosophical anthropologist, will be heeded any more than that of the prophet. The superiority of their grasp on reality may be recognized by those who are not capable themselves of reaching it, but we have no assurance that such recognition will take place, and the application of this knowledge by force rather than by persuasion results in its loss for practical purposes. Plato, after all, failed to reorder Athenian society, but his achievement lives on. The quest for political anthropology based on philosophical anthropology— the science of man as a whole—will continue to be pursued by those gifted theoreticians who are capable of it. The remainder of us must do what we are able to do and hopefully anticipate that their work may become effective for existential society.

III The Philosophical Underpinnings of the Contemporary Controversy in American Political Science

For more than two decades the practitioners of American political science have been engaged in a continuing struggle over the nature of the discipline. Like all such academic controversies the battle has waxed and waned at various intervals; numerous pleas for peace have been made in language more suited to protagonists in a cold war than to potential allies in a common cause; and, like all internal disorders of such apparently grave practical consequences, the upheaval has spread in such a manner as to confuse not only the intellectual boundaries of the conflict but the identity of the loyalties and alignments of the combatants themselves.

Primarily for convenience in dating the joining of the controversy—and note that I do not say the joining of the issues—we may suggest that the appearance of David Easton's *Political System* in 1953 provides as useful a benchmark as any. The groundwork had, of course, been laid earlier: The Social Science Research Council report of 1944 projected the idea of a behavioral approach; the same organization formed a committee on political behavior in 1945, which it reorganized in 1949; and David Truman set forth the basic premises of behavioralism in a report on some aspects of that group's activities in 1951.[1] And one must not neglect to recall the efforts of Rice, Merriam, Lasswell, and others in the 1920s and 1930s, because their "scientific" efforts presaged the developments of the 1940s and 1950s. It is also important to recollect what some behavioralists seem to have overlooked—that the challenge of positivism to prior conceptions of knowledge goes well back into the nineteenth century, and (under a different nomenclature) further back than that. In an even broader dimension it can be said

---

1. David B. Truman, "The Implications of Political Behavior Research," Social Science Research Council *Items*, V (December, 1951), 37–39.

that empiricism as a useful method for the study of politics is at least as ancient as Aristotle, a fact which makes the pejorative use of the term *traditional* even more ironic than it would otherwise be.

But I choose the publication of Easton's book as the critical event because it launched a full-scale attack on the prevailing condition of the academic study of politics, elaborated in some detail the regulative ideas and methodology of what was to become known among adherents as the "new" political science, introduced or refined most of the standard terminology associated with behavioralism, and ascribed to nonconforming efforts the characteristic term *traditionalism*. *The Political System* even went so far as to disengage the study of political behavior—and *behavioralism* in general—from the stimulus-response psychological school of *behaviorism* which had flourished in the 1920s, although not all subsequent discourses on the difference between behaviorism and behavioralism acknowledge even a casual acquaintance with Easton's dissociation of the latter concept from the former.[2] At any rate, if memory serves me adequately, most of the conscious self-identification of persons in the profession as behavioralists or nonbehavioralists, most of the attempts to categorize the works of others in terms of this dichotomy, and most of the tendencies to subject the problem of political understanding to methodological preconceptions have been subsequent to the appearance of Easton's book.

Although no member of the profession could doubt the strength of the feelings aroused over the bifurcation that was taking place, even those most deeply committed could hardly fail to be shocked by the acerbic exchange in the *American Political Science Review* in 1963 between Schaar and Wolin and the contributors to *Essays on the Scientific Study of Politics*, a book which may well have established a new record for titular misdirection.[3] The language of the disputants was not simply acrimonious, it was shrill; not only was the hostility on both sides manifest, but a pervasive sense of

2. David Easton, *The Political System* (New York: Knopf, 1953), 151.

3. John H. Schaar and Sheldon S. Wolin, "Essays on the Scientific Study of Politics: A Critique," and Herbert J. Storing *et al.*, "Replies to Schaar and Wolin," *American Political Science Review*, LVII (March, 1963), 125–50, 151–60; Herbert J. Storing (ed.), *Essays on the Scientific Study of Politics* (New York: Holt, Rinehart and Winston, 1962).

malice was obviously savored by the participants. Such naked ex-
tremism could hardly be countenanced among civilized colleagues; for a time, at least, a predisposition toward tolerance of
opposing views made itself felt, and an acceptance of the common
conditions on which rational discourse depends appeared to be in
the offing.

This is not to say, however, that the breach was closed. Later I
shall say something about the *political* nature of the controversy,
which is a contributing factor to the difficulty of establishing a
rapprochement. Over and above this, fundamental philosophical
disagreement divides behavioralists and nonbehavioralists, and
this point of contention is all the more acute because it is rarely
articulated with any clarity or detail in the massive and still ac-
cumulating literature on the subject, even in those rare cases in
which the philosophical consequences of the argument seem to be
explicitly or implicitly recognized. Furthermore, since the mid-
1960s the opponents of behavioralism have, through rapidly ac-
celerating activity (both in writing and in actual political participation), taken over the role of insurgency in the profession, thereby
reducing the behavioralists to a posture of defensive conservatism. In thus seizing the initiative as proponents of the "advancement" of the discipline (or, in the usual cliché, becoming the group
that is working "at the frontiers of knowledge"), the more recent
(and more vociferous) opponents of behavioralism have rapidly
reversed the previous position in which the behavioralists were in
the forefront of the effort to effect radical change in the orientation
of political science. The "new" political science is no longer behavioralism. In much the same manner that the behavioralists once
attacked the nonbehavioralists, the *anti*behavioralists (or *post*behavioralists) now attack behavioralism.

My intention in this essay is to try to expose the philosophical
differences between behavioralists and nonbehavioralists by examining the implications—or at least some of the implications—
that are attendant upon the assumption of a behavioral or a nonbehavioral position. For this reason I shall try to avoid what I think
are the usual points of controversy in favor of a somewhat broader
and more eclectic argument. I will not, for example, engage in
much discussion of method as such, on the grounds that method
is largely a derivative of epistemological preconceptions, and that

discussions of method without acknowledgment of the underlying theory of knowledge on which the "scientific" or any other method of studying politics depends lead in the current disputes, more often than not, to homilies on the separability or nonseparability of facts and values or some related issue of practice. By the same token, I shall try not to wax eloquent on such questions as the triviality or importance of the work done by behavioralists or nonbehavioralists because these issues, too, are dependent on more fundamental theoretical considerations. I shall try not to give in even to the temptation to point out the many contradictions among both behavioralists and nonbehavioralists about the central concerns of political science, and the difficulty of reconciling these central concerns with proposed methods of studying politics. Anything at all that is added to arguments long since stale from repetition may appear to be supererogatory, but since the dispute is obviously going on, and since much of the argumentative support for one side or the other seems to be more involved with gamesmanship relative to the opposition than with clarification of fundamental issues, it may be useful to try to return to the simplest elements of political experience and to expand that experience to the point at which the current philosophical differences had their inceptions. In this way perhaps the elemental disagreements will be clarified.

William Ebenstein has pointed out—and he is by no means the first to have done so—that all conceptions of politics have their base in a more general philosophy involving conceptions of the world and man's place in it. At the elemental empirical level, anthropologists have found that the members of even the most primitive societies seem to share interpretations of their place in the universe and of all of their "practical" activities that are internally consistent. Indeed, all serious discussions of politics from the most ancient surviving sources right through contemporary writings express, either overtly or covertly, a basic concern with what has been referred to as the "quaternarian structure," namely, the interrelations among man and society, the universe and God.[4] Even if the demise of God is accepted and we pose the problem as triangular,

4. William Ebenstein, *Modern Political Thought* (2nd ed.; New York: Holt, Rinehart and Winston, 1960), 3; Eric Voegelin, *Israel and Revelation* (Baton Rouge: Louisiana State University Press, 1956), Vol. I of Eric Voegelin, *Order and History*, 5 vols. projected.

the effort to integrate (or separate) man, nature, and society in a theoretical way is implicit, if not explicit, in every interpretation of politics that I know. It can be said even more simply, and in a manner considered anachronistic by many commentators, that all plausible attempts at generalization about the nature of politics rest on declared or undeclared sets of premises about the nature of man. Even those who vociferously deny that there is a "nature of man" affirm in the denial a theory of the nature of man; more often than not the internal evidence in the writings or lectures of those who make such denials shows them to assume a relativistic position in which "culture," "nature," or some other causal factor shapes man's pliable being into whatever structure is being described and analyzed.

If elementary introspection reveals anything to us that can be accepted as verifiable evidence by almost anyone who can think at all, it reveals, (in a manner reminiscent of the Cartesian position) a self-identifying, percipient being. And if immediate sensual apprehension (mingled at the source, of course, with perception) can tell us anything that can be accepted as verifiable evidence by virtually anyone possessed of one or more of the five senses, it tells us that we live in a world peopled by other self-identifying, percipient beings. And, just as in our relation to other aspects of the real or ideal external world, we react to those other beings both emotionally and cognitively. Out of these reactions we build up methods of communication by which we try, among other things, to bridge the gap between the self and the other, and to perceive that which is common (*i.e.*, that which in its parts manifests itself as belonging to a whole beyond the self) and that which is individual, and how the two are related. Out of this complex of passions and awareness come the elemental forms of cooperation, the symbiotic or "living-together" process, and eventually the whole architectonic structure of man in society. But here I am anticipating myself by suggesting that what is involved is an enormous creative process, whereby certain capacities in man—his nature, as it were—enable him to transform himself from a percipient individual into a man in society who is capable not only of comprehending the external world in a number of different ways but also of transcending the limitations of the self even to the point of comprehending the basic needs and interests of other sentient beings and entering into a relation of comity with those other sentient beings in whom he recognizes likeness or commonality.

Now it seems to me that, in relation to these elemental experiences as they have been transformed through history into the complexities of contemporary life, and as they have been subjected to a variety of interpretations so prolific as to dazzle the imagination, there are only three basic philosophical positions which one can assume and attempt to validate in a consistent manner. I am not forgetting that the number of philosophical systems is legion or that the refinements within each (and cutting across some of them) are incredibly complex and rich in their diversity. But it must be remembered that an attempt is being made to reach to the elemental level on which the proliferation is based and that, while there is danger in simplifying, the opportunity for undetected error and diversion increases with the level of complexity at which the problems are approached. So at this point I want to suggest that, so far as I can detect, all those who engage in political theory in any form (and any deliberate effort to make politics intelligible involves some theoretical engagement) are positivists or transcendentalists (perhaps the term *idealist* is preferable here) or skeptics. Again, I cannot possibly deal adequately with even the fundamentals of these three philosophical positions, let alone indicate the breadth of their respective theoretical potentialities or practical consequences. Nonetheless I am compelled to suggest certain characteristic doctrines of each, to project some of the methodological presuppositions that follow from these doctrines, and to acknowledge the relation of each position to certain tendencies in the world of pragmatic politics.

Positivism, in its modern version, is largely attributed to Auguste Comte, although its main features were implicit in a number of earlier social and political philosophers and many of its principal tenets are virtually synonymous with the origins of philosophy. Its primary metaphysical assumption—and I cannot accept the positivist claim to having excluded metaphysics entirely from its purview—may be said to be based initially on naïve realism. That is to say, the external world is structured as we perceive it through our senses, and all of our knowledge is derived from observation in one form or another. An element of naturalism runs through positivism whereby it is assumed that all of nature (*i.e.*, the universe) is structured in such a way that causal and noncausal relationships can be discerned, classified, and explained theoretically, apparently because all parts of the universe are subject to laws of uniformity and determined relationships.[5]

Positivism thus adopts what might be called a "flat" or horizontal logic, in which there are no "higher" or "lower" levels of being; instead all objects of perception (including the perceptive and cognitive processes themselves) are subject to the same types of scientific laws and are open to the same methods of investigation. Objects are identifiable in terms of the relative complexity of their organizations, rather than in terms of the differentiation of their basic substances. Truth consists solely of propositions verifiable through cumulative observation, although observation itself may, of course, be aided and refined through the use of more complex tools by which the perceptions may be extended.

The methodology of positivism follows consistently from these conceptions of existence and logic; the positivists tend to be radical empiricists. They deal only with "facts," *i.e.*, with data which may be observed in the same form by anyone, and they frame hypotheses in a form which is subject to empirical verification and to replication by any other investigator. They take as their model the methods of the natural sciences and insist that knowledge is valid only insofar as it conforms to the canons of scientific procedure.

Persons who may be identified as transcendentalists, on the other hand, take an altogether contrary view of man, nature, and the universe. In a simplified form, they may be said to make a basic distinction between the objects of the external world and the intelligence which comprehends that world. This is one of the reasons I have suggested that some might prefer the use of the term *idealist* rather than *transcendentalist*, although philosophical idealism as a "school' has been more concerned with the logical co-

5. Alfred North Whitehead, *Science and the Modern World* (New York: Mentor Books, 1948), 19–20, discusses the relation between "faith in reason," which lies at the basis of the trust of modern science in the nonarbitrariness of the ultimate nature of things, and the deeper faith of the Western tradition.

herence of concrete experience as a whole than with the sources and meaning of the special human capacities for comprehension of existence as such.[6] At any rate, the transcendentalist tends to accept the structure of the external world as being determined by its own laws and open to abstract comprehension through the analytic quantitative methods of science, but holds that man and society are different substantively, insofar as man is at least partly self-determining and creative and is therefore able to rise to some extent above his natural limitations—*i.e.*, to transcend the limits of his own sensory modes of perception so as to grasp (albeit limitedly) truth, beauty, and goodness as existent realities. Although some transcendentalists may be pure idealists (in the limited sense of accepting ideas as the sole basis of reality), as a general rule they are more likely to be metaphysical dualists.

By contrast with the "flat" logic of the positivist, the transcendentalist tends to adhere to a hierarchic logic. In many, although not all, cases this is derivative from Aristotelian logic, with its hierarchy of being extending in a steadily ascending scale from the lowest level of inanimate objects up through man and ultimately to God. Each successive stage is characterized not only by increasing complexity but by its having transcended all the lower forms and by having added thereto its own special form and substance. Causality is similarly differentiated, and all levels of being move toward their own particular ends as well as toward the end of the whole.[7]

Naturally the methodology of the transcendentalist differs in many respects from that of the positivist. For our purposes the main distinction is that the transcendentalist does not accept the restrictions imposed by the scientism of the positivist. Knowledge

6. See, for example, W. H. Greenleaf's discussion of idealism (essentially *British* idealism), in *Oakeshott's Philosophical Politics* (New York: Barnes and Noble, 1966), 8, in which he holds that idealism has no ontology or cosmology and generally tends to eschew the problem of the ultimate meaning of life. However, Greenleaf seems to me to be generalizing from a special case; theorists of politics of all varieties tend to display implicit ontologies and cosmologies and to be concerned with the ultimate problems of life. And idealism's basic premise of the logical coherence of experience carries with it strong transcendental intimations.

7. G. R. G. Mure, *An Introduction to Hegel* (Oxford: Clarendon Press, 1948), Chaps. I–VI, is the clearest exposition I have seen of the Aristotelian logic whch forms the basis for much of modern philosophical idealism.

for him does not consist solely of the accumulation and hypothetical ordering of observed "fact"; it also consists of rational or even suprarational processes by which, in Kantian terms, those things which belong to the realm of the practical understanding can be comprehended as forms of reality; and it is by means of this comprehension that we order our private and public life. Thus such questions as the "good" or "right" or "justice" are not mere abstractions belonging to the area of preference or opinion, but are precisely the type of problems that men are required to confront and solve in their creative process of living together. The laws of society for the transcendentalist are not naturalistic, but are prescriptive, although the objective prescriptions must take into account certain necessities of the natural world which impinge upon the choices that are available. Although empiricism can provide much useful information, to the transcendentalist man and society are differently constituted as compared with the objective world of nature and therefore must be approached in a different manner. This differentiation between man and nature (over and above the elements in common) is the source of the trancendentalist's concern with ethics, with history (as a continuum of the creative effort of man to live symbolically with his fellow man and his environment), and with legal and other institutional "carriers" of major ethical and political attributes.

The skeptic, by way of contrast with the positivist and the transcendentalist, makes no claim to objective comprehension of the real world. On the contrary, his skepticism consists precisely in the denial of any real connection between cognition and the reality of the external world. Hume is, of course, the modern prototype of the skeptic. If his arguments are accepted, the ground is cut from under both the positivists and the transcendentalists, although with the usual human propensity toward the cunning legitimation of doctrinal persuasion, both the positivists and the transcendentalists have selected from Hume those proofs which support their respective positions and ignored the rest. By and large the positivists accept Hume's separation of fact, reason, and value, but disregard his negation of knowledge of causality and, to some extent, his limitations on the use of reason. The transcendentalists, on the other hand, are likely to embrace the arguments against facticity, while they overlook the negative implications of Hume's theory of reason and value.

Skeptics avoid commitment to the logic of either the positivists or the transcendentalists. Since the world is unknowable in its real form it is equally futile to talk of a uniform logic embracing all experience or a hierarchically structured logic embracing various levels of experience. The function of reason in the Humean sense is limited to inferences from unverifiable propositions.

By the same token, if knowledge is not possible, it is futile to talk about method in any definitive sense. Science can proceed to its practical results on the basis of probability; in the social milieu the skeptic is inclined toward a conventionalist view, although in extreme cases (and especially those in which intellectual skepticism takes place within a disintegrating society) skepticism may culminate in nihilism. Ordinarily, and again following Hume, the skeptic will accept the necessity for making practical decisions from day to day in the area of social and political life, but will confine those decisions to an extension of the traditional or conventional way of doing things within the special context of his own society, taking it for granted that the conventions have a certain utilitarian value based on experience with their use. The skeptic's method (if it may be called method) is inclined in the social sciences toward historical empiricism or social pragmatism. What the skeptic denies philosophically, he frequently tends to restore through common sense in his confrontation with the necessities of practical existence.

All of the foregoing descriptions may appear to be somewhat arcane in relation to the division of the political science profession into behavioralists and nonbehavioralists. So the time has come to try to establish the connection or, as the behavioralist might say, to attempt to "validate the hypothetical linkage."

Even in the cases in which they have not openly declared themselves to be such, the overwhelming internal evidence of their writing points to the conclusion that the behavioralists are thoroughgoing positivists. Although the attempt to characterize the behavioral "persuasion" or the behavioral "mood" by the behavioralists themselves is so discursive that I had to turn to a nonbehavioralist for a succinct characterization a few years ago, some

excerpts from the behavioralists will illustrate the positivist underpinnings. David Truman, for instance, points out that the study
of political behavior attempts to state "all the phenomena of government in terms of the observed and observable behavior of men."
He elaborates on behavioral method by pointing out that "research must grow out of a precise statement of hypotheses and a
rigorous ordering of evidence" and that primary emphasis must
be placed upon "empirical methods." Furthermore, "the ultimate
goal of the student of political behavior is the development of a
science of the political process." And in another broader illustration, Easton quotes Beard in a headnote to *The Political System*
(presumably with approval) as follows: "No one can deny that the
idea is fascinating—the idea of subduing the phenomena of politics to the laws of causation, of penetrating to the mystery of its
transformations, of symbolizing the trajectory of its future; in a
word, of grasping destiny by the forelock and bringing it prostrate
to earth."[8] Again, we should note, for purposes of illustration, how
often we run into the phrase "a predictive science of politics" in
the behavioral literature, and I can discern little indication that
the authors have in mind a mere projection of probabilities; they
seem almost invariably to be speaking in absolute terms.

It would be possible to extend these examples almost indefinitely, but I think the main point is now clear: The underlying
philosophical assumptions of behavioralism, the logical system
which it projects, and the methodological conformity on which it
insists are positivistic. Behavioralists differ among themselves in
a number of ways, which we cannot pursue here, but philosophically there is a substantial orthodoxy and the substance of that orthodoxy is in direct conflict with nonbehavioral political science
because of the latter's antipositivist foundations.

Most nonbehavioral political science in the United States tends
toward the transcendentalist view, and perhaps the gravest charge
that can be made against a large portion of those who belong in
this category is that they are not aware of their own philosophical
commitment. Two groups of transcendentalists stand out as hav-

8. Dwight Waldo, *Political Science in the United States of America* (Paris:
UNESCO, 1956), 21 ff.; Truman, "The Implications of Political Behavior Research," 37 ff.; Easton; *The Political System*, [vii].

ing clearly accepted the role: The Aristotelian or rational transcendentalists on the one hand, and the theological transcendentalists on the other. Most prominent among the former are Leo Strauss and the whole Strauss school; among the latter could be included John Hallowell, Reinhold Niebuhr, and possibly Eric Voegelin. But I would argue that many other nonbehavioralists are implicit or unacknowledged trancendentalists. Quite a few of the orthodox constitutional law people, as well as many institutionalists and students of political processes of all varieties, reflect a sort of unselfconscious transcendentalism. In most instances the latter types disagree with the behavioralists emotionally, but cannot seem to explain why, so they are usually accused of being too intellectually worn to retread for the long behavioral road to a science of politics. The new antibehavioralists are also trancendentalists in their assumptions about objective experience, and by reason of their acceptance of the idea of the possibility of the transformation of man and society through the self-conscious setting of new moral and political ends.

Transcendentalists, acknowledged or unacknowledged, disagree with the positivists primarily on the grounds previously cited in distinguishing the two philosophical traditions. They regard man and society as belonging to an order of things different from that pertaining to the structure of the natural world, and they therefore regard the study of the two realms as requiring different regulative ideas and different methods. While not rejecting the uses of empiricism, they do not wish to exclude the attempt to validate the "good" objectively; indeed they think the most important questions of politics belong to the area of practical reason and relate mainly to ethical questions such as What is a good man?, a good society?, etc. With Aristotle they accept it as "the mark of an educated man to look for precision in each class of things just so far as the nature of the subject admits,"[9] and they perceive in human behavior all the uncertainties attendant upon the conflict between necessity and free choice, emotional predispositions and rational decisions, and aspiration and natural limitations. Consequently they will nearly always regard the possibility of a

9. Aristotle, *Nicomachean Ethics*, Book I, 1094b.

predictive science of politics as utopian; they will accept the notions behind probability theory, but will continue to regard man's
capacity to make decisions freely as an overwhelming limit on all
but the most tentative extrapolations about the future. In this respect they share with the skeptics some serious doubts about the
attainment of complete knowledge.

It is doubtful that there are very many full-blown skeptics among
American political scientists. However, in the interest of providing concrete examples of each of the three philosophical positions,
I would cite two groups who seem to me to fit into this category.
One is the existentialists, and the other consists of Michael Oakeshott and a small (but possibly enlarging) group of persons influenced by Oakeshott. The nature of existentialism largely precludes any coherent explanation of politics, unless one wishes to
include Camus among its adherents, even in the face of his explicit
rejection of the designation. In Oakeshott, however, we have a clear
and even eloquent expression by the skeptic as political theorist.
And for him, as for Hume, the solution to political problems lies in
the practice of politics. Empiricism, rationalism, or any other
method will not provide knowledge of politics. Both causal theory
and the possibility of objective knowledge of the moral or theological grounds of right action in politics are rejected. Although politics is ubiquitous and apparently necessary, it is not derivative,
but in Oakeshott's own words is a "self-moved manner of activity"
whose meaning is exhausted in the doing. We learn how to maintain the system through experience with it, but of its creation or
its roots in reality we can apparently know nothing.[10]

One of the charming, if exasperating, attributes of man is his capacity for inconsistency. So we should never really expect his actions to follow his explanations with relentless fidelity. And so we
would not accuse the devotees of a particular systematic philosophy of intellectual dishonesty if they fail to act on all of the implications of that philosophy in practical affairs. Nevertheless, it may

10. Michael Oakeshott, *Political Education: Inaugural Lecture at the London
School of Economics* (Cambridge: Bowes and Bowes, 1951), is probably the best
succinct statement of Oakeshott's overall view of political understanding and its
relation to the practice of politics. Although Oakeshott is, by philosophical heritage, an idealist, his doubts about the possibility of comprehensive knowledge of
politics amount to a basic epistemological skepticism.

be helpful in explaining the cleavages among the philosophical schools we have been discussing to see something of the courses their representatives are inclined to follow in the area of contemporary political practice.

Among behavioralists I note—and I am far from the first to have done so—a strong proclivity toward the adoption of a value system that is purposive and authoritative, despite the tenuous basis of these concepts in their philosophical predisposition. Scratch a behavioralist, and nine times out of ten you will expose a liberal social democrat, regardless of the fact that one might expect to find either an uncommitted man or a classical liberal of the variety of Jeremy Bentham or Herbert Spencer. After all, the empirical nature of his pursuits encourages the behavioralist to fix on the individual as the unit to be analyzed,[11] and the aggregate of individuals in a society might be expected to conform to natural laws of interaction about which man can do nothing deliberately. The explanation for this seeming contradiction lies, I believe, in the unarticulated reasons why many political scientists adhere to behavioralism. Such persons are, in my opinion, basically progressivist reformers, and their faith in science as the progenitor of technological change leads them to an implicit assumption by analogy that society can be transformed through the perfection of social knowledge by means of imitating science in the study of society. This point has been well elaborated by others,[12] so I mention it only in passing here.

The transcendentalists are a more diffuse lot in social outlook, but they, too, often contradict in practice the implications that are inherent in their pronouncements from the professorial chair. Let me cite examples. Some of the more conservative among them (especially the neoconservatives such as Russell Kirk and the academicians attached to the *National Review*) tend to defy the logic

11. Group theory, which enjoyed a great vogue in the early 1950s, following the publication of David Truman's *Political Process* (New York: Knopf, 1951), might be considered an exception, but the emphasis on "interest" as the basis of group coherence makes most group theories, from Bentley onward, essentially dependent on the elemental collectivization of individual behavioral tendencies.

12. See, for example, Mulford Q. Sibley, "The Limits of Behavioralism," in James C. Charlesworth (ed.), *The Limits of Behavioralism in Political Science* (Philadelphia: American Academy of Political and Social Science, 1962), esp. 83 ff.

of their emphasis on free choice and the notion of common good by adhering to a conception of economic policy much more suited to the mechanistic naturalism of the positivist than to the idealism of the transcendentalist. And some of the more reformist types among them appear sometimes to forget the tenuous nature of the social structure and the inherent limitations in the human situation in their enthusiasm for sweeping practical change. The academic exponents of the New Left (about whom more is said below) are the most immediate case in point, and this group constitutes the core of the new *anti*behavioral mode.

Among the skeptics, existentialists such as Sartre seem to me to confound all expectation by joining the mood of despair and an emphasis on the absurdity of existence to a Marxian concern for the common man and for the perfectionist possibility in history. But Oakeshott and his followers seem to me fairly consistent in following Hume's lead in the direction of a bemused, genteel, and tolerant conservatism, although in his affinity with the economic and property doctrines of classical individualistic liberalism Oakeshott comes close to ideological closure around a naturalistic assumption.[13]

In the latter connection it seems to me that Oakeshottians have a useful lesson for application in the philosophical controversy between the positivists and the transcendentalists. Skeptics such as Oakeshott are not too much inclined to militancy in action, they possess the capacity to criticize without destruction, and they are prepared to judge a political action on the basis of its results rather than on advance claims. Surely the profession in this country could take a lesson in practice from this set of attitudes. I suggest that if each shoemaker is allowed to work at his own last, some useful products will be forthcoming from all the different types of artisans and, just as surely, we will be able, unless we deliberately turn a blind eye to results, to tell the difference between a delicate pair of dancing slippers and a set of clodhoppers.

And now mainly because both behavioralism and the current form of antibehavioralism, by their own interpretations, are relatively new and pose such strong challenges to one another and to

13. See, for example, Michael Oakeshott, "The Political Economy of Freedom," *Rationalism in Politics, and Other Essays* (New York: Basic Books, 1962), 37–58.

political science as a whole, it may be useful to point out a few mis-
directions that each is prone to take. I have already indicated that
there are those on both sides of the controversy who are boorish in
their argumentative behavior, but I do not believe that either party
has had its attention as forcibly called to its elemental sins of
omission and commission as it has to those extraneous characteristics that are relatively easy to dramatize in controversy.

Among the behavioralists, the first questionable practice that
should be cited is the tendency to transform the behavioral movement from a scientific into an ideological political movement. Of
course, all movements, scientific and otherwise, have their political implications.[14] And one has only to look at the bent of the Social Science Research Council to see how great the effort has been
to spread the doctrine. One cannot fail to be conscious, moreover,
of the openly admitted attempt to capture the professional journals, the social science sections of foundations, and even whole departments. No less an eminence than Robert Dahl referred to the
behavioral movement as a "revolt," and a successful one at that.[15]
From personal experience I could cite many examples of both
veiled hints and open suggestions that one had better get into line
or suffer the consequences. In a minor key, one was earlier aware
that many departments were beset by pressures to look specifically for a behavioralist rather than the best person available
within an established field, just as we are now becoming aware
of the necessity to seek out an exemplar of the new *anti*behavioral type.

But I am less concerned about these kinds of activities—because they can be accommodated or defended against on their own
terms—than I am about another aspect of the ideological struggle
that may do violence to intellectual pursuits as such. I refer to a
rather common tendency to rely on the *authority* of science to es-

14. Sheldon Wolin has written an interesting paper on this question in which
he utilizes T. Kuhn's idea that a "scientific community" is constituted and held together authoritatively by the existence of a "paradigm" of scientific practice which
determines the validity of individual efforts. See Wolin's essay "Paradigms and Political Theories," in Preston King and B. C. Parekh (ed.), *Politics and Experience*
(Cambridge: University Press, 1968), 125–52.

15. Robert A. Dahl, "The Behavioral Approach in Political Science: Epitaph for
a Monument to a Successful Protest," *American Political Science Review*, LV (December, 1961), 770.

tablish a claim to knowledge rather than allow the results of scientific procedure to speak for themselves. The philosophical danger in this tendency is acute: Severe limitations are placed on the
possibility of interpreting experience in the variety of modes in
which it manifests itself and of making some sense of the consciousness of experience as a whole. If one abstracts from experience only those things which may be handled quantitatively, any
possibilities of validating other epistemologies and methodolo-
gies are foreclosed, as are the possibilities of raising certain types
of questions which seem introspectively to be fundamental to the
understanding of politics. Let me cite some specific, and varying,
manifestations of this tendency. The following "classification" of
political scientists is a case in point:

> We are content to identify (1) political theologians, (2) political histo-
> rians, (3) political engineers, (4) political anecdotalists, and (5) political
> behavioralists. All differ markedly in their intellectual concerns, in the
> audiences they write for, in the things they read, and in the goals they
> have set for themselves.
>
> Political theology is concerned with such questions as "How should
> men live together?," "What is a good man?," and "What is a good so-
> ciety?" Theologians formulate and defend answers to questions such as
> these. . . .
>
> The political historian seeks factual information. One form of history
> popular with political scientists is intellectual history. . . . Another
> equally honorable branch of political historiography concerns the
> doings and decrees of jurists. . . .
>
> The task of the political engineer is to reform the present. Plans for
> "efficiency and economy," and legal, constitutional and organizational
> change spring from this tradition in political science. . . .
>
> Under the rubric of anecdotalists we classify those who are, in the
> main, historians of the present. These political scientists see as their goal
> the reconstruction of "what happened." This branch of political sci-
> ence bears the closest resemblance to journalism. . . .
>
> On the whole, political behavioralists can be distinguished from their
> fellow political scientists by the close attention they are apt to pay to
> what is going on in one or more of the other social sciences: social psy-
> chology, psychiatry, sociology, economics, and anthropology. . . . A sec-
> ond characteristic of political behavioralists is, as we have said, their
> attempt to explain political events "scientifically." Let us move, then,
> to a brief description of what is meant by a "scientific" approach to the
> study of politics.

"Science" is in one sense a way of organizing information, in another a series of directives about how to proceed in gaining new knowledge, in another a social institution embracing many members who have a special code of behavior. When knowledge about a particular subject matter is organized "scientifically," when new knowledge about the subject is gathered according to "scientific" rules, and when students of the subject obey the "scientific" code of professional behavior, we call the subject matter a "science."[16]

Now I submit that no empirical procedure could lead to a classification of political scientists into the typology indicated here, because no groups of political scientists that I know of conform to the elementary patterns described or work in the manner laid out here. Furthermore, the old logical fallacy of "poisoning the well" is so blatantly committed that only one emotionally charged with ideological commitment could find the characterizations plausible. Finally, the characterization of "science" and the "scientific approach" is a near-perfect example of the point I have attempted to make about the necessary conformity of all knowledge to the authoritative canons of a particular way of pursuing knowledge which is characteristic of behavioralism.

Let us take two more examples, one negative and one positive, of a related use of political rather than scientific canons for establishing the validity of behavioralism. More than ten years ago, Bernard Crick wrote a provocative critique of behavioralism entitled *The American Science of Politics*.[17] Yet the only references and reviews that I have seen by behavioralists have dismissed his criticisms out of hand by charging him with a "straw man" argument or by asserting (which amounts to much the same thing) that Crick concentrated on the earlier examples of the movement and failed to take into account the later and more refined contributions. These criticisms may be valid, but they can only be shown to be so by confronting Crick's arguments directly and not by a display of pique.

On the positive side, a *Journal of Politics* article by James W. Prothro and Charles M. Grigg has frequently been cited in behav-

16. Nelson W. Polsby, Robert A. Dentler, and Paul A. Smith (eds.), *Politics and Social Life* (Boston: Houghton Mifflin, 1963), 2–4.
17. Bernard Crick, *The American Science of Politics: Its Origins and Conditions* (London: Routledge and Kegan Paul, 1959).

ioral literature as an example of the successful application of the empirical method to disprove the necessity of a consensus in the operation of a democratic society. I reread this article quite carefully in the course of preparing this essay and was again dismayed that those who insist so strongly on the proper framing of hypotheses and on precision of investigation should accept at face value the purported results of the investigation. The possible criticisms are legion: Virtually every question raised is begged and the overall conclusion is dictated by the procedure followed. The standards for establishing consensus are so high as to be literally unobtainable in any except a society of total conformity, the abstract standards of democracy are primitively conceived, and the barest lip service is paid either to the fact that an affirmation of a general principle on the part of those interviewed is as often as not contradicted in detail, or to the possible validity of the notion of negative consensus. Beyond all this, the whole problem of the acceptance by individual respondents of conventional forms of authority as a deterrent to action which does not conform to underlying societal beliefs is not effectively touched on. I suggest that the reception accorded this article is a prime example of the use of the symbol of science as the basis for political authority in establishing behavioralism as a procedure appropriate to the acquisition of knowledge. Behavioralists above all should be concerned to criticize the inadequate application of their own tenets as these inadequacies are reflected in the results. Science, too, develops by means of criticism, especially from among its own practitioners.[18]

A second tendency that should be touched upon is the threat to the corruption of the language posed by some behavioral literature. Although science may require a special language either as a

18. James W. Prothro and Charles M. Grigg, "Fundamental Principles of Democracy: Bases of Agreement and Disagreement," *Journal of Politics*, XXII (May, 1960), 276–94. Among numerous citations (almost invariably in concurrence with the conclusions reached in the article) is that of Dahl, "The Behavioral Approach in Political Science," 771 n. 21. A quick perusal of a number of "readers" emphasizing behavioral materials suggests that this must be one of the most widely reprinted items in the entire literature of the profession. I have seen only one critical analysis of the Prothro and Grigg article (among other anticonsensus positions) and that by a nonbehavioralist. See Fred M. Wilhoite, Jr., "Political Order and Consensus: A Continuing Problem," *Western Political Quarterly*, XVI (June, 1963), 294–304.

shortcut in exposition or, more important, for precision in differentiating concepts, it is to be used only where its utility clearly outweighs its disadvantages. It should not be adopted as a substitute for thinking, or to complicate relatively simple concepts in the interest of displaying erudition, or as a presumed concession to demands of a political nature. As a shortcut on my own homework, I have cribbed the following example from a review by Henry Kariel in the *American Political Science Review* a few years ago:

> It is this thrust toward the devitalized and the dehumanized, the formal and the abstract, that justifies, in my judgment, a reservation about the health of American political science. My scruple may be given point by considering the rhetoric, the literary style (not to say grammar), of those who so earnestly pray for "formalization." . . . Hardly anything is to be gained . . . from coming to terms with the radically . . . simple pronouncement (it is Peter H. Rossi's) that "in the course of pursuing a task, groups of individuals, who had hitherto no enduring relationship to each other, rapidly develop a social organization the nature of which affects the way in which they come to decisions and the sort of decisions made" (p. 377). This is as wholly true—who would doubt it?—as the conclusion T. M. Newcomb manages to extract from one body of research: "within certain limiting conditions communication is most likely to occur when there is less rather than more similarity of orientation among potential communicators, and its consequences tend to be those of increasing similarity of orientation" (p. 251). "It seems highly unlikely," another writer informs us, "that a decisional unit could survive constant falsifications of motives" (p. 32).
>
> Snyder duly warns us not to succumb to those who would press us to paraphrase and thereby to vulgarize our findings. Yet how are we to resist when we affirm, for example, that "individuals seem to have characteristic limits within which they can tolerate the strain of perceived dissimilarity with attractive others, at least within a given topical area" (p. 255)? Doesn't this virtually beg for restatement? And, in restated form, is the statement genuinely engaging? Is it relevant to our burdens, our cares, our hopes? . . .
>
> We are put off—certainly some of the contributors themselves are put off—by the trimming and perversion of language. It may be convenient to speak of operationalizing concepts. But must we refer to the fractionation of field? Is it really necessary to say, in so many words, that "only when molar assumptions prove to be flatly contrary to what is known molecularly does the molar principle lose tenability" (pp. 218–19); or that "the whole fabric of society—its institutions, its sub-groups, and its role structure—hinges [yes, hinges] upon the possibility of sim-

ilar orientations to objects (including persons) of common concern" (p. 251); or that in cities "informal participation in friendship relations, with individual friends or friendship circles, is an extremely frequent occurrence" (p. 332)?[19]

To show that I am not altogether lacking in resourcefulness, here is a sample of my own selection: "In the behavioral study of politics, on the other hand, the individual remains the empirical unit of inquiry, but the theoretical units of analysis may be role, group, institution, organization, culture, or system, and so on, whatever conceptual tools may be most adequate for the purpose of a particular investigation."[20] I submit that quite apart from the dubious grammar of that sentence it not only does not tell us anything precise but is internally confused. I doubt, for example, that a "role" may be properly considered as a unit of analysis comparable to those other units with which it is grouped and I am sure that the last clause does not fit logically into the preceding part of the sentence.

Politics is a subject of such eminently practical consequence that we should be even more wary of departures from the language of common discourse than we would be in most other subjects. One sometimes longs to turn a forthright linguistic analyst (or logical positivist) loose on some of the supposedly precise language of the behavioralists.

Finally, I should like to warn against the *ahistorical* propensity of much of behavioral science, although this is an area in which an increasing tendency toward self-correction seems to have developed among the behavioralists themselves. So far as we are aware, man is the only creature to develop a conscious history, and many areas of his behavior cannot be analyzed except through the aid of historical understanding. My own research in voting patterns in Louisiana, for example, revealed that issues long since apparently dead can be dredged up under appropriate circumstances and made viable because there is something like Durkheim's collective

19. Henry S. Kariel, Review of Roland Young (ed.), *Approaches to the Study of Politics*, in *American Political Science Review*, LIII (March, 1959), 186.

20. Heinz Eulau, "Segments of Political Science Most Susceptible to Behavioristic Treatment," in Charlesworth (ed.), *The Limits of Behavioralism in Political Science*, 31.

consciousness at work in the historical dimension.[21] History and contemporary practice (with all of its complex institutional, conventional, and ideological foundations) are the two most important forms of experience that philosophy has to reconcile interpretatively if we are to achieve any sort of theoretical understanding of politics in relation to the whole of experience. To exclude history from the purview of political science is the easiest way to arrive at a concept of natural social causality, because history provides whatever data are pertinent to the concept of society as a creative act of human mind and will.

The philosophical deficiencies and excesses of the new *anti*behavioral movement are less subject to precise documentation than those of the behavioralists because the literature is still so diffuse. Although some names and a few books and articles can be specifically identified with the genre,[22] much of the expression thus far has been negative (in the sense of being severely critical of behavioralism, with positive alternatives stated mainly in the form of broad generalizations). In many respects the point of departure is so close to that loosely structured ideology generally identified as the New Left that one might easily mistake antibehavioralism as synonymous with the Left Hegelianism of Herbert Marcuse. But the base is considerably broader than that, since it draws on sources that have been identified as politically more moderate (or even conservative) than Marcuse and others associated with the revolutionary Left. What follows, therefore, is more a reflection on discernible tendencies than an effort to come to grips with precisely articulated doctrines.

21. On the self-corrective tendency, see the strictures in Dahl, " The Behavioral Approach in Political Science," 771–72. William C. Havard, Rudolf Heberle, and Perry H. Howard, *The Louisiana Elections of 1960* (Baton Rouge: Louisiana State University Press, 1963).

22. Among the more important names identifiable with the beginnings of the critique of behavioralism and the emergence of the new directions of the antibehavioralists are Christian Bay, Peter Bachrach, and Morton S. Baratz, although many others, of widely varying backgrounds and prior work in political science, are now associated with this intellectual "movement." The most representative collection of writing reflecting the set of attitudes that informs the movement seems to me to be Charles A. McCoy and John Playford (eds.), *Apolitical Politics* (New York: Crowell, 1967). Much of what follows in this discussion draws on the main theme of this volume of essays.

The main criticisms directed at behavioralism set much of the tone of antibehavioralism. The principal charges are that the behavioralists demonstrate a strong—though perhaps unconscious—bias in favor of the values associated with the political status quo, despite their methodological emphasis on scientific objectivity; that they are elitist rather than democratic in their view of the problems of political leadership and political participation; and that they have tended to neglect or ignore the vital issues of public policy. On the first point, it is said that the behavioralists have stressed the fact-value distinction, but that the content of their work shows their basic political bias to be liberal in the classical sense of that term. That is, they assume the continuity of a given political system which has a self-corrective tendency toward equilibrium resulting from the countervailing political pressures through which the interests of individuals and groups are expressed. The pluralistic bias implicit in this position tends to display itself in the form of an expectation that all of society's classes and other groupings, and their respective interests, are effectively represented and reconciled in the continuing political process. The effect is a conservative attitude which limits change to a gradual adjustment within the framework of existing institutions and objectives. The unreflective identification of what is with what ought to be (the naturalistic fallacy, as it were) leads the behavioralists to the further acceptance of the efficacy of the elites who assume the leadership of the more influential groups in contemporary society and, through the domination of these groups, actually control the content of political decisions. Finally, the assumptions of a political equilibrium and of elitism apparently lead to a tendency on the part of the behavioralists to sublimate the idea of a more comprehensive "participatory" democracy, and to the failure to deal with the vital issues of public policy (including the continuation of the war in Vietnam, poverty, racism, the environment, and repression) because the system to which they give theoretical support largely excludes these issues from its purview.

The particular charges of the antibehavioralists against the behavioralists (as I understand them) are set forth here because of the implications they contain for the positive aspirations that the exponents of the new position have for political science. As is often the case with fundamental philosophical positions, the refutations of the antibehavioralists seem to me to be much less ambiguous than their affirmations. But one thing seems reasonably clear, and that is that their positive position is necessarily transcendentalist in its philosophical implications. No limit seems to be placed on the capacity of man to transform himself or his society through the potential for creative action in politics. The logical frame is hierarchic; human ends are the ultimate objective; and these are expressed, more often than not, in such abstract moral terms as *equality, social justice, participatory democracy*, and *freedom*.

Unfortunately, when one looks for the epistemological foundations on which the implicit metaphysics, ontology, and ethics of the "new" antibehavioral political science are erected, they are extremely difficult to discover. And this is the major defect of omission of this intellectual movement. If the behavioralists tend to confine the epistemological foundations of political science to the narrow limits of a particular methodology, the antibehavioralists make no efforts to explain the basis in knowledge of their assertions about the nature of society, political power, institutions and processes, and the imperatives of social and political change. In reading the somewhat fugitive literature of the movement one looks in vain for an indication of an awareness among its proponents that an enormous historical, philosophical, and theological literature exists—beginning with classical antiquity and continuing to the present—that is pertinent to the ontological, metaphysical, and ethical questions implicit in the critique of the behavioralists and in the program for redirection of the profession. Instead, reliance seems to be placed on an ethics of *ressentiment* and a visionary utopianism as the basis for opposing the status quo and projecting the appropriate future trends for the discipline.

And this brings up a second (and closely related) problem discernible in the "new" political science: the self-conscious political activism of the movement. When the first signs of the counteroffensive began there was little indication that the controversy was to extend much beyond the intellectual concerns that were already at issue between behavioralists and nonbehavioralists. Even when the Caucus for a New Political Science mounted its major drive for membership at the meeting of the American Political Science Association in Washington in 1968, political scientists of a wide diversity of philosophical and political perspectives either joined the caucus or seriously considered doing so, apparently with a view to maintaining (or restoring) the eclectic quality of the profession. But whether affected by the temper of the times, with its propensity toward politicizing practically every human concern, or by other influences, the caucus rapidly accelerated its activities both as a partisan organization aiming at enhancing its influence in the association (or perhaps even at controlling it) and as an advocate of a political ideology which is designed to reorder American politics and public policy. In the 1969 and 1970 elections of officers for the American Political Science Association the caucus presented its own electoral slate, and advanced an election platform which, though directed toward activities of the association, was compounded in about equal parts of doctrines of political and academic reform and proposals of means by which the association might implement these reforms in the act of reforming itself. The prefatory statement in that document furnishes the flavor:

> The Caucus for a New Political Science is nominating a slate of candidates to run for the APSA offices and Council seats that will be filled at this year's APSA convention elections. We are presenting a slate, and are conducting an electoral campaign, to express and make known our conviction that a *new* political science must now be developed. We have chosen this election as a means of presenting our views because we believe that:
>
>   1. The political science profession has invested its energies primarily in celebrating and supporting the economic, social, and political status quo, both here and abroad.
>   2. The American Political Science Association, more than any other force, shapes the nature and direction of political science in America.
>   3. The resources of the APSA must be used to re-direct some of the energies and expertise of the discipline to encourage the development of a *new* political science—devoted to radical social criticism and fundamental social change.

The platform then goes on to outline the type of research program that should be supported by the association, the type of educational reorganization that should be developed, some political support activities that the association should move into, and the way in which the association should alter its membership patterns and governance.[23]

The main danger that seems to inhere in this tendency to turn political science into a political activity is the effect that it is likely to have on the pursuit of knowledge. Although we may freely admit that politics is a practical activity, the quest for an understanding of politics is a form of intellectual rather than political action. And as Aristotle reminds us, the *bios theoretikos* is the highest form of action because it is action which is complete in itself. The successful pursuit of knowledge requires some distancing of the subject from the object of its thought—a measure of objectivity, if you will. If the behavioralists made a fetish of objectivity, and turned the authority of science into an ideology by which they assayed the collective control of the intellectual activity, the antibehavioralists seem no less bound to try to limit the understanding of politics to the orthodoxies prescribed by them for political practice. If the behavioralists attempted to consign values to the area of opinion and thus to circumscribe too narrowly the experiential data of political theory, the new antibehavioralists tend to suborn the philosophical and historical search for existential truth to the felt needs of the times. The transcendentalist, above all others, is obliged to recognize that the ultimate values his pursuit of truth subserves are always beyond his absolute grasp, and that this condition is a restraining influence on the total activism of a politics which aims at the perfection of man and society as an end. Many of the political nightmares of the twentieth century were stimulated by this gnostic type of vision.

These objections are not intended to suggest that the scholar should be denied, in his practical life, the opportunity to be a political participant. They do suggest that it is necessary for the scholar to maintain an openness that ideological commitment necessarily limits narrowly or even precludes altogether.

23. Caucus for a New Political Science, "Election Platform" (Mimeo., undated), 1. A recent endorsement and refinement of the aims of this platform may be read *in extensio* in Lewis Lipsitz, "Vulture, Mantis and Seal," *Polity*, III (Fall, 1970), 15 ff. It is interesting to note that Lipsitz enters the following caveat despite what seems to me to be strong evidence to the contrary: "The Caucus does not propose to turn the profession into a political action group, but rather to recall it to a deeper concern with its own values and to the troubling problems of our time" (p. 16).

Having said all this, I conclude by reiterating an earlier stricture: The understanding of politics can be assisted by work carried out under the regulative ideas and methods of any of the philosophical schools discussed in the foregoing comments. But it should simultaneously be said that a viable theory of politics cannot be realized on the basis of a closure of inquiry, either in the name of science or in the cause of political activity. The debate on the meaning of politics requires that we accept as a minimum common ground the openness of the questions and the willingness to face the criticism to which a given philosophical position exposes one when he poses his questions and attempts to answer them. Only on this understanding (which is in itself a value of civilization) can our mutual criticism be constructive. And I assume that all of us, including even the skeptics, are more eager for affirmation than negation.

IV The New Lexicon of Politics; or How to Engage in Research Without Really Thinking

In 1946 George Orwell, a master of the simple English prose style whose writings are object lessons in clarity of expression, published a short essay "Politics and the English Language." By now that essay should be familiar to every political scientist who is not so heavily engaged with the "professional literature" (in itself a contradictory phrase) that he has lost touch altogether with the real world. Yet rereading the essay today forces one to the dismal conclusion not only that the injunctions set forth there have been violated with impunity but that the improvement in status of social scientists over the past twenty-odd years has been in part a reward for grosser and more frequent transgressions than those cited a generation ago.

The main charge pressed by Orwell is the use of language that apparently has no immediate meaning for the writer and therefore conveys little or nothing to the reader. In his own words:

> Modern writing at its worst does not consist in picking out words for the sake of their meaning and inventing images in order to make the meaning clearer. It consists in gumming together long strips of words which have already been set in order by someone else, and making the results presentable by sheer humbug. The attraction of this way of writing is that it is easy. . . . If you use ready-made phrases, you not only don't have to hunt about for words; you also don't have to bother with the rhythms of your sentences, since these phrases are generally so arranged as to be more or less euphonious.[1]

The bill of particulars lists the use (or abuse) of "dying metaphors," "operators, or verbal false limbs," "pretentious diction," and "meaningless words." As examples, Orwell quotes passages from Harold Laski, Lancelot Hogben, an essay on psychology from

1. George Orwell, "Politics and the English Language," *A Collection of Essays* (New York: Harcourt, Brace, 1953), 164.

Politics, a communist pamphlet, and a letter that appeared in *Tribune*, thus covering a considerable range of political rhetoric. While Orwell admits he might have found even worse examples, the contemporary reader, especially if he is a social scientist and thus inured to jargon, will find little to fault in the passages quoted until Orwell analyzes them for him. True, Laski's syntax is not felicitous, at least in the passage quoted, and he deliberately uses double negatives as positives, presumably for emphasis. Certainly, the other excerpts contain hackneyed and even mixed metaphors, clichés and words deprived of precision through overuse and excessive generality, and too many inflated words with Latin roots in too close proximity to each other. And as one might expect, the quotation from the communist pamphlet is full of stereotypical invective. But compared with what passes for English composition in most of today's journals, the items that Orwell extracted might stand as illustrations of fair to middling prose. The ideas are expressed so that they may be comprehended without undue labor by the reader, and most of the passages are emphatic enough to convey some measure of the intensity felt by the writers.

It should be understood that I am far from being as exacting in my demands as Orwell. I have an admiration for the periodic structure of the eighteenth-century sentence, a fondness for the triple-phrase or triple-clause balance in construction, and a preference for even a commonplace metaphor over nonmetaphorical usage. I also think that latinized English may aid rather than hinder the search for precision, and that well-conceived special terms can provide linguistic shortcuts that do not threaten the life of ordinary political discourse among political scientists. But even if Orwell's standards are lowered by the concessions I am willing to make, the amount of contrived obscurity, meaningless repetition of "in" words and phrases, tortured construction, and sheer ugliness of expression in current professional writing about politics is sufficient to drive to despair anyone who has not already lost all zest for politics itself and long since ceased to be fascinated by the "noble structure of the English sentence."

The sources from which examples may be drawn are so profuse that one becomes frustrated in attempting to choose the most fitting. Consequently, I decided to resort to an experiment of an elemental sort: I took the last three issues of the *American Political*

Science Review and thumbed through them at random. A superficial glance at the passing columns of type was enough to confirm the potential of this method of securing illustrations. In fact one might be blindfolded, use a pencil as a pointer, and still come up with only slightly less impressive results. Presuming on your tolerance, I will quote three paragraphs—from as many issues of the *Review*—that were extracted by the technique of casual perusal.

Paragraph No. 1:

> The central thrust of our argument has been that reformed governments differ from their unreformed counterparts in their responsiveness to socio-economic cleavages in the population. Logically, if the presence of one feature of the "good government" syndrome had the impact of reducing responsiveness, the introduction of additional reformed institutions should have an additive effect and further reduce the impact of cleavages on decision-making. We therefore decided to treat "reformism" as a continuous variable for analytic purposes and hypothesized that . . . the higher the level of reformism in a city, the lower its responsiveness to socio-economic cleavages in the population.[2]

Paragraph No. 2:

> A most interesting variable in this system is the relationship represented by the concept of compatibility. Compatibility is a concept for judging the feasibility of demands made by the national system on the external, operational environment: it assesses the structures and opportunities of that environment with respect to a range of goals. As the system becomes highly penetrated, and as the distinction between foreign policy and domestic policy diminishes, the concept of compatibility necessarily begins to apply to feasibility relationships in an operational environment that is simultaneously "external" and "internal." This provides an opportunity to bridge the gap between concepts pertaining to goals and the *international* system and those pertaining to goals and the *national* system.[3]

Paragraph No. 3:

> The Hess and Torney argument thus represents a major departure from the more traditional view. They see the family's influence as age-spe-

2. Kenneth P. Langton, "Peer Group and School and the Political Socialization Process," *American Political Science Review*, LXI (September, 1967), 713.

3. Wolfram F. Hanrieder, "Compatibility and Consensus: A Proposal for the Conceptual Linkage of External and Internal Dimensions of Foreign Policy," *American Political Science Review*, LXI (December, 1967), 981.

cific and restricted in its scope. In effect, the restriction of the family's role removes its impact from much of the dynamic qualities of the political system and from individual differences in political behavior. The consensual qualities imparted or reinforced by the family, while vital for comprehending the maintenance of the system, are less useful in explaining adjustments in the system, the conflicts and accommodations made, the varied reactions to political stimuli, and the playing of diverse political roles. In short, if the family's influence is restricted to inculcating a few consensual attributes (plus partisan attachment), it means that much of the socialization which results in individual differentiation in everyday politics and which effects changes in the functioning of the political system lies outside the causal nexus of the parent-child relationship.[4]

One is reminded by these paragraphs of Aristophanes' notion that "exalted ideas of fancy require to be clothed in a suitable vesture of phrase." From these passages one could quite easily pick out all of the faults ascribed by Orwell to political writing, including pretentious diction, jargon, and words rendered meaningless through overuse or lack of any discoverable object. But what irritates me most is that after muddling through this thickly planted maze of verbiage, I can only conclude either that the authors have expressed relatively simple ideas in an unnecessarily pompous and obscurantist form or that I am too simpleminded ever to be able to grasp the subtleties of political analysis. Being about as intellectually arrogant as the next man, I refuse to entertain the latter possibility. My commonsense understanding of these three passages is as follows: The first tells me that the more intense the concern with what I presume is structural reform of government within a city, the less likely it is that the city government will be concerned with the social and economic problems that confront its population. The second conveys to me the idea that there is a reciprocal relation between foreign and domestic politics within a given country, and as foreign politics becomes more important in the political life of the country, the ends sought in domestic and foreign policies will tend to merge. The final passage suggests that family influence has more to do with helping children adapt to ex-

4. M. Kent Jennings and Richard G. Niemi, "The Transmission of Political Values from Parent to Child," *American Political Science Review*, LXII (March, 1968), 170.

isting political institutions and practices than with preparing them for participation in efforts to change the political arrangements or to adjust to the changes that actually occur. Professor Frederick Schuman has expressed the dilemma of interpretation even more effectively when he concludes after reading an article in the *Review* that covered eighteen pages of neologisms, nonsense terms, equations, graphs, and charts that, in English translation, what really was said was "States have closer relations with some States than with other States."[5]

The problem of interpretation is not the only one that arises from the attempt to cope with the literature. Bad writing habits almost inevitably develop from reading bad prose. Orwell notes at one point that he has probably already committed all the faults that he deals with in the article on political writing, although my enthusiasm for the essay is based partly on the judgment that he is invulnerable against his own criticism. On the other hand, rereading my writings after a suitable lapse of time always has an effect similar to the one that occurs every time I look up something in Fowler's *Modern English Usage*: I am assailed with a sinking feeling which tells me that my critical faculties will never measure up to the task of overcoming accumulated writing faults. But I am old enough and settled enough in my ways not to try to turn these faults into virtues in order to cater to what seems an implicit demand that one either adopt the usages that I have been talking about or cease to publish in some professional journals or with certain publishers.

Among the more disagreeable linguistic excesses in these sources, we may isolate the following: (1) the unnecessary complication, (2) the palpable truth expressed as a new discovery, and (3) the compound-noun phrase. The examples that I have already given are probably sufficient to establish unnecessary complication as the most grievous of these sins, but I cannot forbear to cite at least one more. When I was still in grade school, it was commonplace to list agreement among scientists as a basic means of validating scientific discovery. Professor Heinz Eulau has restated this proposi-

5. Fred L. Schuman, "Letter to the Editor," *American Political Science Review*, LXI (March, 1967), 149.

tion as follows: "The critical characteristic of the scientific culture is its cognitive intersubjectivity: that is, the agreement among scientists that the observed phenomena are, in fact, what they are alleged to be."[6]

The palpable truth is so ubiquitous that it scarcely requires the emphasis of specific illustration. However, in the interest of comprehensiveness, here is a minor example from Lewis Coser: "Conflict with another group leads to the mobilization of the energies of group members and hence to increased cohesion of the group." What middle-class American who has ever attended a high school football game can doubt such a maxim, even if he has never had occasion to express it in so imposing a sentence?

The compounding of noun-based phrases and the use of nouns as adjectives are among the more vulgar contemporary constructions. The most common encounter is with the word *situation* in conjunction with some modifying noun. The one that frequently leaps out of the page is "conflict situation." Although proof is always problematic in such cases, I suspect that this phrase has its origin in the tendency of those who use it to supplement their reading in the literature of political science by scanning the sports pages of the daily newspapers of middle-sized cities and following the televised commentary on college and professional football. The "third down situation" is a constantly recurring theme in these sources; and I cannot really accept the alternative explanation that the sportswriters may have picked the terminology up from the political science journals. I find it equally difficult to impute such barbarities to Arthur Daley or Red Barber. There are, of course, more elaborate variations, such as Gabriel Almond's "interest articulation structures." Or, to repeat from one of my prime sources, I could point to Heinz Eulau's statement that one of the more difficult problems of behavioral research is to uncover the "meaning content of behavior."[7]

Even if one becomes accustomed to language of this sort through

6. Heinz Eulau, *The Behavioral Persuasion in Politics* (New York: Random House, 1963), 68–69.
7. Gabriel A. Almond and G. Bingham Powell, Jr., *Comparative Politics: A Development Approach* (Boston: Little, Brown, 1966), 74; Eulau, *The Behavioral Persuasion in Politics*, 69.

constant exposure, he may still be taken aback when he discovers the extent to which it has entered the workaday conversation of social scientists. In this respect political scientists are far outdone by sociologists and psychologists. I recently attended a meeting to discuss the possibilities of changing the core curriculum in the social sciences within one of the residential colleges at my university. On three or four occasions a psychologist who was participating made passing remarks that were cast in terms virtually interchangeable with those in the passages that I quoted from the *Review*. With typical southern indirection, I cautiously pointed out that the problems under discussion were really not complicated enough to require such precise formulation, whereupon I was met with the hostile glare ordinarily reserved for the most committed anti-intellectual. During the remainder of the meeting, I did my best to curb my sardonic tendencies in the interest of good interdepartmental relations, but I am afraid that the possibility of future communication with this man has been placed in jeopardy. From his perspective I have probably betrayed my professional commitment; while I in turn maliciously suspect that he not only talks jargon but thinks in gobbledygook.

Up to this point, I have said very little about the use or misuse of metaphor in political writing, partly because metaphor is seldom deliberately used in contemporary professional literature. Yet nearly all important communication about politics is, in my view, metaphorical. Politics, like language, is a human creation that serves quite practical purposes. As such, politics not only concerns the external behavior of people but also reflects the inner life of individuals, including their emotions, imaginations, and wills. In most cases, the intensity and subtlety of subjective experiences that are pertinent to the understanding of politics cannot be conveyed effectively except in mythic or poetic expressions heavily involved in metaphor. Even Hobbes, a forefather of behavioralism, provides us with a most poignant example. Few passages in the literature on political ideas surpass in subtlety of distinction or breadth of introspective vision the one in which Hobbes denies the ability of egoistic individuals to understand one another. He expresses this limitation of the egoistic consciousness in his metaphor of the Greek dramatic mask, through which each person speaks as representative of himself or some other. All that we try to convey through modern and looser terms such as *alienation, anomie, isolated self-consciousness, nihilism,* and scores of other words may be grasped in its immediacy in the still fresh insight dramatized by Hobbes in this particular figure of speech.

Again, one thinks of the political explanations achieved through metaphors drawn from medicine, a form which has been extant since the early classical period. The idea of the sickness of man's soul, or the sickness of a society whose health can be recovered only through a combination of the arts of diagnosis and prescription, in conjunction with some empirically based knowledge of external factors affecting the organic balance, has, at the hands of the better political writers, continued to remind us that description and even analytic perception are not sufficient to preserve order and well-being in society.

One can hardly deny that metaphor is present in the contemporary writing of political scientists, even if much of it is unintentional. The central issue is whether the people who write about politics in a professional way today are aware of the implications of their own metaphorical usages. If the biological metaphors of an earlier period are rejected out of the suspicion that they may involve support of the idea of the organic state, it seems plausible to suggest that many political scientists do not seem to be conscious of the extent to which metaphors in their writings are bound to the supposedly outmoded concept of the purely mechanistic state. Surely such voguish terms as *systems analysis, political process,* and even *models* are suggestive of a dependence on naturalistic analogy to the physical sciences or even to technology. What is striking about these unconscious uses of metaphor involving physical science and technology is the manner in which they manage to suggest the dehumanization of politics in their abstraction, in their focus on mere descriptions of aggregate uniformities as opposed to personalized, ethically oriented, policy questions, and in their implicit denial of the uniqueness and creative potential of the human spirit. The pursuit of this theme, however, is a task better left to the political philosophers; in this context such a commentary is a contrived digression from our immediate concern with the words and phrases of politics.

F. M. Cornford, the English classical scholar, once wrote a monograph advising young men on getting ahead in the academic world. Following his example, I think this occasion a suitable one for tendering some advice to the newer members of the profession on the successful application of the new political lexicon. Although a few political scientists of my acquaintance have made instant reputations by attacking the giants of the profession with carefully aimed intellectual slingshots, this tactic is a highly dubious one. In the pursuit of success, it is far better to don conventional armor and attempt to join forces with those who have already established themselves on the commanding heights. For this purpose, one needs only to control a couple of dozen key words and phrases and observe a few very simple rules in the disposition of these potent verbal fortresses.

With very little advance reflection, one can go quite far toward satisfying publication requirements at an early stage of his career by adopting a terminology that requires minimal supplementation with common conjunctions, prepositions, and intransitive verbs. It is best to start with some of the simpler terms and repeat them often in the early stages of writing. One should not dally too much with the question of what constitutes serious problems in political science; almost any topic can be handled within the confines of an appropriate vocabulary. The selection of a correct methodology takes a little more time, but it, too, may be borrowed from the better exemplars of the new political linguistics.

The elemental words must be carefully cultivated. The term *hypothesis* is a must, and it should always be used as early in an article as possible; it is better applied in the plural, and except on rare occasions, it should be preceded by the modifier *testable*. The use of *hypothesis* should always be followed closely by a discussion of the data on which one is relying for proof; preferably these should be *hard* data. At one time it was necessary for the political writer to begin with an explanation of his *frame of reference*, but this phrase is now somewhat archaic and one would be well advised to talk about his *conceptual frame* or *conceptual scheme*, or better still about his *model*. The dynamic model is much to be preferred to the merely static one. The astute beginner will always make appropriate reference to his *research strategy* or his *research design*, and will stress that he is striving to make some contribution to the development of *empirical theory*. One should always ignore the suspicion that the very term *empirical theory* may be a logically contradictory one. Appropriate modesty may sometimes compel the admission that what is really aimed at is *middle-range theory* rather than something more comprehensive. Among the elemental words, one need only add to the foregoing list the indispensable term *variables*. But it is well to bear in mind that a distinction should always be drawn between dependent and independent variables. If emphasis is required, the variables may become *critical*. Although *factor* was once an important designation, and in some cases may be still appropriate to a given mathematical formula, it has now fallen into disuse and may even be looked upon with scorn as traditional. It is considered useful to indicate the way in which you have *operationalized* your research, but you should be wary of other words ending in *ize* or *ized*, such as *finalize* or *finalized*. One of the best devices of one-upmanship is to refrain from the latter expressions in order to ascribe their origins to Madison Avenue.

Having laid these terminological foundations, you may now proceed to the erection of the superstructure. A wide latitude exists in the materials that may be used at this point. For the most part the appropriate choices depend on the particular method or conceptual scheme within which one works. The following suggested terms are far from definitive, but others may be picked up from almost any of the recognized works within a given *modus operandi*. One should seldom refer simply to politics, or the political, or anything else that takes place within political institutions without appending the word *process* or *system*. Although somewhat prosaic, terms such as *shared values* or *shared characteristics*, *norms*, *political development* or *political modernization*, and *inputs* and *outputs* can be tossed about with relative abandon. A somewhat more complicated set of terms may also be added, such as *socialization*, *salience* (or preferably *saliency*), *interaction*, *linkage*, *political actors*, and *role*. The term *role*, in fact, is extensively adaptable, especially when hyphenated with *identification* or *perception*. *Functional* and *dysfunctional* also belong in this category, and they are especially applicable when one is involved in structural-functional analysis. However, since Talcott Parsons is not in good repute in all circles of political science, the site must be carefully selected before one resorts to these resources. *Probability*, on the other hand, is nearly always acceptable, and *probabilistic* is even better.

If one masters the use of the terms suggested above, and a few related ones, everything else can be considered decoration. Again, only a few suggestions are appropriate, since the decorative terms from which one may choose are virtually unlimited. What is more, if one wants to be really enterprising he may invent new ones. The more common examples of decorative words are *parameters*, *reify*, *replication*, and *heuristic*. To these, I would add *homology*, especially since it is susceptible to a number of impressive variations. A word of caution, however, is in order. *Homology* is a term with a biological reference and, although biological analogies are already coming back into vogue in anticipation of the next great leap in science, they are not yet sufficiently established to be indulged in carelessly.

Diogenes warned us that "men ought not to investigate things from words, but words from things"; and Daniel Bell has recently noted that "since new words are like newly minted coins, writers, like collectors, are eager to grab them, and heavy use soon brings tarnish." But these strictures need not worry us excessively since, like the variety of ideologies through which the older members of the profession have already passed, the new lexicon of politics is almost indefinitely extensible. So even if we eventually have to reject some of the prevailing terms in favor of new ones, we can continue to build plenty of fabricated word bridges on which to circumambulate.

V A New Rousseau

For those of us who have been struggling to gain some coherent perspective on the metaphysics, teleology, logic, method, and rhetoric of the New Left, this collection of Noam Chomsky's essays is a godsend. Although he notes that "the revival of Anarchist thinking in the 'New Left' and the attempts to put it into effect are the most promising developments of the past years" (p. 19), I am not aware that Chomsky specifically identifies himself as a New Leftist. But the exaggerated pronouncements of those who declare themselves to be the vanguard of this movement could be derived from Chomsky as easily (and more clearly) than from acknowledged sources such as Marcuse. On the surface, *American Power and the New Mandarins* (Pantheon Books) is deceptive: The subtitle is *Historical and Political Essays*, the paraphernalia of scholarship is well displayed in the extensive quotations and copious footnotes attendant on most of the essays, and both the titles of the essays and the publisher's blurb show evidences of conventionality. But as one begins to feel the cumulative impact of reading these previously fugitive pieces of dissent from the academy as a sustained statement, the clarity of the message can no longer be called into question.

Many spokesmen of the New Left seem to have adopted a monocausal basis for their uncompromising attack on the failures of American society and American politics. Everything begins and ends with the Vietnam conflict and no issue is too trivial to escape being turned into a consequence of the war. Although Chomsky, too, takes as his point of departure the Vietnam issue, his critique fans out from that central incident in at least two major, but related, dimensions. The first of these is historical. He does not see the Vietnam War as something into which we drifted as a naïve, unthinking response to a combination of Wilsonian idealism and *realpolitik*. Instead, his perception is of a society and a political system undermined at their historical roots by their propensity for materialistic imperialism. By the time he has projected this ethos back into the nineteenth century and beyond, throughout the twentieth century, and into the future, one is left with a vision of an America without any redeeming moral or political virtues. A Calvinistic sense of total degradation pervades most of the book.

The second extended dimension is the attack on the ideological commitment of those (especially the intellectuals among them) who control the institutions through which monolithic American power is exercised. The phrase "the new mandarins" is taken from a political scientist at MIT, Ithiel de Sola Pool, who recently suggested that behavioral and social scientists will have to become the mandarins of the future in the planning and development of a modern mass society. Chomsky regards this claim to expertise, based on the pseudoscientific pretensions of the social and behavioral sciences, as a camouflage for the "liberal intellectual" or "pragmatic liberal intellectual" who gains his own power by serving the ends of an imperialist policy which is effected by unlimited application of force.

It would be futile in a short space to attempt to illustrate the polemical skill with which Chomsky advances his critical attack on men and ideas. In any case, I am less concerned about his escalation of emotive language and the insertion of his bracketed, ironically condemnatory phrases into and alongside quotations than I am about the implications of both the style and the content of his argument. We are involved here with nothing less than the major intellectual division in Western society between the two cultures of the sciences and the humanities, a division which first clearly manifested itself in the eighteenth century. The massive glorification of human sentiments, the scathing attack on the social scientists for being concerned only with pragmatic means to the corrupted ends of contemporary society, and the outraged pleas for "honesty and indignation" are part of a pattern. The arguments are reminiscent of nothing so much as Rousseau's "Discourse on the Arts and Sciences." Nor should it be forgotten that, in Peter

Gay's apposite comment, Rousseau was a "world-historical neurotic."[1] Obviously there is much that is worthy of criticism in the materialism, the dogmatic positivism, the pure instrumentalism of reason, and the moral relativism that are characteristics of the scientific culture at its worst. And certainly the agonizing involvement in Vietnam is sufficient in its effects to call us to a reexamination of our own national purposes and of the policies that we have pursued or failed to pursue in the effort to realize these purposes. But a criticism which suggests that one of the few viable political orders in history is virtually unfit to survive, the scarcely veiled reversion to a primitive, naturalistic irrationalism, and the virtual abdication of the attempt to reconcile the values of science with a reasoned morality are unlikely to do much to preserve and enhance the humanistic culture.

The latter features of Chomsky's style and attitude are implicit in his suggested solutions for the problems which he rightly identifies as critical for contemporary Western man. Again like many New Leftists, Chomsky assumes no particular responsibility for explaining the ontological and epistemological bases on which a new and perfected society might be grounded; it seems enough to bring down the violent society in which we live. Whatever may replace it will be a natural improvement.

A spirit of romanticism pervades Chomsky's visions of a new society, at least to the extent to which he alludes to any positive features of that society. Beginning with an ethic of *ressentiment*, in which a feeling of repression is sufficient to evoke moral outrage, Chomsky moves naturally toward a position of revolutionary anarchism. "Transformation" of man and society and "spiritual transformation" brook large in his lexicon. Some interesting paradoxes emerge as a result. While accusing others of bias and distortion in their service to liberal goals, Chomsky does not even bother to consider the evidences of violence and terrorism among revolutionary anarchists in the past, or the Viet Cong's acknowledgment of violence and terrorism as appropriate means. Similarly, while condemning the self-anointed intellectual elite, he

1. Peter Gay, *The Enlightenment: An Interpretation* (2 vols.; New York: Knopf, 1966), I, 271.

lauds the emergence and growth of a new "moral elite." Again, while condemning the elaborate doctrinaire rationalizations of the pragmatic liberals, he apparently does not balk at the notion of forced indoctrination when he suggests that what America needs is a de-Nazification program. And when he objects to the liberal practice of a politics of accommodation, one can only wonder whether the alternatives may not be a politics of selective annihilation. Finally, but by no means exhaustively, while he acknowledges that one of the advantages that the resisters have in this country is free speech, he notes time and again that certain subjects are not debatable or not arguable and that certain means or instruments of democracy are "a monstrous irrelevance in the face of the effort required to raise the level of culture in Western society to the point" of providing for economic development and "true" democratic institutions in the third world and at home (p. 348). In light of such statements even the nonparanoid might infer that certain indispensable attributes of democratic procedure would not be very safe in his hands.

Chomsky notes in his introduction that "if any self-righteousness creeps in, it is unintended and, more important, unjustified" (p. 8), and he suggests in other parts of the book that he is by inclination a nonactivist. But we now have many extensions in practice of the views expressed in his book, particularly on college and university campuses. As a result, some of the pragmatic consequences of the ideology of the New Left are becoming clearer, and certain of the moral omissions from its catechism are simultaneously revealed. One of the latter is the ancient proposition that it is not institutions alone that corrupt; the problem is essentially one of the internal capacity for both good and evil in man himself. Another is that we must assume moral responsibility for our actions, even when those actions have consequences that we did not foresee. The historical future is uncertain at best; when we undermine the values which have sustained a public order we can feel no great security in our knowledge of what will replace them. In a sense Chomsky has faced up very well to the arrogance of power of the enlightened intellectual; he has hardly come to grips with the moral hubris so manifest in his own position and in the activism which grows out of it.

VI   Voegelin's Changing Conception of History and Consciousness

The ideological leaders of contemporary youth movements, who argue that time is on their side in the struggle against their seniors, have apparently not yet learned from experience about the tyrannical relativity of time in the purely subjective sense. For my part, it is not easy to comprehend the fact that Eric Voegelin is over seventy years of age, or that I am now more than a decade older than he was when I first met him thirty-odd years ago, or that the transition in my life from late youth to middle age has taken place since the preparation of an essay for the earlier festschrift, *Politische Ordnung und Menschliche Existenz*, in honor of his sixtieth birthday.

Perhaps my contracted perspective is merely a result of belonging to a generation that is more conscious than young adults today of the implications of the Fifth Commandment. But I prefer to think it is because I continue to experience the same pupil-teacher relationship with Eric Voegelin that I have enjoyed for more than a quarter of a century. And I intend that statement as a compliment to him, though some undoubtedly will regard it now, as they did in my undergraduate and graduate years, as evidence of a natural intellectual dependence, or even subservience, among those of us who attempted, as neophytes, to defend his contributions to philosophy and political science. For no matter how much one may grow and develop himself, he must, if he has remained in touch with the literature at all, stand in awe of Voegelin's continuing feats in mastering an ever-expanding volume and variety of historical and philosophical materials and assimilating these materials recurrently into a more refined and comprehensive theoretical structure.

Gregor Sebba, who published in *Southern Review* in 1967 the best brief overview of Voegelin's theoretical position that I have read, has noted (in the Winter, 1968, issue of *Polity*) that two things have prevented the appropriate recognition of the emergence of a new theory of politics as a result of a "radical reconsideration of the question: "What is political reality, and what cognitive avenues lead to its critical understanding?" The first is that the advancement of that theory "is largely the work of one independent thinker, Eric Voegelin, who published his first book four decades ago . . . and is still forging ahead at a pace which leaves his best readers behind." The second is the "enormous demand" which the Voegelinian achievement makes on the "newcomer to such studies." Not only must the reader be able to follow abstract reasoning at its highest level; he must also know the history of ideas, philosophy (in all its dimensions), theology, the full sweep of history from prehistory to modernity, and the present development of scholarship in fields as widely separated as anthropology, biblical criticism, comparative literature, and psychology. But Sebba also recognizes that "all this is very far from the concerns of the practicing political scientist today."

Perhaps the real measure of the neglect of Voegelin's efforts by American political scientists is the fact that he has not been ignored nearly as often as he has been dismissed with categorical labels, most of which indicate that the labeler either has not bothered to read him or, if he has read him, has not taken the trouble to understand him. Even if one admits to difficulties with Voegelin's neologisms or the frequent use of German constructions in his writings in English (more prevalent in *The New Science of Politics* than in *Order and History*), anyone who can purport to have read and comprehended the *American Political Science Review* with regularity in recent years has no reason to plead tortuous prose as an excuse for a distorted representation of what Voegelin has said.

Voegelin's problems in this respect extend farther back than his residence in America. It is still possible to locate books by Nazis in which references to him are accompanied by the parenthetical notation "*Jude!*" just as it is possible to find works from the same period in which he is accused of being a Nazi sympathizer, if not indeed a Nazi. In more moderate language suitable to less chaotic times, Voegelin has been called a Platonist, a Hegelian, a writer from a purely confessional position, and even a Calvinist. A highly reputable scholar once asked me whether I considered Voegelin a "clerical fascist." The general run of American political scientists, from their less-than-sophisticated perspective of citizen-as-liberal, scholar-as-behavioralist, have often contented themselves with dismissing Voegelin as a conservative and a metaphysician.

Voegelin's books and articles have had a fairly wide distribution in this country; he has been invited to lecture or to teach as a visiting professor at a sizable number of leading American universities; and several clear, concise accounts of various aspects of his work have been published by scholars who have a firm grasp on what he is about. Most of the latter materials have appeared fairly recently, however, and have been directed mainly toward the central problem of *Order and History* and the collected essays published under the title *Anamnesis*. Since Voegelin's work is complex, and is directly contrary to the positivist tendency that has been dominant in philosophy and the social sciences virtually throughout his active scholarly life, it is perhaps useful to offer a simplified survey of the intellectual high points in the development of the philosophical position which Voegelin is still engaged in articulating.

In view of what has already been said, it hardly needs repeating that this is a tenuous undertaking. But if much of what follows is also highly personal, it is because so many of Voegelin's critics seem to me to have contested his scholarship on ideological or *ad hominem* grounds that a corrective is badly needed. And, again needless to say, my perception of him, which may be equally biased in the other direction by the regard in which I hold him as an original scholar and as a person, is quite different from that of the many academicians who seem to have *heard* of him without really bothering to learn anything about him or his work at first hand.

Although some philosophers start with a basic conceptual system and devote their subsequent efforts to its details, the case of Voegelin is much more complicated. His is an intellectual record of changing perspectives, a constant openness to new influences, and the accumulation of vast stores of empirical historical information which, though systematically collected, often appear in the published theoretical works only in such allusive form as he feels necessary to carry his argument.

It may surprise some contemporary "behavioral scientists" to learn that Voegelin started from a philosophical position that is not substantially different from their own unexamined first premises. He took his doctorate in the Faculty of Law in the University of Vienna in 1922. His earliest published articles were in the areas of sociology and economics. They were written at a time when he served as assistant to Hans Kelsen, the originator, under the influence of neo-Kantian positivism, of the "pure theory of law" and the principal draftsman of the Austrian constitution of 1920. In 1927 Voegelin published a laudatory article on Kelsen's legal theory in the *Political Science Quarterly*. He noted in that piece that "by transferring the legal system into an ideal realm of meanings and reducing it to an instrument Kelsen destroys any undue respect for existing legal institutions. The content of law is shown to be what it is: not an eternal sacred order, but a compromise of battling social forces—and this content may be changed every day by the chosen representatives of the people according to the wishes of their constituents without fear of endangering a divine law." The pragmatism and instrumentalism that had grown out of the earlier forms of positivism, the complete rejection of any transcendent meanings in the legal institutions created by man out of his efforts to establish social order, and the assumption that the practical reason is no more than a means for coping with conflicts arising out of the most elementary motivations—all present or implied in this statement—might easily be used by a contemporary critic as a refutational antithesis to some of the major themes of Voegelin's later theories.

Voegelin was not to remain bound by the rigid attempt to separate politics from legal science, institutions from the ideas which inform them, and behavioral description from the totality of experience which gives meaning to it. He soon came to realize that he was engaged in a reductionist treatment of his subject matter; it was not sufficient to deal solely with the logic of the law in terms of its purely categorical assertions. Law—considered apart from the historical and ontological purposes behind its origins and regarded solely as a set of operative definitions of behavior that set in motion correlative enforcing actions—is a mechanical instrument which has no relation to the substantive human experience that produced it and on which it depends for its effectiveness. As part of his studies in sociology, Voegelin had naturally read Max Weber, and by the mid-1920s he had written at least one essay on him. At the same time that he began to question the foundations of his own legal studies, Voegelin also began to see a similar reductionist problem in Weber's work. Weber's fact-value distinction derived largely from his lack of knowledge of classical philosophy and Christianity; in excluding these fundamental influences on the value structure of Western civilization, Weber was able to evade the omnipresent questions of the meaning of existence and to confine his analysis to uniform occurrences in social behavior and in history. Unlike many of his successors, Weber was not led by his epistemological self-limitation into trivial work; he studied problems that were relevant to a science of order even while he rejected the idea that such a science is possible. Voegelin would later enlarge upon these problems in Weber in his introduction to *The New Science of Politics*.

These critical reappraisals never produced a simple negation of his former position; positive influences were also at work, making him aware of the fields of inquiry into which he needed to move in order to cope with some of the problems that had been read out of consideration by Kelsen and Weber. In reading the romanticist Othmar Spann, who was busily engaged in laying the theoretical groundwork for the forthcoming Austrian experiment in the corporative state, Voegelin became aware of the necessity for learning classical philosophy and Greek philology. In the early 1930s he learned Greek as part of his effort to deal with his enlarging historical perspective and his increasing regard for the subtleties of language in the formation of consciousness.

Broadened personal experiences, too, were working their effects on him. As a Laura Spelman Rockefeller fellow from 1924 to 1927, Voegelin was able to spend a considerable amount of time in the United States and France, as well as some briefer periods in England. During his residence in the United States, he was impressed by the variety of personality types striving to cope with the essentials of an emerging political tradition that was largely inherited from British experience, but which also, in part, had to be fabricated in order to accomodate the diversity of peoples seeking representation in the idea of a common nationhood. Again, not too many people seem to be aware that his first book, *Uber die Form des Amerikanischen Geistes* (1928), was an interpretation of American society largely based upon case studies of representative intellectual influences. Voegelin was particularly impressed by such people as John R. Commons, the labor economist at the University of Wisconsin, whom he regarded as "a Lincolnesque figure." Commons was a scholarly midwestern frontier type, writing from the perspective of a society in transition from an agricultural to an industrial order. George Santayana, a philosopher whose paternal Spanish background and broad acquaintance with the traditions of European culture never quite permitted him to be reconciled to the new and unformed America in which he resided throughout most of his formative years, was another figure who attracted Voegelin's attention. An even more direct and purely intellectual influence was Voegelin's attendance at some of Alfred North Whitehead's lectures at Harvard, a contact that helped to draw him away from his former concern with logic toward the awareness that inquiry into the problems of existence inevitably involved one with metaphysics. In Paris a similar influence was exerted on him by his reading of Lucretius and Paul Valéry.

Another experience from the same era that is directly discernible in some of Voegelin's later essays and lectures was his discovery in England of the writings of Thomas Reid, the Scottish "common sense" philosopher. Although I have long known that Voegelin's view of practical politics is based largely on the application of common sense to a working political tradition, it is only recently that I have come to recognize the extensive use he makes of commonsense principles in his general analysis of historical problems. Not long ago, in fact, he told me that he had purchased and read Reid's works in the 1920s. He had, he said, been constantly aware since that time of the dual implications of Reid's perspective as (1) an appropriate starting point for almost any philosophical reflection and (2) the articulation of a perspective that has furnished an important stabilizing influence on the successful maintenance of the order of the British and American democracies. Reid—in his insistence on the unified nature of experience, in his rejection of the radical distinction between immediate perception and cognitive judgment, and in his refusal to distinguish between appearance and reality until solid observationally based grounds have been given for doing so—provided an epistemological antidote to both the abstractness of Berkeleyan idealism and David Hume's skepticism, as well as serving as a check on the tendency to ignore the incontrovertible limitations inherent in the human condition. For Voegelin, with his constant reminders of the need for awareness of man's finiteness and the other limitations of existence, Reid's common sense seems to serve an important function as a set of regulative limits on both speculative philosophy and man's conscious pursuit of the *vita activa*.

The horizons of Voegelin's concerns were also substantially enlarged by the events occurring in Europe generally and in Austria particularly from the late 1920s to the mid-1930s. By 1927 the impending advent of national socialism in Germany gave Voegelin some incentive to study biology in an effort to understand how the race idea could emerge and develop into a full-blown social myth from so scanty a background of fact. Although he published two monographs relating to these problems in 1933, the plan for publishing a comprehensive treatise on the origin of the race idea was suppressed. Only in 1940 did some of his conclusions on this topic appear in the *Review of Politics* in a long article entitled "The Growth of the Race Idea." It appears to me that Voegelin's active scientific interest in the origin and role of the myth began with this analysis of an elementary experience in the conscious construction of a social myth that occurred while he could observe the process at first hand. His awareness of the myth as a means of symbolizing the meaning behind a society's cohesion was to receive increasing attention later as he explored the nature of myths in a wide variety of historical eras and circumstances.

Another external event that played a major role in the development of Voegelin's view of consciousness and history was the political upheaval in Austria in the late 1920s and early 1930s, which culminated in the substitution by the Dollfuss regime of a Catholic corporative arrangement for the 1920 constitution. In his book *The Authoritarian State* (1936), Voegelin indicated that the political divisions in Austria reached a complete impasse because there was no experiential substance to which the polarized political parties in Austria could turn for mutual accommodation. A structure of instrumental legal institutions such as the one created by the 1920 constitution was insufficient for holding a society together. Opposing political parties in Austria had become organizations which demanded the total adherence of the individual in all aspects of life; commonsense reality had been subsumed by ideology. The inadequacy of procedural arrangements alone was revealed by the fact that Otto Bauer, the intellectual leader of the Social Democrats, had indicated in his program that democratic electoral procedures would be followed until the Social Democrats obtained 51 percent of the vote; and the *substance* of "social democracy" would be installed with no possibility of electoral reversal. Actual events took an entirely different turn, because it was the Catholic party that was successful in restructuring the political order on the basis of its own substance, the full augmentation of its power being completed by the promulgation of the corporative constitution of 1934. Engelbert Dollfuss and other political and intellectual leaders of the movement drew heavily on the papal encyclical *Quadragesimo anno* as the authoritative support for the social doctrines of the new order. Living under such a regime—and even playing a minor role in its bureaucratic structure as a civil service examiner—stimulated Voegelin to inquire into the contents of many of the major papal encyclicals, and from that he moved into a more extended study of Christianity in general. His fundamental concern with the religious underpinnings of his own and other civilizations thus took its point of departure from direct experience, as is indeed the case with most of his historical pursuits.

In 1938, with the overthrow of the Austrian government by Hitler, Voegelin was fired from his position at the university only shortly after he had been made an Extraordinary Professor. To avoid arrest he quickly fled across the border to Switzerland and eventually came to the United States. After brief stopovers at Harvard and Bennington, he went to the University of Alabama as an assistant professor in 1939. In January, 1942, he moved with the rank of associate professor to Louisiana State University, where he remained for sixteen years, during which time he was promoted to a Boyd professorship.

When I first encountered Eric Voegelin, soon after his arrival in

Baton Rouge, I was an extremely naïve, eighteen-year-old sophomore at LSU. Fortunately, my freshman record had been good
enough to place me in a special (presumably "enriched") section
of the introductory course in American government, scheduled at
that time as a full-year sequence at the sophomore level. It may
sound strange to academic types who have come to the profession
lately to hear that Voegelin, a political philosopher not long out of
Europe and with a secondary field in comparative government,
should have been assigned to teach an introductory section of
American government during his first semester at LSU. But such
an occurrence was not at all unusual in those days; in fact, until he
left to take the chair of political science in Munich, in January,
1958, Voegelin continued to teach introductory courses in both
American government and Western European comparative government. During most of those years he taught a full twelve-hour
load, sometimes involving four different course preparations.

My impression of his first appearance in class remains vivid in
my memory, although it has undoubtedly been colored by imagination. He was, to say the least, a striking figure to my provincial
eyes. He was dressed in what I considered extremely formal fashion; he wore a tight-fitting black coat, striped trousers, and heavy
black semi–brogue shoes that made his presence felt before his
coming because they squeaked rather loudly when he walked down
the hall. Voegelin was, and is, a robust man—thick-chested and
prominent-featured, with a florid complexion and sandy hair that
could have been quite red in his youth. His hands, which he uses
with expressive grace in his lectures (and occasionally in conversation), form something of a complement by contrast to his features and frame; his fingers are long and tapered, with just a hint
of delicacy about them. He carried himself most erectly and invariably walked at a brisk pace with his head thrown well back, as
he still does. At that time he wore close-fitting, round, steel-rimmed
spectacles; and then, as now, he was rarely seen without a cigar.

It was not long before I came to consider Voegelin as striking in
his capacity as a teacher as he then seemed to me to be in appearance. He brought to American government a perspective that was
totally unanticipated by those of us who had been brought up on
orthodox institutional description. Although I am sure that most

members of that class were as unsophisticated as I was, nearly all of us very quickly realized that Voegelin was a man of extraordinary intellectual power, a man possessed of that rare quality of being able to look at things with a special vision not open to others until he had guided them toward it. Under his tutelage one came to appreciate the enormous complexity of the interplay between ideas and institutions, as well as the subtle way in which historical experience manifested itself long after the original events that produced specific social responses in the form of ideas, patterns of habitual action, or a set of institutions had been lost to immediate consciousness. The classical sources on which the Founding Fathers drew so heavily were clarified both in their original meanings and in the impact they had on the legal and institutional structure of the Constitution. A commonplace arrangement such as the separation of powers was placed in the perspective of its historical origin in the long-drawn-out struggles in the Middle Ages between the plenitude of power of the head of state and the emergence of consultative checks on these powers; and the tensions that remained in the religious sphere in America, even after an apparent resolution of the problem had been achieved through church-state separation, were elaborated within the context of the omnipresent search for religious truth in forms both theological and secular in all human settings.

As a teacher Voegelin never engaged in pyrotechnics; his effectiveness sprang solely from the impressive breadth and depth of his learning and the analytical powers of his mind. If one stood just beyond the point at which his actual words could be understood, his lectures could sound monotonous, because the flow of his sentences and his lack of inflection would create a deadly evenness in one whose ideas are less exciting than Voegelin's. Having sat through his classes and seminars as an undergraduate, as a graduate student, and later as a junior colleague, I was always surprised when I heard other colleagues speak disparagingly of his "arrogance" or his "rigidity."[1] I have always found him excep-

1. Ideologues constantly throw up blocks against the concept of an expansion of consciousness by refusing to accept the possibility of a nonideological theory of man and society. On one occasion a fellow graduate student (now a rather prominent social scientist who has shown great skill, as Voegelin said with reference to Har-

tionally considerate with students, patient with their problems of understanding, and in some ways a rather soft touch in the matter of grades. In supervising research he is an exacting critic, as one might expect; but he is also generous with both his time and his ideas. He has a pixyish sense of humor that comes through somewhat unexpectedly in light of his German accent, until one remembers that the Austrians are as much southern Europeans as they are Germanic in the more subtle aspects of their culture.

I think there may be some basis in fact for the differing perceptions of Voegelin's manner and comportment among those who have been his students or colleagues and those who know him only through professional meetings and books and journals. That difference derives largely from the fact that he expects more of those who are supposed to be his scholarly peers than they are usually able to deliver, with the result that, while he always observes the amenities, he can be devastating in his analysis of inadequate scholarship and questionable logic. Since he is also so far removed from the prevailing orthodoxy in political science, it is not surprising that many of his colleagues should feel compelled to attack his position vociferously, and the attacks are not always adequately reinforced by a careful comprehension of what he has said about a particular subject or by very much caution in detaching the criticism from ideological considerations.[2]

---

old Laski, "in his expert surf-riding on the wave of the future") remarked, after hearing Voegelin examine the pragmatic necessity for social democratic reforms under certain historical conditions, "I didn't know the man was a Socialist; I always thought he was a reactionary." The neoconservatives have often attempted to secure an identification with him on similarly mistaken grounds.

2. A senior colleague for whom I have great respect once astonished me by bluntly asserting that he could not make the written tribute to Voegelin for which he had been called on because "Voegelin never said anything against the Nazis after he came to this country." It continues to puzzle me that so well informed a man could have missed Voegelin's articles "The Growth of the Race Idea" (in which the racial myth is brilliantly exposed as a pseudoscientific symbol that achieved its effect under special historical circumstances), "Extended Strategy" (the most perceptive discussion I have read of the way in which Hitler's expansionist tactics succeeded because the Western democracies were incapable of perceiving the total removal of normal moral and political restraints that was characteristic of the new revolutionary consciousness of the Nazis), and "Some Problems of the German Hegemony." Yet all of these articles were published in highly reputable professional journals in 1940 and 1941. See Eric Voegelin, "Extended Strategy," *Journal of Politics*, II (1940), 189–200; "The Growth of the Race Idea," *Review of Politics*, II (1940), 283–317; and "Some Problems of the German Hegemony," *Journal of Politics*, III (1941), 154–68.

I remember one occasion when someone at a professional meeting challenged Voegelin to demonstrate that his use of the word *transcendence* had any meaning that could be connoted in common form to anyone in the audience. To illustrate the extent to which men's judgments are constantly made in transcendental terms, Voegelin referred the questioner to virtually any newspaper headline involving what were then the early stages of the space race between the United States and the Soviet Union. The meanings attached by the protagonists in this competition were invariably cast in terms that extended far beyond the pragmatic results of getting the rockets into outer space; in almost every instance, cosmic significance was attached to the achievement in relation to one or the other great power's view of itself. Much more than the actual state of science and technology was at stake: Both countries were dealing in symbols that transcended the ordinary, immediately observable state of existence; each was articulating its meaning as an entity that had an existence beyond the finite men and materials temporarily engaged in a particular activity. Voegelin's answer simply called attention to a basic fact open to observation at the most elementary empirical level: Man is continually reaching beyond the limits of his finite existence, regardless of whether this experience in transcendence is at the higher levels of philosophy or revealed religion or is associated, as in the illustration at hand, with a less conscious, but no less real, projection of a state of pragmatic action into a judgment involving transcendental implications. If, however, one chooses to ignore the relevance of such observations to social theory, because of either a failure of discernment or a prior closure against the admission of the epistemological validity of any experience of transcendence, one cannot even question the meaning of such experience for the problems of individual and social existence. Having become aware of the data in the form in which they are presented to the conscious mind, one may then proceed to develop the means appropriate to an inquiry into variant forms and their relations to one another.

Voegelin's work habits are also worth commenting on briefly. I have never known any man with his combination of physical energy, capacity for sustained concentration, and the dedication of will necessary to work at the pace and with the degree of continuity that he manages to achieve. While he was at LSU, for example, his usual pattern was to come to the campus for classes, return home for a brief nap, and then work until the small hours of the morning. He held a seminar in his home one evening a week, and even after three or four hours of intensely analytical discussion, he hardly paused before retreating to his study for several hours of research and writing. When he was concentrating on a particularly difficult problem he would forgo all social engagements for weeks at a time. My impression of his behavior in other settings is that much the same pattern prevailed, although in later years (despite increasing demands on his time for administration and public appearances) he has seemed to be under less internal pressure and a bit more leisurely than in the earlier years.

When I first met him, Voegelin was working, under an agreement with a commercial publisher, on a history of political ideas. Although he had already reached the point at which he was approaching the elements of a philosophy of history by way of the "problems of harmonization between the histories of theory and of politics which arise for the modern period," I believe he was still looking for patterns of history and parallel theoretical sources somewhat after the manner of Oswald Spengler and, more important, of Arnold Toynbee. But the inadequacies of this method, too, loomed larger as he worked through the materials for the history of ideas.[3] It is not easy to identify the elements leading to this change chronologically, because the influences themselves do not follow a straight-line pattern. Even before 1940 Voegelin was reaching beyond the origins of Western history in the Hellenic area; he was increasingly absorbed with earlier influences on modern Western civilization and with other parallel civilizations. For example, he began to study Hebrew while he was still at Alabama in order to comprehend the prehistory of Christianity. And when he worked through the history of ideas up to Friedrich Wilhelm Joseph von Schelling, he found that Schelling's philosophy of myth

3. Voegelin wrote literally hundreds of pages of well-integrated commentary on the political philosophers from the Greeks to the present, all enriched by his capacity to set each thinker in his appropriate historical background. In his courses on the history of ideas in the 1940s and 1950s he taught from these manuscripts, which, if published in their present form, would far surpass any of the standard commentaries in accuracy of detail, comprehensiveness, and internal coherence.

and revelation made it imperative that he learn more about myth as a historical form of symbolization of the existence of social and political entities.

It was becoming increasingly clear to him in all this that ideas are not entities in history; the real entities are societies, which express their existence in history through an enormously complex set of symbols. With this realization Voegelin abandoned the idea of writing a history of ideas and began his inquiry into the variety of symbolic manifestations through which historical societies express their existence, the way in which these differing symbolic forms are related to one another, and the problem of discerning the extent to which the experiences symbolized approach reality and thereby provide a basis for order. This is the source of what Gregor Sebba refers to as "new theory" and Voegelin is inclined to call the work of "retheoretization."

When I returned to LSU for my first year of graduate work after World War II, Voegelin was deeply engrossed in this new set of problems. He had already begun to rework Plato within the framework of the transition from myth to philosophy, which represented a major shift in symbolic forms under the influence of an expanding human consciousness. This changing focus seems to me to have been the point of departure for the eventual development of *Order and History*.

To those of us who were in his classes and seminars and who worked on research problems under his direction during this period, these new concerns manifested themselves most clearly in his emphasis on the Aristotelian concept of the nous (the rational soul), the noetic virtues identified with this philosophic symbol, and the problems of Gnosticism. It was the latter theme—the adaptation of the Gnostic heresy as a concept for analyzing the problems of modernity—that furnished the theoretical foundation for *The New Science of Politics*, which was published in 1952, after having been presented as the Walgreen Lectures at the University of Chicago in 1951, under the general title "Truth and Representation."

Voegelin preferred the title of the lectures to that later given the book, and with good reason. His use of *representation* refers to the way in which a society represents itself symbolically in order to establish its existence in history. Although he deals briefly with other forms of symbolization of experience in *The New Science of Politics* (thus foreshadowing the expanded theoretical treatment in *Order and History*), his main concern is the self-interpretation of the Western world that took place through the Christian experience and the subsequent distortion of those symbols in the modern era in ways that had been identified at the very outset of Christianity (through the original definition of Gnosticism) as a dangerous threat to the truths of the revealed Christian religion and the order which grew out of it. *The New Science of Politics* might be perceived in retrospect as a compressed case study of the way in which a symbolic self-interpretation on which an order (both of the individual psyche and of the society) has been based can break down when the experiences in which its truth is grounded are no longer present in the consciousness of the intellectuals and rulers who articulate the variations on the original symbols. The case just happens to have been our own civilization in its recent historical and contemporary setting, with the Christian symbols of a salvation beyond temporal history being transmuted into immanentist ideologies (and revolutionary mass movements based on them) promising a perfection of man and society within the future confines of world history.

By the time *The New Science of Politics* made its appearance, Voegelin was far advanced in his comprehensive study *Order and History*, the first three volumes of which appeared in 1956 (*Israel and Revelation*) and 1957 (*The World of the Polis* and *Plato and Aristotle*). Six volumes were planned originally; the last three were to be concerned mainly with the developments in Western civilization (empire and Christianity, the Protestant centuries, and the crisis of Western civilization), although the projected fourth volume was supposed to include an analysis of the simultaneous rise of several empires beginning about the sixth century B.C., each based on the notion of its universality and each paralleled by the appearances of religious prophets or philosophers whose teachings "raised humanity to a new level of consciousness." As the work progressed beyond the first three volumes Voegelin concentrated on these ecumenical imperial movements. He gradually excluded altogether the idea of carrying the work to completion by means of a chronological, periodized history of the order and disorder of

Western civilization alone. For several years, down to about the mid-1960s, he thought about rounding out *Order and History* with a single concluding volume on the ecumenical civilizations. The corpus of ideas that was to be included in this fourth volume was outlined in his Stevenson Memorial Lecture, "World Empire and the Unity of Mankind," delivered in London in 1961 and published in *International Affairs* in 1962. This change of plans was related to a change in theoretical perspective; his historical studies revealed an even larger and more complicated set of problems associated with man's interpretation of his existence. The patterns of history produced through external phenomenal description (a residue perhaps from his early contacts with philosophies of history from the eighteenth century to Toynbee) were perceived as theoretically subordinate to larger questions of human consciousness which made their appearance in several different forms in virtually all phases of human history. As in all successful efforts to move from the virtual infinity of potential materials to explanatory theory, Voegelin was ordering his vast empirical knowledge of history into broader and broader conceptual generalizations. And more and more, these generalizations were related to the central question that Henri Bergson had delineated as the "opening of the soul" to transcendent divinity.

Order and History contains the more patterned explanations of the historical developments of this openness to the ground of existence; the work in which Voegelin is now engaged is an exploration of the phenomenon as it occurs in the individual consciousness of a variety of human types, including philosophers, artists, mystics, and theologians, in widely different settings. He is thus in the process of moving from a study of the order of history, which can be apprehended by an examination of the history of man's search for order, to an inquiry into man's conscious experience of the transcendental source of his existence. Although he expresses it more obliquely, Voegelin is moving from the formulation of a philosophy of history to an exposition of the "drama of humanity."

In *Order and History* Voegelin summed up the major theoretical components of his earlier studies (many of which turn up in sequential parts in various "minor" publications scattered over a long period of time). Beginning with man's omnipresent inquiry into the relations among man, society, God, and the universe, Voegelin proceeds to demonstrate the forms which have been used to symbolize the experiences which have grown out of this search for meaning. The earliest form was the myth, which manifested itself variously as cosmological, theogonic, or anthropogonic, and moved from compact to differentiated expressions. The other symbolic forms, which, because they express the experience of further opening of the soul toward the ultimately unknowable transcendent ground of existence Voegelin refers to as "leaps in being," are philosophy and revelation. But closure is also a historical phenomenon. The symbolic forms lose their meaning through detachment from the experiences out of which they were generated. As in the case of Gnosticism, a "second reality" (as Robert Musil put it) overlays the reality of existence and disorients and disorders man and society. Since man's existential dilemma consists of a quest for that which is unattainable in its ultimate form, the historical setting in which the quest takes place is an open one; the end of history is beyond history rather than with it.

Order and History could not be finished, either in its original intended form or in its curtailed form, for a variety of reasons.[4] The origins of Christianity were much more complicated than had initially been supposed. The ecumenic empires were not simply cosmological in their symbolism; one has to go back farther into their prehistories to understand the complexities of their symbolic expression. The straight line from Judaism through Christianity to Gnosis is not the only pattern of symbols and distortions that needs to be analyzed in the Western experience; the philosophic symbols growing out of Platonism (and the later distortions of these symbols by Neoplatonists) parallel the interpretations of Christianity and its Gnostic crisis throughout Western history. The rapid development of the fields of archeology, the ancient Orient, Far Eastern studies, African studies, comparative religion, and the

---

4. This comment, and the foregoing remarks generally, should not be construed to mean that *Order and History* is not to be "finished." A fifth and final volume, *In Search of Order*, is being prepared. It will consist of a series of studies (some previously published) of ecumenic empires, of Christianity, and of the eclipse of reality; the projection is a work that will serve the dual purposes of completing *Order and History* and preparing the way for the further theoretical perspectives to be developed separately as the "drama of humanity."

philosophy of symbolism has thrown up new problems. All of these, and other influences, broke the pattern intended for *Order and History*, not by outmoding what was done there, but by enlarging the scope of the inquiry and requiring a broader historical source from which to generalize about man's experiences with the transcendent basis of order and its immanentist variations.

This new departure is well illustrated in Voegelin's analysis of Henry James, which appeared in the *Southern Review*, in January, 1971. The enlargement of perspective between the original letter and the postscript is typical of Voegelin's expanding analytical facility. In the first piece, the rather obscure symbols are clarified in light of the historical legacy of Calvinism and the influence of Sigmund Freud. In the postscript the earlier work is not vitiated, but the analysis is deepened by the penetration to the very formation of James's consciousness under the influence of the immanentist developments of later modernity; and the obscurantism of the symbols not only is revealed but is extended into the subsequent stages of the deterioration that James has prefigured.

At least one other study of recent vintage is an extended essay in *Studium Generale* (1971) entitled "On Hegel—A Study in Sorcery," in which Voegelin analyzes (again with overpowering command of the sources) the stages by which Georg Wilhelm Friedrich Hegel misuses his formidable knowledge of philosophy to convert its symbols into a "second reality" in which Hegel himself becomes the Logos through which history is shaped, thereby literally transmogrifying himself into Christ.

In light of this all-too-sketchy review of the changes in the focus of Voegelin's historical inquiries over time, it is to be expected that other studies of consciousness similar to those on James and Hegel will be forthcoming. It may also be expected that the new ventures in the "drama of humanity" will evoke, as his work always has in the past, new theories that are at once more expansive in what they explain and more precise in the detailing of the direct influences from which the generalizations are drawn. But like the compulsion of humanity toward the ground of existence which the existential condition of man places ever out of reach, we may also expect that the love of wisdom (the literal *philosophia*) that impels Voegelin's quest will go on without his reaching that definitive end which also remains constantly beyond the reach of man.

VII Notes on Voegelin's Contributions to Political Theory

From time to time one runs across or hears about a rank-ordered listing of outstanding American political scientists, usually consisting of about ten names. Rumor even has it that on one occasion two of the eminences who had been singled out for a distinction of this type were engaged in a dispute over some matter having to do with the state of the discipline, and one of them closed out the argument (without regard to the substance of the issue) by pointing out that his position should carry the day because he stood a place or two ahead of the other in the rankings. So far as I know, Eric Voegelin's name has never appeared on such a list. Indeed, with some regularity he has been tacitly excluded from serious consideration in the debate over the nature of the discipline and the relative standings of the contributions of various scholars to it by the implication or the outright assertion that he is not a political scientist at all.

The foregoing paragraph is not intended to be totally facetious. For a number of reasons any adequate assessment of Voegelin as a political theorist, especially in the present context, will also have to be—at least inferentially—an assessment or critique of the state of political science. In the first place, Voegelin's professional self-identity has always been as a political scientist, however puzzling this may seem to colleagues who, though not quite sure what political science is, or what its practitioners should be doing, are sufficiently uncomfortable with Voegelin's language and conceptual concerns to want to label him as something else. But his teaching appointments in American and German universities for some thirty years have been in political science, and he has boldly affirmed the dependence of any science on the existence of a collegial working relationship, for "science is not the singlehanded achievement of this or that individual scholar; it is a cooperative effort. Effective work is possible only within a tradition of intellectual culture."[1]

Despite these apparent identifying characteristics as a member of the political science profession, Voegelin is rightly suspect in that role by those who are somewhat uncertain about the possibility of a science of politics, and even more so by those who are positive that a science of politics based on the methods of the natural sciences not only is possible but has been or is about to be achieved. For one thing, Voegelin persists in the use of a terminology that does not convey the immediate meaning that orthodox political scientists ascribe to it. He talks for instance, about the "science" of man and society and its origins in the *episteme politike* of the classical philosophers, whereas they understand "science" in the reductionist sense which Voegelin identifies as a

> scientistic creed . . . characterized by three dogmas: (1) the assumption that the mathematized science of natural phenomena is a model science to which all other sciences ought to conform; (2) that all realms of being are accessible to the methods of the sciences of phenomena; and (3) that all reality which is not accessible to sciences of phenomena is either irrelevant, or in the more radical form of the dogma, illusionary. The creed implies two great denials: it denies the dignity of science to the quest for substance in nature, in man and society, as well as in transcendental reality; and in the more radical form, it denies the reality of substance.

Stranger still, Voegelin talks about the empirical basis of theory even when his references are to meanings in history, experiences of transcendence, symbolism, and such abstract "values" as order. Every "scientist," on the other hand, knows that scientists are supposed to do their work without resorting to value judgments, that values are subjective and are properly advanced as "preferences" which are outside the bounds of cognitive validation, and

---

1. In "Autobiographical Notes," taped by Ellis Sandoz, Voegelin explains his selection of a career in political science in preference to other possible choices as "partly economic, partly . . . principle" (p. 3). Sandoz has graciously permitted me to use the notes as "reinforcing" references in this essay. Relying on other sources, I have discussed some of the early influences on Voegelin as a political scientist, as well as his "position" vis-à-vis neo-Kantian positivism, in my essay "The Changing Pattern of Voegelin's Conception of History and Consciousness," *Southern Review*, New Ser., VII (Winter, 1971), 52. Eric Voegelin, *The New Science of Politics* (Chicago: University of Chicago Press, 1952), 23.

that science is based on "facts" apprehended by observation of external (objective) phenomena.[2]

It is a disturbing experience for those whose language symbols derive from the "climate of opinion" (which Voegelin frequently cites as Alfred North Whitehead's term) within contemporary culture to be confronted with a language which suggests that they are operating from a closed "position" with respect to problems of epistemology and methodology, rather than from an openness to the exploration of reality based on an abiding tradition of inquiry reaching at least to classical antiquity. It is not surprising, therefore, that most political scientists (and American ones, particularly) should react defensively in the face of this threat to the substantiality of their self-contained intellectual world. It is far easier and more in keeping with the nature of the problem as Voegelin has addressed it to make dogmatic assertions about the meaning of science and to relegate Voegelin to the status of a "metaphysician" or worse, than to try to come to grips with the direction of his inquiry and its results. During the roughly twenty years (*ca.* 1950–1970) when the struggle within the discipline was between an aggressive behavioralist movement, solidly united under the positivist creed, and an amalgam of groups (mostly rather passive and generally aphilosophical) commonly designated by behavioralists as "traditionalists," Voegelin tended to be assigned to the latter category by the behavioralists, although there is not much evidence of his having more than a *pro forma* acceptance by most of the diffuse elements of traditionalism. In their standard work on the profession, Somit and Tanenhaus have summed the matter up most appositely: "On the other side of the ideological fence, there was Eric Voegelin's impressive but less widely read *The New Science of Politics*."[3]

---

2. Eric Voegelin, "The Origins of Scientism," *Social Research*, XV (December, 1948), 462. Voegelin often makes the distinction between a generic understanding of science as *episteme*, which is open to any question pertinent to human experience, and the appropriation of the term *science* by those who wish to limit the questions which may be legitimately asked to those which can be responded to by the methods of the sciences of natural phenomena. Perhaps the earliest extended discussion in the strict context of the social sciences is in Voegelin, *The New Science of Politics*, esp. 3–13.

3. Albert Somit and Joseph Tanenhaus, *The Development of Political Science: From*

Voegelin's understanding of theory also tends to differentiate him as a political scientist from those who might be considered more representative of the state of the discipline in its current self-conception(s). In reading Voegelin's books and essays I do not think it is possible to abstract a firmly fixed concept of what theory is out of the totality of the inquiry in which he is engaged. For one thing, he is wary of everything that smacks of a definitional fixture of any of the experiences he examines. He does not use the terms *theory, theoretical,* and *retheoretization* as familiar language symbols to connote a logically coherent, but inadequately tested, explanation to be used as a framework for directing experimental inquiry, or a synthesized explanation of the results of empirical analysis, or a union of these two cognitive functions which forms a paradigm according to which science proceeds. Even if theory has a guiding role with respect to science and is also, in a special sense, the sum of the state of affirmed knowledge at a given time, it is much more than this. Although the term is not altogether satisfactory, one might say that theory, for Voegelin, is more a process than a logical construct abstracted from the whole experiential activity which produced it. A scientist is involved with theoretical activity from his confrontation with the first stimulus to inquiry, through the framing of the questions which he seeks to answer, into the methods appropriate to the inquiry, and on to the framing of the symbols by which he interprets and communicates the experiences which both direct this process and are the objects of its investigation.

This implied union of subject and object, through which the theoretical process moves, however, pushes us beyond the limits of the present argument and into the more substantive problem which Voegelin delineates as man's awareness of being a participant in

---

Burgess to Behavioralism (Boston: Allyn and Bacon, 1967), 188. Although neither Voegelin nor the behavioralists would be likely to accept the designation of their work as "ideological," a good many of the more vigorous proponents of behavioralism have exhibited some of the behavioral characteristics of persons engaged in an ideological cause. Voegelin has had followers, to be sure, but he has continued his work (including some cogent discussions of the nature of ideology) without propagating doctrine by means of a claque organized as a "movement." Neither his mode of behavior nor his animadversions on ideology have prevented others from ascribing to him a wide range of ideological positions, and most of these ascriptions blatantly contradict one another.

the structural reality of which he is a part. For the moment it is sufficient to stipulate that the structure of reality is such that man's participation in it by way of the theoretical activity is never complete. Although the constant object of the search may be identified, knowledge is not accessible in final form to man as subject-participant because realization of this aspiration would transgress the limits of man which result from his being part of the natural world as well as consubstantial with the divine ground of that world. The condition of man, then, is an essential source of his theoretical activity, as well as a limit on the results to be achieved by theory. Not only may the theoretical activity be misdirected, but because it takes place within the flux of history, its achievements may be misplaced or lost over time and have to be recovered by way of recollection and retheoretization, which involves re-creating the experiences through which the theoretical attainments were realized rather than a mere recovery of the symbols by means of which they were expressed. Realization of the limit-end of the quest is as much a fact of the theoretical activity as are any of the other logically analyzable, but practically inseparable, components of the whole of this activity.

Although the term *theory* has not been clearly or consistently delineated in the literature of American political science, a cursory examination of the recent tendency to modify the noun (often with other noun-adjectives) provides some insights into the prevailing inclinations toward a scientific orthodoxy, an orthodoxy quite at odds with Voegelin's theoretical contribution. The separation of "empirical" theory from "normative" theory, for instance, further illustrates the point made earlier about the extent to which the dominant trend has been toward the acceptance of the natural sciences as the definitive model for the science of man and society and, beyond this, the extent to which method has come to displace theoretical relevance as the determinant of the choice of objects to be studied in the pursuit of a science of politics. I do not want to dwell too long on this subject, but it should be noted that the context in which "empirical theory" usually appears includes the assumption (more often implicit than explicit) that politics has an objectively ordered structure analogous to the order of nature, which has been successfully penetrated by the mathematized natural sciences.[4]

The further modification of *theory* into the stratified conceptions of "explanatory" (the lower order) and "causal" theory (the higher order) implies a progressive development, the culmination of which is a predictive science of politics. Although disappointment has been expressed from time to time about the slowness with which the massive enterprise that American political science has become in recent years is moving toward this perceived goal, little evidence can be adduced to show that the proponents have seriously addressed the question of what a definitive knowledge of politics predicated on such foundations would imply. Would a technology of manipulative control over man and society emerge from such a completed theoretical pursuit? And would the results of that potential dominance over the scientifically revealed structure of man and society produce a utopia or a nightmare? Thus far, the failure of a science of politics modeled on the natural sciences to produce even an explanatory theory, let alone a causal one, has led (at least within the discipline) to little more than the suggestion that, in the period of waiting for the Godot of grand theory, the profession should concentrate on "middle-range" theory. Apparently such a pursuit would ensure a continuation of the positivist mode, and perpetuate a concern with problems which do not disturb either the political "system" within which the theoretical activity takes place or the kind of theory which makes no effort to cope with politics as part of the full range of human experience.

From the appearance of *The New Science of Politics* onward, Voegelin has been engaged in a theoretical effort at its highest level. That effort has involved two tightly interrelated activities: First, he has offered a devastating criticism of political science as it has virtually destroyed our grasp of political reality through the positivist reduction. In the course of this criticism he has also demonstrated how positivism opened the way for immanentist ideol-

4. For a reasonably succinct discussion of the confusing range of meaning ascribed to "political theory," see Neil A. McDonald and James N. Rosenau, "Political Theory as Academic Field and Intellectual Activity," *Journal of Politics*, XXX (May, 1968), 311–44.

ogies to replace a science of man and society based on ontology. Second, he has produced an increasingly complex and authoritative articulation of what is involved in the restoration of the theoretical content of politics that explores the reality of politics from the perspective of the generality of human experience. Gregor Sebba has characterized Voegelin's participation in theoretical activity in these terms:

> The question: What is political science? is being answered anew out of a radical reconsideration of the question: What is political reality, and what cognitive avenues lead to its critical understanding?
>
> Two factors have so far stood in the way of recognizing this extremely rapid development of new theory, quite apart from its newness. The first factor is that, in contrast to behavioral social science, it is not the result of many theoretical and technological research advances initiated by a number of social scientists and continued by a host of workers backed by enormous institutional support; it is largely the work of one independent thinker, Eric Voegelin, who published his first book four decades ago, launched his major enterprise a dozen years ago and is still forging ahead at a pace which leaves his best readers behind....
>
> The second factor is of course the enormous demand which the new development makes upon the newcomer to such studies. To gain an adequate understanding—not even a critical one—he must be able to follow some of the most abstract philosophical reasoning found today, he must have a thorough knowledge of the history of thought, philosophy, metaphysics, epistemology, religion and theology, of political theory, and of political history from the Sumerians to the present; he must know the present state of scholarship in fields like anthropology, biblical criticism, comparative literature, psychology—the list is by no means complete. All this is very far from the concerns of the practicing political scientist today.[5]

This summation provides more than a brief assessment of the extent of the separation between Voegelin's new science of politics and the new science of behavioralist politics which is still in the ascendency in the profession; it also suggests some of the difficulties of attempting even a simple exegesis of Voegelin's work, let alone trying to draw on his achievement to provide a sustaining core of theory around which an intellectual culture devoted to *episteme politike* might be developed. Some of these problems of

5. Gregor Sebba, "The Present State of Political Theory," *Polity*, I (Winter, 1968), 263–64.

interpretation and potential extrapolation can be understood only in light of the interplay between certain biographical events and the chronological development of topical concerns in Voegelin's work. Obviously an analysis of this type cannot be attempted here, but at least a cursory exposition of some of the features of his scholarship and writing may furnish a useful background against which the substance of his theoretical contribution may be made a little clearer.

The unity of Voegelin's work is not to be found in an emphasis on historical chronology, a particular object of study (whether it be a historical unit of social or political organization or the meaning of an abstract concept in its concrete manifestations), or a focus on any one method appropriate to an understanding of man's experience with politics. The constancy of the search is, of course, the most obvious feature of his *bios theoretikos*, and one might say that the evocative pull exerted by the literal *philosophia* is undoubtedly the motivation behind the total dedication to scholarship he has demonstrated both in his teaching and in his voluminous and complex research productivity. But this is a personal quality that does not necessarily culminate in theoretical coherence on a scale worthy of being designated a science. One can point to other scholars who worked tirelessly to produce reams of books and articles, some of which have become minor classics on special subjects, but whose cumulative results do not seem to be informed by any principles that would enable them to lay claim to a theoretical achievement on this level.[6]

6. Walter Lippmann affords an example which is almost too easy—and not, as some academic political scientists would have it, because he was just a "journalist" (although the pressure of keeping abreast of, and writing about, public affairs on a day-to-day basis may have played a part in limiting his potential as a political theorist). Even when Lippmann's books attracted the attention of serious students of international politics, public opinion, and political philosophy by reason of his obvious analytical craftsmanship, he never reached the point of breaking through to the unifying reality behind his insights into particular problems. Not only did he move through several varieties of ideology (most of them within the general framework of liberalism) without going much beyond the treatment of each set of problems as sequential correctives of each other, but even when his critical faculties were at their best and he perceived that fundamental gaps existed in the "public philosophy," he saw rather more the results of the deficiencies than what kind of theoretical inquiry would be needed to understand and correct them.

Throughout Voegelin's work, one can detect the persistence of the questions designed to establish theoretical relevance, the abiding nature of the general topics one has to elucidate in the course of the inquiry, and the way in which methods emerge from and are applied to the problems thus identified. Because these constants do not always stand in the same relation to one another within the various parts of the work, and because the constants themselves are always being sharpened and extended in relation to their particular applications to the historical materials on which he works at a given time, Voegelin appears to some who have not read him carefully to range over an impossibly large source material which he interprets almost capriciously on the basis of abstract conceptions which have little concrete meaning. On the contrary, the work is cumulative in a dual sense: Each new subject addressed expands the scope of the empirical inquiry (usually in terms both of historical extension and of the variety of symbolic forms examined) and simultaneously displays a refinement of the larger theoretical context within which the particular problem is set. Critical analysis is thus guided by the state of theory previously developed, even as the expanded range of criticism is extending, sharpening, and reinforcing the general theory on which a science of politics is predicated. As Dante Germino has noted: "To Voegelin political science and political theory are inseparably bound together."[7]

The point can be illustrated by a brief overview of the order in which the work has unfolded. In this context it is worth noting that the internal patterns of Voegelin's theoretical development closely parallel some of the preconditions and subsequent developments in his general interpretation of the way in which a science of order has emerged under various historical circumstances. In *The New Science of Politics*, where he first explains at some length the nature of his general quest, he points out that the expansion of political science to its full grandeur "as the science of human existence in society and history, as well as the principles of order in general, has been typical for the great epochs of a revolutionary and criti-

---

7. Dante Germino, *Beyond Ideology: The Revival of Political Theory* (New York: Harper and Row, 1967), 163.

cal nature." At that point he identifies three great epochal crises in Western history, each marked by the production of a major theoretical development: the foundation of political science by Plato and Aristotle in the Hellenic crisis, Saint Augustine's *Civitas Dei* in the crisis of Rome and Christianity, and Hegel's philosophy of law and history in "the first major earthquake of the Western crisis." In between, minor epochs occurred and secondary restorations took place—for example, Bodin in the sixteenth century.[8]

This conception of the stimulus to a theoretical science of order in man and society, or the restoration of the principles of such a science, out of a crisis in the existential order of man and society is a constant, but its application, so to speak, changes in the context of the unfolding analysis of a larger and larger field of empirical historical materials. Among other examples that might be cited, two seem to me to stand out. In his later treatment of Hegel, Voegelin had moved so far away from the epochal theme (which implies historical regularity in the responsive relation of science to crisis) and had developed his own critical theory to such an extent (through further studies of pre-Socratic philosophy, Gnosticism, and the seventeenth-century Neoplatonists, among others) that he was able to discern in Hegel's response to the crisis of Western modernity as manifested in the French Revolution a perversion of the ordering symbols of philosophy in the form of an egophanic revolt against reality, which was less a restoration of a science of order than a symptom of how deep the Western crisis of order had become. On the other hand, the conception is given new content and vigor when Voegelin applies it once again in his remarkably compact analysis of the classical experience of reason, where he is not dealing "with the 'idea' or a nominalist 'definition' of reason but with the process in reality in which concrete human beings, the 'lovers of wisdom,' the philosophers as they styled themselves, were engaged in an act of resistance against the personal and social disorder of their age." Once again we see the concept in application in a fuller dimension than ever, following the intervening work on the polis, Plato and Aristotle, and the elaboration of a philosophy of consciousness in *Anamnesis*. Here we have

8. Voegelin, *The New Science of Politics*, 2.

the originating influence of personal and societal disorder closely related to the penetration through the symbols to the experience of reason as the substance and source of understanding of reality, and the bold interpretation of the philosophers as being in revolt against the disorder of their age as the starting point for their discovery of reason.[9]

Voegelin's awareness of the disorders of the age as they manifested themselves in the ideologies of the twentieth century, and the wars and revolutions into which mass movements based on these ideologies debouched, was also the point of departure for his search for a science that might explain not only how such disorder came about but also what sources one might draw on for a restoration of order. As a student in Vienna in the early 1920s he was apparently fairly well adjusted to the "climate of opinion" of the time and place. For a time the neo-Kantian positivist circle influenced him, especially since he was an assistant to Hans Kelsen. But other experiences, too complex to go into here, pushed him in new directions which led eventually to the study of order and history. The process was in close keeping with his suggestion that science starts from an assessment of the concrete political events in the immediate range of one's experience. The value neutrality of the pure science of law (and of Max Weber) was no defense against the insurgency of ideologies, so Voegelin increasingly became interested in political ideas as manifestations of ideology.

The books and monographs of the 1930s—on the race idea, the authoritarian state, and political religions—were part of the effort to come to grips with these problems. His subsequent assessment of these works follows the pattern of his retrospection at any given time on almost any of his earlier work: They were all right as special studies, but were not sufficiently well informed by some theoretical principle or principles revealed through later work to be more than tentative. The study of the authoritarian state, for example, which was his first attempt to penetrate the role of contemporary ideologies, Right and Left, was written before Voegelin had fully analyzed the distortion of language characteristic of ideolo-

9. Eric Voegelin, "On Hegel—A Study in Sorcery," *Studium Generale*, XXIV (1971), 355–68; Eric Voegelin, "Reason: The Classic Experience," *Southern Review*, New Ser., X (Spring, 1974), 237.

gies. The term *authoritarian* itself is too closely related to ideological ways of characterizing regimes to serve as an adequate theoretical category for examining the effort of a state to assert its
authority against ideological movements bent on imposing themselves by using constitutional arrangements which they then destroy. Similarly, the study of political religions relied on a literature which treated ideologies as secular varieties of religions, a
usage which tended to distort the experiences by mixing them with
problems of dogma and doctrine, and by lumping together a number of phenomena which should have been differentiated more fully
for comparative purposes.[10]

The interplay of the rising interest in the history of political ideas,
the broadening of contacts with the intellectual world beyond Vienna (especially the time spent in the United States, England, and
France under a Laura Spelman Rockefeller grant in the 1920s), and
the course of political events in Austria in the early 1930s led Voegelin into the study of Christianity and classical antiquity. Shortly
after his move to America in 1938 he started to work on a history
of Western political ideas; at first the project was conceived as a
textbook, but the scope of the materials soon outran that objective. The history was written in large part by the late 1940s, and it
covered the typical period from the Hellenic origins until well into
the nineteenth century. The theoretical focus which emerged in this
work was the concentration on Christianity and classical philosophy as the experiential substance out of which Western civilization emerged, and which constituted the sources of order for Western man and society. The critical standard against which the ideas
of major figures in Western thought were examined was Voegelin's exegesis of Plato and Aristotle and the major sources through
which the Christian experience was interpreted. If one applies one
of Voegelin's categories from another context, the understanding
of Christianity and classical philosophy, which he was to differentiate more fully in the later works, was already there in compact

10. "Autobiographical Notes," 41, 50–55. A slightly more extended discussion
of the relation of *The Authoritarian State* (1936) to both the 1920 Austrian constitution (Kelsen was the principal draftsman) and the Dollfuss corporative constitution of 1934 is to be found in Havard, "The Changing Pattern of Voegelin's Conception of History and Consciousness," 56–57.

form (and was actually in the process of differentiation in the various revisions of the history).

By the late 1940s Voegelin was uncertain about the future course of the history. As usual, he felt compelled to push his inquiries far beyond the boundaries set by the project as originally conceived, and as altered from textbook to multivolume interpretation of the patterns in the history of Western civilization revealed by way of political ideas. The studies of both Christianity and the classics required further consideration of the deeper historical background of their origins, so the Hebraic studies and the exploration of the historical sources on the ancient Near Eastern empires were begun. In the course of the work on Schelling, Voegelin also began to question the conception of a history of ideas as a means of elucidating political reality. If I read him correctly, Voegelin began at this point to see the necessity for getting beyond "ideas" to the symbols through which societies expressed their meanings for existence in history, and then to penetrate the symbolizations in order to understand the experiences of reality that the symbols express. The problem of the relations of ideas to symbols and of symbols to experience is an extremely difficult one which cannot be discussed in any detail here, so for the moment it is sufficient to leave it that the perception of this problem, together with the expansion of the historical perspective to other civilizations, led to the abandonment of the history of political ideas as a method of grasping political reality.[11]

11. Although materials developed from the history have been worked into *The New Science of Politics; Wissenchaft, Politik und Gnosis* (Munich: Koesel-Verlag, 1959); *Anamnesis: Zur Theorie der Geschichte und Politik* (Munich: R. Piper Verlag, 1966); and four volumes of *Order and History* (Baton Rouge: Louisiana State University Press, 1956, 1957, 1974), Voegelin refused separate publication of the history of Western ideas, in whole or in part, until the appearance of *From Enlightenment to Revolution*, ed. John H. Hallowell (Durham, N.C.: Duke University Press, 1975), which selectively covers the period from Voltaire through Marx. I think that Voegelin underestimates the importance of the history, not only as a major factor in leading him into more penetrating methods of theoretical inquiry, but also as a source for understanding his theories of man and society and his philosophy of history. The theories are embedded in the historical criticism: Even if "ideas" are twice removed from experiences of reality, the language through which they are expressed is a symbolic form which Voegelin analyzes with great skill to demonstrate the distortion of reality or, in some instances, the effectiveness of the symbolization of reality embodied in the expressions of ideas. In "Autobiographical Notes" he indicates the variations in points of time at which various influences made their

The invitation to give the Walgreen Lectures in Chicago in 1951 offered the opportunity to formulate some of the theoretical principles that had emerged from the historical studies which had resulted in his placing the history of ideas in abeyance. The lectures were published as *The New Science of Politics*, and the book is in many respects an attenuated version of the theory that has been unfolded in the subsequent twenty-five years. I do not wish to summarize the book at this point, but rather to place it in the context of the theoretical development. By this time Voegelin had gone far beyond the origins of the search in the disorders of his own time and was expressing in cryptic form the ways in which Western society had symbolized its existence in history, how those symbols had differentiated over time, and how the symbols which most closely approximated reality had been deformed to the point of producing the present crisis of order. Once again it is possible to see the major conceptions in early stages of elucidation relative to the later explorations. Included (among a host of lesser themes) are the forms of representational symbols embodied in the cosmological myths of the earliest civilizations, the representational symbolization of transcendence through Greek philosophy, revelation in Israel, and the soteriological truth of Christianity. All of these subjects were to be explored in detail and under more completely worked-out theoretical principles in *Order and History*.

Perhaps of most importance in this particular volume was the examination of Gnosticism as the particular source of explanation for the conversion of the Christian symbols of transcendent reality into immanentist interpretations which are distortions of reality and sources of disorder. In *The New Science of Politics*, Voegelin discusses the way in which Gnosticism developed during the course of the struggles which attended the decline of the ancient world and the growth of the new multi-ethnic ecumenic empires, with Christianity emerging as dominant in the West. In view of Christianity's symbolization of the realms of existence as being divided

---

initial, if still unformed, impacts on his thinking; many of the fully developed theories are thus discernible in their incipient (and sometimes more than incipient) stages in the history, which itself has undergone many revisions. Elsewhere I have argued that the best approach to Voegelin by the neophyte is through *From Enlightenment to Revolution*. See my essay "Voegelin's Diagnosis of the Western Crisis," *Denver Quarterly*, X (Autumn, 1975); 133–34.

between the eternal, transcendent realm of God and finite, mundane realm of man, with salvation for man possible only beyond the world, the Gnostic vision of the world as a place of total chaos which was itself to be transformed into a world of perfected, durable order by divine or human intervention was, of course, in its manifestation within Christianity, heretical. As Voegelin indicates, Gnosticism persists in various forms through the entire course of the Western Christian Era, but was generally contained until the erosion of the meaning behind the Christian symbols permitted Gnostic symbols of reality to take over the representational function among the nation-states of the Western world. The result is a steady acceleration in the intensity of the revolt against God and man in the attempt to realize one or another of the Gnostic dreamworlds that have become the new versions of reality. The path has been from progressivism through utopianism to totalitarianism.

A problem of interpretation arises here that again illustrates the difficulty of entering into a serious discussion of Voegelin's theory with the general run of political scientists. Even some of his closest readers have had difficulty perceiving in the application of the concept "Gnosticism" to the analysis of the political disorders of modernity anything more than a useful analogical tool (and an exceptionally loose one at that) for characterizing and categorizing historical events.[12] It is difficult enough to comprehend that the Christian (and classical philosophical) symbolizations of reality have been sufficiently evocative of the experiences of reality to be able to touch the consciousness of so large a segment of mankind as to form the basis of reality for a civilizational order persisting through two millennia. But the notion that that entire history was acted upon by a persisting doctrinal conversion of those symbols (including especially the trinitarian symbols of sacred history and eschatological expectation, both of which were immanentized) and

12. In his essay "Order and History: The Breaking of the Program," *Denver Quarterly*, (Autumn, 1975), 122, John Corrington says that Altizer once observed to him that "Professor Voegelin finds everything to be Gnostic." Corrington thought at the time that the remark was defensive (in light of Voegelin's comments on "death of God" philosophy and theology), but he admits that he sees some substance in it after having read *The Ecumenic Age*. The problems, in other words, tend to enlarge as Voegelin moves from historical studies toward the elucidation of "pure" theory.

that these deformations of reality evoked mass movements that constantly threatened, and eventually broke through, the whole structure of society was not easy to assimilate, even for those not already living within the representational interpretation of one of the "second" realities. For the latter, Voegelin is apparently a sort of intellectual anachronism who is trying to apply the outmoded internecine arguments of the Christian Middle Ages to a modern secular ("scientific") world in which they have no place.[13]

In a manner that should now be familiar to all who have followed his intellectual odyssey, Voegelin chose the occasion of his inaugural lecture at Munich (1958) to elaborate the meaning of Gnosticism in its recent context and to illustrate by an analysis of some major German thinkers (Hegel, Marx, Nietzsche, and Heidegger) how their gnostic speculations differ from a philosophy of politics.[14] In the introductory material Voegelin carefully explains that Gnosticism was not an arcane Christian heresy which he had

13. In a review article,"The Science of Politics: New and Old," *World Politics*, VII (1955), 479–89, Robert Dahl complains that "Voegelin reifies endlessly" and says that he will follow suit (p. 486). The statement was made as a criticism of Voegelin's reference to the fact that pre-Christian societies symbolized themselves as representatives of transcendent truth (an antecedent of the later analysis of the cosmological myth as a "compact" symbol of the undifferentiated conception of the quadripartite structure of man and society, God and the universe). The point is that Voegelin was not reifying anything: every society exists as part of reality by reason of its symbolic interpretation of what it is, and everybody who deems himself a member of that society participates to a greater or lesser degree in the experiences behind the representative symbols of the society's truth of existence.

Dahl offers so many other arguments in the review that are characteristic of the difference between Voegelin's conceptions of science and theory and those of the orthodox political scientists that the entire discussion could be used as a foil for an analysis of the ways in which contemporary political science fails or refuses to come to grips with Voegelin's theory. One is tempted to digress into an analysis of this piece, but one or two self-evident examples should suffice: Dahl notes at one point that one of three parts of *The New Science of Politics* is "a historical examination of the rise of *what Voegelin calls* Gnosticism" (italics added). And he concludes the review, without paying even passing regard to Voegelin's discussion of the post-Cartesian reduction of the meaning of science, by demonstrating how he participates in that reduction when he says that Voegelin "has not only un-defined science; he has un-scienced it" (p. 489). I do not mean to cap this note with an *ad hominem* argument when I say that the review is a good illustration of the appropriateness of Dahl's place (usually at the top) on lists of the type referred to at the beginning of this essay.

14. The lecture was published, with an introduction on the nature of gnosis and an added section "Der Gottesmord," under the title *Wissenchaft, Politik und Gnosis*. A previously published essay, "Ersatz-Religion," was included in the American edition, *Science, Politics and Gnosticism* (Chicago: Henry Regnery, 1968).

chosen for analytical convenience. He points out that "the idea that one of the main currents of European, especially of German, thought is essentially gnostic sounds strange today, but this is not a recent discovery. Until about a hundred years ago the facts of the matter were well known." He goes on to cite the earlier literature, as well as the revival of interest in the subject in the 1930s as part of the general (if not widely recognized) revival of the historical sciences over the past several decades, which have contributed so much to his own work. He also further identifies the problem of the recovery of science when he notes that, in America, the gnostic nature of ersatz religions was recognized by William James early in the twentieth century, and that James also knew that Hegel's speculation was the culmination of modern gnosticism, but his critical opposition had little effect because today intellectual movements of the gnostic type dominate the public scene in both America and Europe. "The attempt to come to grips with the problems of personal and social order when it is disrupted by gnosticisms . . . has not been very successful because the philosophical knowledge that would be required for the purpose has itself been destroyed by the prevailing intellectual climate. The struggle against the consequences of gnosticism is being conducted in the very language of gnosticism.[15]

The treatment of Gnosticism is rich in meaning, not only in itself, but for its elucidation of the manner in which Voegelin's achievements as a theorist are realized. Several items deserve mention, if only in passing. First, it is obvious that the participants in the intellectual culture in which he works are historians, philosophers, theologians, anthropologists, and others, and not "social scientists." His mastery of the literature, primary and secondary, is extraordinary, not only for its breadth, but for his control of it. Second, his own objections to "positions" as starting points for speculations that culminate in closed "systems" which resolve by exclusion all problems that do not fit into the internally self-sustaining "model" of reality are amply borne out by his example: He not only responds to questions raised about the lacunae in his presentations (including those recognized through his self-

15. Voegelin, *Science, Politics and Gnosticism*, 3, vi.

criticism) but is constantly making the new departures necessitated by the openness of science.[16] Third, the question of Voegelin's language, much complained about by those who wish to de-
pict him as an obscurantist, and a source of difficulty at times even
for those who have scrupulously attempted to comprehend him, is
clarified both by implication and by direct reference. Here and in
subsequent work it is made plain that he is not inventing a technical language of his own, but is seeking to recover the precise
meanings of the language appropriate to philosophical discourse.
The purpose is dual: to circumvent misinterpretation by not relying on a language that has been corrupted by the deculturation
of our times, and to assure (through textual and contextual accuracy) that more of the nuances, let alone the broader expressions,
of the philosophers are not lost in the interpretations. Again, the
critical and reconstructive efforts go forward together. Increasingly, Voegelin has indulged those who have followed him open-
mindedly, and implicitly answered those who have regarded his
language as wholly contrived,[17] by carrying the Greek (or occasionally other language) terms in parentheses alongside the English equivalent.

The New Science of Politics was a prefiguration of the study of "the
order of history [which] emerges from the history of order."[18] *Order and History*, in a manner similar to the history of ideas, has gone
through a metamorphosis which is still in process. It was originally planned as a six-volume work ranging over the civilizations
of the ancient Near East through the Hellenic civilization, into the

16. For example, Voegelin, in *Science, Politics and Gnosticism*, vii, refers to the
study of modern gnosticism as "inevitably work in progress" in the present state
of science, and then goes on to point out his own extension of the study into the
subject of alienation.

17. Much of the commentary on Voegelin which aims at broadening the general
basis of understanding of what he is about tends to track his terminology (and
sometimes even his syntax and idiomatic usage) so closely that its interpretative
value is depreciated. This tendency is understandable, however, in light of his frequently repeated strictures on the debased uses to which "language symbols" may
be put, and the steadily enlarging vocabulary which his philological skill brings
into his writings as he enlarges the scope of his inquiry.

See Dahl, "The Science of Politics," 484, for a precise example of criticism on the
basis of contrived language.

18. This is the sentence with which Voegelin opens the initial volume of *Order
and History, Israel and Revelation* (Baton Rouge: Louisiana State University Press,
1956), ix.

multicivilizational empires since Alexander, the Christian empire in the West, the Protestant centuries, the emergence of the modern national states, and the development of gnosis as the symbolic form of order. The first three volumes—*Israel and Revelation, The World of the Polis*, and *Plato and Aristotle*—appeared in 1956 and 1957. Pursuing the object of identifying from historical sources the ways in which the various societies symbolized the meanings of their existence, which included the quaternarian community of being (man and society, the universe and God), Voegelin found the earliest societies expressing their meanings through the cosmological myth in which the elements of the community of being were not differentiated. The major "leaps in being" through which consciousness of the experience of existence found symbolic expression were revelation in Israel, philosophy in Hellas, and the soteriological truth of Christianity.[19] The first three volumes of *Order and History* analyze, with the usual mastery of historical material combined with theoretical rigor, the varieties of mythic symbols, the crises that evoked the noetic experiences of the philosophers, and the revelatory experiences of Moses and the prophets, and the ways in which the experiences of participation in the structure of being affected the order of the civilizations under consideration. It was anticipated that the course of Western civilization would be pursued down to the present in the final three volumes.

Eighteen years elapsed between the publication of Volumes III and IV of *Order and History*. In the introduction to *The Ecumenic Age* Voegelin explains that a "break" occurred in the program he had originally laid out for the projected six-volume work. As the work proceeded "the structures that emerged from the historical orders and their symbolization proved more complicated than . . . [he] had anticipated." The principle of the study (that the order of history emerges from the history of order?) was not wrong, but the expansiveness of the project carried it beyond the originally es-

19. This sentence is a synthesis based on prefatory comments in *Israel and Revelation* and sections of *The New Science of Politics*, esp. 76–77. Although I think it is adequate for the state of the work now being considered (*ca.* 1950–1960), later published work, including Volume IV of *Order and History—The Ecumenic Age* (Baton Rouge: Louisiana State University Press, 1974)—raises some questions about the relation between the noetic experience of philosophy and the pneumatic experiences of Christianity that are not completely resolved.

tablished boundaries. The mere quantity of empirical materials resulting from the continuing rapid advancement of the "historical sciences" would have necessitated that the three additional volumes be expanded to at least six, and the five types of order and symbolization set forth at the beginning (the ancient Near East and the cosmological myth, Israel and the revelatory form of existence in history, Hellas and the development of philosophy, the multi-civilizational empires and the emergence of Christianity, and the modern national state and Gnosticism) were "regrettably limited." That situation was awkward enough.

> What ultimately broke the project, however, was the impossibility of aligning the empirical types in any time sequence at all that would permit the structures actually found to emerge from a history conceived as a "course." The program as originally conceived, it is true, was not all wrong. There were indeed the epochal differentiating events, the "leaps in being," which engendered the consciousness of a Before and After and, in their respective societies, motivated the symbolism of a historical "course" that was meaningfully structured by the event of the leap. The experiences of a new insight into the truth of existence, accompanied by the consciousness of an event as constituting an epoch in history, were real enough. . . . Still, the conception was untenable because it had not taken proper account of the important lines of meaning in history that did not run along lines of time.[20]

Without complicating the issues unnecessarily at this point, we might refer tersely to some of the consequences of this broadened perspective on the historical order. For one thing Voegelin discovers that, even in the cosmological civilizations, history is not conceived as simply cyclical; the very genesis of the historical imagination involves the symbolization of the existence of the concrete

20. Voegelin, *The Ecumenic Age*, 2. The comments about the epochal nature of the "leap in being" are intriguing in light of some of the later interpretations. The Greek philosophers, for instance, not only developed philosophy as a symbolic form to express a differentiation of experience beyond the form of the myth, they were conscious that this symbolization constituted a new epoch in history (the awareness of a break in linear time which would thenceforth establish a "Before and After" conceptualization of history). In light of some later suggestions about the "equivalence" of various symbolic forms without respect to temporal sequences, one wonders whether the engendering experiences are the same in the equivalences, and whether the effectiveness of the symbolizations is the critical element in constituting and sustaining the concrete existences of societies. If so, the "leap in being" is not so much a differentiation of experience as an advance in the communicative expression of the experience.

society as originating in the infinity which preceded time, and as continuing indefinitely into future time and even beyond time. Second, the appearance not only in the West but in the Far East of ecumenical civilizations involves the consciousness, even within the confines of nonuniversal concrete (tribal and ethnic?) societies, of the universality of mankind (we have no *historical* experience of a world empire, only the conception and, apparently, complex and repetitive aspirations for such an order). Finally (but not definitively), the complications of the relations between the symbolizations of the experiences of order and the ways in which those symbols are drawn upon for representational purposes in the societies themselves seem to be much greater than in the earlier work. The movements to establish multi-ethnic (ecumenic) geographic empires by conquest, for example, may be described as rising out of almost pure power considerations (*libido dominandi*) on the part of the conquering imperators, with the ecumenical religions (and their symbolizations of spiritual order) being conveniently at hand to be used, not as the substantial foundations of order, but as palliatives for the disorders of the society. The contingencies in experience that follow from the nature and condition of man make even the most fully differentiated experiences of the noetic and pneumatic forms less than complete (any other construction of the problem would be gnostic); the necessarily inadequate translation of the experiences into communicative symbols involves still further loss of immediacy in the experience of reality (*vide* Saint Paul and the reception of the symbol of eschatology in the form of expectation of the return of Christ within the era of the living); and the historical circumstances attending the reception of the symbolizations make for the possibility of concurrent perversion of the symbols, not to speak of the process of deformation over time.

One other consideration that affected the shift in the structure and context of *Order and History* (although not as fully discussed in the introduction to Volume IV as the historical factors) was Voegelin's intense concentration on the philosophy of consciousness in the interim between the first three volumes and the latest one. That shift in interest was manifested most clearly in the publication of *Anamnesis* in 1966. Although some of the discrete studies that make up this volume originated in earlier periods of Voegelin's career, and he notes that he was interested in the subject as far back as the 1920s, the core pieces (some previously published) were written or substantially modified in the decade prior to the appearance of the book.[21]

Perhaps the change in focus that this new direction in Voegelin's research brought to *Order and History* is most succinctly summarized in the following statement: "History is not a stream of human beings and their actions in time, but the process of man's participation in a flux of divine presence that has eschatological direction. The enigmatic symbolism of a 'history of mankind,' thus, expresses man's understanding that these insights, though they arise from concrete events in the consciousness of concrete human beings are valid for all men." The change seems to imply that while the search for history of order continues as part of man's ineluctable search for the meaning of existence, the order of history will not emerge from the welter of events of history. There may be concrete *orders* in history, but there is no overall order beyond the discernment of the orders and disorders in the souls of men which recurrently manifest themselves in symbols through which the panoply of political orders are more or less fully represented in the flux of history.[22]

The contents of Volume IV, as well as the suggested contents of the projected fifth and final volume of *Order and History*, reflect this changed emphasis. Like *Anamnesis* these volumes are a series of discrete examinations of a tremendous range of problems that are loosely unified by their origins in the experience of consciousness in man. The organizational principle has changed from one directed as much by the perception of a "course" of history as by the constancy of the object of the quest for ontological meaning, to one directed by the evocative urge to probe deeper and deeper into the experiencing psyche behind the symbols by which man has expressed his experiences of participation in the divine ground of

21. Although no English-language edition of *Anamnesis* is available, two essays which concentrate on the book are among the better commentaries on Voegelin (the closing section of Germino's piece excepted). These are Dante Germino, "Eric Voegelin's Anamnesis," *Southern Review*, New Ser., VII (Winter, 1971), 68–88; and Ellis Sandoz, "The Foundation of Voegelin's Political Theory," *Political Science Reviewer*, I (Fall, 1971), 30–73.

22. Voegelin, *The Ecumenic Age*, 6.

being. Some of the pieces of Volume IV and those projected for Volume V are explorations of some of the broadest conceptions of experience (for example, historiogenesis, immortality, equivalences of experience and symbolizations, the classical experience of reason, etc.); others are explorations of the experiences and ways in which the experiences were symbolized by representative individuals (for example, Saint Paul, Hegel, Schelling, Henry James, etc.). Although extracted from history, and in some instances taking the experience of history itself as a theme, these studies are more nearly approaches to a pure theory of being than they are to a study of order and history as such.

Voegelin's contribution to political science cannot be understood, in my view, without some insight into the process out of which his theoretical attainments have emerged, hence the foregoing sketchy summary. But it is also obligatory, especially under the present circumstances, that some effort be made to formulate the content of his theory a little more coherently. One way of engaging in so risky a venture in so brief a compass is by taking his own criteria of a theory of politics and assessing the extent to which he has met them. In this framework, three dispersed statements seem to me to constitute the sum of what he includes as expectations from *theory*, although it is well to keep in mind my previously expressed reservations about discovering in him any "fixed" meaning of the term. One of the requisites for political theory that one finds explicitly stated at numerous places in his works, and implied in others, is a fully articulated philosophical anthropology, or concept of the nature of man. A second criterion is established in the opening sentence of *The New Science of Politics*: "The existence of man in political society is historical existence; and a theory of politics, if it penetrates to principles, must at the same time be a theory of history." Finally Voegelin's foreword to *Anamnesis* begins as follows: "The problems of human order in society and history originate in the order of consciousness. The philosophy of the consciousness is therefore the core of a philosophy of politics." A philosophical anthropology, a theory of history, and a philosophy of consciousness, then, are essential to a theory of politics.[23]

23. Some of Voegelin's most cogent presentations are to be found in his lesser-noted critical works. For that reason the following example of his often stated at-

An adumbration of Voegelin's philosophical anthropology is difficult for two reasons. The first is a problem of surface simplicity: I have no reason to doubt the possibility of extracting from a variorum treatment of Voegelin's comments on the subject a fairly clear set of propositional statements that summarize his concept of the nature of man. Such a summary starts with the most elemental distinctions and moves to more differentiated conceptions of an ontology. Robert Penn Warren stated what could be the opening proposition with devastating succinctness when he said that man is a machine with consciousness. Although conscious of the finiteness of his existence within the world, man is also conscious of participation in the structure of being of which he is a part. Human existence is beset by the tension of living in an "in-between" state (the Platonic *metaxy*) in which the confinements of life in the world are all too present (mortality, disorder, alienation, meaninglessness), but in which there is also the pull toward transcendental reality (the divine ground) as the source of the intimations of immortality, order, and consubstantiality with being. The order of the individual soul is dependent on the orientation toward the ground of being, and the order of society depends on its analogy to the structure of order in the soul of the well-ordered man. The possibilities for man's orientation toward the ground of being as a source of order in his own soul (and thus of his awareness of the possibility of order in society and history) is not, however, something that can be made simply a matter of doctrinal prescription, or dogmatized. It takes place within the individual consciousness, and the process is one which has to be experienced by the individual. Nonetheless, the process of attunement to the divine order has been symbolized in widely differentiated ways: in classical philosophy through the concept of nous (that is, reason as the differentiating attribute of mankind and the one through which man shares as a participant in being; the terms *noetic* and *noesis* derive from *nous*), in Saint Augustine through the dichotomy of the *amor Dei* and the *amor sui*, and in Bergson through the

---

tachment to the principle of a philosophical anthropology is taken from his review of Hannah Arendt's *Origins of Totalitarianism*, in *Review of Politics*, XV (January, 1953), 68: "It is difficult to categorize political phenomena properly without a well developed philosophical anthropology." Voegelin, *The New Science of Politics*, 1; Voegelin, *Anamnesis*, 7.

contrast between the opening of the soul to transcendence and the closure of the soul against ultimate reality.

Here the propositional statement must end, because we are already beyond the point of the surface simplicity of a description, and into the necessity for penetrating the symbols in the effort to reconstitute the experiences themselves. The second difficulty in summarizing Voegelin's philosophical anthropology arises out of this transition from a description that is more or less familiar to us from doctrinal sources in metaphysics and religion to Voegelin's philosophical reconstruction of the experiences of consciousness, especially as they were symbolized through the origins of philosophy in Plato and Aristotle. In two long essays, "Was Ist Politische Realität?" and "Reason: The Classic Experience," Voegelin extends the content of philosophical anthropology to the point of making it virtually one with his philosophy of consciousness. Although the essays are long, they are so compact that they virtually defy summary exegesis. They must be read in their entirety to realize the full import of Voegelin's theoretical reconstruction. The problem is further compounded by the fact that, although they select from the entire corpus of classical philosophy, they are not simply recapitulations of key concepts in Plato and Aristotle, but philosophical reconstructions of the experience of consciousness in its noetic manifestations.[24]

If these key essays cannot be summarized here, the range of their contents may be indicated without distortion. They cover the origins of philosophical inquiry in the effort to separate philosophy (love of wisdom) from philodoxy (love of opinion), explore the ways in which the dialectical argument proceeds, reconstruct the process by which the noetic potential is explored to its depths and heights (with particular emphasis on the search for the divine ground and the ultimate luminosity which the noetic consciousness brings to its own oneness with being). They then move on to the experience of order in man's psyche and the articulation of that order through symbols which are representative of the noetic potential shared by mankind.

Some of the implications of these explorations for a science of

24. Eric Voegelin, "Was Ist Politische Realität?," *Anamnesis*, 283–354; Voegelin, "Reason," 237–64.

politics will be considered later. For now it must be sufficient to mention one or two. First, not every human being will live the noetic life, or be the fully ordered or mature man characterized by the Aristotelian concept of the *spoudaios*, but the noetic order is open to all men, at least to the extent of the capacity to be drawn to it when perceived in others, and the philosopher, in particular, will represent in his person the attainment of the order of reality open to all men. The possibilities for the order of society arise out of these ordering potentials in man. A further extension of the noetic potential at the pragmatic level is to be found in the capacity of every man for the exercise of common sense in relation to most aspects of both private and public life.[25] The ordering potential of the noetic consciousness also provides the means of critically understanding the nature of disorder to the point of psychopathology. The way in which the foundations for criticism of the disorder in society are developed through the grasp of the closure against the noetic meaning of reason in man is also analyzed in the essay on reason. Since existence in tension is not abolished by its discovery, noesis has educational, diagnostic, and therapeutic functions.

Because of what seems to me to be a change in focus from a philosophy of history as such in the earlier works to a philosophy of consciousness in relation to critical historical events in the later ones, not much need be said here about the theory of history as part of Voegelin's overall commitment. At a minimum it may be noted that history is the field in which the "drama of humanity," involving the quest for order in man and society, takes place. The science of man and society, then, is necessarily involved with the historical sciences. The materials of empirical history are the sources from which societies may be seen to emerge out of the symbolizations of order which constitute their self-interpretations, as well as the sources through which the disorders of man and society are perceived. Furthermore, the "leaps in being" through which man has differentiated his consciousness of reality are events in history which are epochal in the sense that they change the order of his-

25. The part played by the apprehension of the philosophy of common sense of the Scottish school (especially Thomas Reid) in Voegelin's theory is an interesting problem, which cannot be pursued here.

tory and are recognized as being epochal by those who symbolize them.

A theory of history is necessary also because the conception of history is part of man's interpretation of his order of being; in the very apprehension of history man makes it a part of the self-inter-pretation of man and society in their existential reality. But his-tory, or at least the symbols which include history as part of the representative order, can also become part of the disordering es-cape into unreality. Gnosticism, for instance, is characterized in part by its projection of an apocalyptic end of history. All attempts to make history a closed conception are stigmatized as derail-ments from reality into "second" realities. *Episteme politike*, then, is a science of man, society, and history.

At the outset I indicated that an assessment of Voegelin's con-tributions as a political theorist would necessarily involve an as-sessment of the political science profession. That judgment was made largely on the basis of his virtually single-handed effort (at least among contemporary political scientists) to develop a sci-ence of politics grounded in theory which is both epistemologi-cally and methodologically at odds with the positivist orientation now dominant in the discipline.[26] The question, then, is whether or not Voegelin has produced a sufficiently comprehensive and co-hesive theoretical foundation on which those who aspire to be part of an "intellectual culture" could build cooperatively to extend and perpetuate a science of politics. If so, what has he provided in their theory that makes it a more effective way of understanding polit-ical reality than the alternative, and how does one work from it as a "paradigm"? These questions can be addressed by an appraisal

26. This is not meant to imply that all practicing political scienctists are posi-tivists. It is rather to say that most of those who have self-consciously engaged in, or looked forward to the possibility of, the formulation of a comprehensive theory of politics have had positivist orientations. Others have worked on political prob-lems in eclectic ways without displaying much interest in theoretical issues. Ger-mino has identified the principal figures who have made recent contributions to the revival of political theory on a nonpositivist basis—particularly Oakeshott, Ar-endt, Jouvenel, and Strauss, in addition to Voegelin—but he seems to me to have placed Voegelin in a unique position in his book, not only in terms of space devoted to him in comparison with the others, but also in the greater emphasis placed on the critical work of Oakeshott *et al.*, as contrasted with the focus on Voegelin's the-oretical constructiveness. Germino, *Beyond Ideology*, esp. Chaps. 7–8.

of four aspects of Voegelin's work: the generality of his theory, that is, the coherence of his conception of politics as a constant in human existence, and the relation of the political experience to experience as a whole; the effectiveness of his criticism of other concepts of political reality as the means of opening the way to understanding politics through the reconstruction of *episteme politike*; the suitability of his formulation of theoretical principles as a guide to what we seek in a science of politics; and the issues in his theoretical conclusions that require further clarification if the theoretical foundations themselves are to be extended. Once again, only the briefest excursions into these vast areas of inquiry are possible within the limits of this essay.

On the issue of the generality of his theory, the central point to be emphasized once again is that Voegelin has not attempted to explain politics as a special or limited form (in Michael Oakeshott's terms, a "mode") of experience. A theory of man and society which is not solidly related to an ontological theory cannot explain anything more than the ephemera of politics, because politics arises out of man's special place in the chain of being, and that place involves man's participation in the structure of which he is a part. The source of the structure of society, like man's own structure, is not a given which one can comprehend solely from an external perspective. The ontological understanding of man can take place only from within; its appropriate method of inquiry involves an examination of the experience of consciousness, and the results are expressed through philosophical symbols. Since politics is a part of man's temporal existence, man himself is the creative source of his political experience. In Oakeshott's terminology, politics is self-moved manner of activity. But the nature of that self-moved activity depends on what man is as a participant not just in politics but in the totality of existence. The order of society that man seeks to structure through politics depends on the experience of order he is capable of realizing as part of the order of being. And that order, of course, while not infinitely open to man's comprehension because its source is the ground of being of which man is only a part (although a consubstantial part through participation in the noetic consciousness), is sufficiently open to man to enable him to structure the order of his being through reason (nous) as he explores the order of consciousness through the tension toward that ground. The order of society, then, depends on the symbolization of the order of being as an analogue of the man whose soul is in order. Although awareness of participation in the order of being takes place only in individuals, and in various levels in different persons at that, reason is the universal substance which differentiates man in the structure of reality. The capacity to symbolize the experience of participation in the order of reality through philosophy affords a measure which makes a universal science of politics possible. At the same time the limits of man's existence in the world as expressed by the Platonic *metaxy* mean that the states of order in man and society are in historial flux, and the theoretical activity which seeks to comprehend that order is never complete.

That we are not accustomed at present to thinking in terms of an ontological foundation of politics is part of the problem that gives rise to Voegelin's critical achievement. Most of the debate over a science of politics takes place at the level of "political ideas" and not at the level of the meaning of politics in the structure of noetic reality. Even the relatively undistorted symbols of political reality which are the means of expressing the existence of a particular society in history tend to become doctrinalized and dogmatized in a way that does not evoke the experiences which constitute the order of reality the society represents. And where those symbols have been deformed in the service of an ideology, the loss of reality is so complete as to constitute a crisis of order.

Voegelin's criticism started, as indicated, from the crisis of our times, with its activist movements having been generated through ideologies (which in his most extended characterization Voegelin refers to as revolutions against man and God). It then moved back through the history of ideas to the forms of symbolization, and from there to the effort to reconstitute the experiences which produced the symbolizations. The vast body of criticism which was produced in the course of these explorations is a most valuable source for approaching the theoretical principles; but even for those who do not have the philosophical urge to penetrate to theoretical principles, it constitutes a body of regulative ideas which may prevent more pragmatically oriented political scientists from making some of the grosser theoretical errors common to the profession.

The clarity and comprehensiveness of the criticism are impressive in their own right; furthermore, some of the best of it can be found in reviews and journal articles which have not been reprinted as part of the larger studies.

One of the best examples (especially because it does not have the coruscating effect of some of the attacks on the Gnostic depredations) is the essay "The Oxford Political Philosophers." It will be remembered by his readers that Voegelin indicated in the closing paragraph of *The New Science of Politics* that the American and English democracies, through their institutions, most solidly represented the truth of the soul, and were at the same time the strongest powers, thus providing some hope for "repressing Gnostic corruption and restoring the forces of civilization." But in the essay under consideration he was concerned to point out how the prevailing tradition of political philosophy in Oxford fell short of meeting the tests of theoretical relevance. By taking British institutions as a model for a valid general theory of politics the various philosophers (with the single exception of G. R. G. Mure) narrowed the object of theory from a civilizational whole to a particular national state, tended to treat the various political movements within the contemporary national state as movements on the level of secular power politics (which they are not), and failed to penetrate to principles because they engaged in debates about the rights of man and what institutions are best instead of elucidating the larger problems of a philosophical anthropology. In appraising the specifics of the theory of several leading figures, Voegelin shows how each tended in his own way to turn the secularized institutions in Britain into a civil theology (without analyzing the symbols they lauded for establishing political order in British history), and then turned the principles on which this special set of political institutions was based into the principles of politics as a whole. Here, as in all of Voegelin's criticism, the concrete presentation of the materials under scrutiny is informed by the "aim, however dimly seen, of developing a [more embracing] theory."[27]

The criticism of the Oxford philosophers, though pointed, is mild

27. Voegelin, *The New Science of Politics*, 189; Eric Voegelin, "The Oxford Political Philosophers," *Philosophical Quarterly*, III (April, 1953), 99.

because it represents the examination of a stage in political science in which some of the symbolic manifestations of the public
order in Britain are protected against erosion or deformation by
elevating them into doctrine or dogma, which in some ways is to
be commended. But it is still a digressive defense as well as an inadequate one; what is needed in the face of the revolutionary ideological threats to the ordering institutions on which the Oxford
philosophers concentrate is a penetration to their sources in reality.

In more extended criticism Voegelin analyzes the way in which
the secular creeds advance their destructive work, moving from the
milder forms of progressivism and liberalism to utopias based on
ever more demonically closed systems of thought, and on into the
revolutionary movements of nihilism, national socialism, and
communism, all of which have as their eventual purpose the
transformation of man and society in the name of an immanentist
reality, rather than the preservation of an environment in which
man will have the opportunity to live a life attuned to the order of
reality.

The standards of criticism which Voegelin exhibits in his own
work are sufficiently supple to be used at almost any level of analysis from simple institutional description to the more complex abstractions embodied in ideas and symbols. The application to political science as practiced by both the positivists and the Oxford
philosophers has already been noted, with special emphasis on the
respective ways in which they limit the objects of inquiry and dog-
matize certain symbols and ideas. One can extrapolate by noting
how Voegelin's critical analysis might be extended to the movement within American political science which has lately challenged behavioralism's claim to be the "new" political science. I
refer, of course, to the activist movement which is generally identified with the Caucus for a New Political Science. In many of their
criticisms of the discipline (especially as it has been tending toward behavioralism), the leading spokesmen for the caucus share
a good many perspectives with Voegelin: the argument, for instance, against a slavish imitation of the natural sciences on the
grounds that the human experiences most pertinent to politics are
excluded by such a commitment, and the view that the value neu-

trality of behavioralism covers a role that is strongly supportive of the status quo. Voegelin might also find the consciousness of the crisis of liberalism among some members of the caucus a potential stimulus to inquiry into the loss of meaning in some of the symbols of the existing political order. But he would also discern in a number of the tendencies among those who claim to be the proponents of the newest insurgency in political science little more than a profusion of leftist ideology and a plea for activism as a surrogate for the restoration of theory. In many ways the latest wave of the future within the discipline is even more symptomatic of the crisis in both politics and political science than the rather innocuous addiction of behavioralists to scientism.

The body of theoretical principles which Voegelin has been articulating over the past quarter century or more includes some of the subjects which have already been touched upon briefly. Included among these are a philosophical anthropology that differentiates man as a participant in the structure of existence in history and the search for the experiences of order in man out of which those symbols were produced as the main objects of inquiry, and the application of methods directed by the content of the philosophical anthropology and the objects of inquiry (these being mainly an empirical examination of order in history and a philosophical probe into the order of consciousness).

At this point, however, it seems useful to stress once again the limits imposed on the efforts to restore a science of politics that is grounded in such theoretical principles. These limits, too, should be included among the principles themselves. The first is the limit of knowledge that is open to man by reason of his "in-between" place in the structure of being. The consciousness of having to live with the tensions of existence rather than being able completely to overcome them by an act of egophanic revolt is the main defense against the ideological and activist inclinations toward the destruction of the existential order. The second is the limit on the extent and duration of order in concrete society. Societies are nonnoetic, even though their respective orders depend on the noetic symbolization of their existence. The noetic life can be lived only by individual human beings, and this means that a noetic response to disorder is the only possibility for evoking a restoration of *episteme politike* out of a crisis of social order. Since the order of society is not a self-correcting "system," but is the result of the infusion of order through a symbolization involving the noetically ordered man writ large, the principles of a science of order in man and society will not be fixed for all time, but must be constantly in process of restoration and extension. Finally, and in a sense closely related to the constancy of the theoretical activity, the noetic life itself imposes limits on the pragmatic political activism of the theorist. It is the philsopher's obligation to engage in the theoretical activity, and to seek to bring the results of that activity to bear on the order of society by expressing them in open debate on principles. But the philosopher's symbols of order cannot be imposed by actions which effectively reduce them to doctrines to be exploited in the struggles for existential power. Persuasion, not the will to power, is the only effective way of the philosopher as seeker after truth. (Socrates is still the symbolic model for the obligations attaching to the person engaged in the *bios theoretikos*.)

In his own general theory and the criticism which led into it, Voegelin has also set a virtually limitless array of problems on which to work. Not least of these is the problem of analyzing his own theoretical achievement. In large part this essay has concentrated on the process which has taken him to the current state of his theoretical generalizations about politics. Since the perpetual openness of the inquiry has been stressed so heavily, it is time to provide a sample of the type of questions growing out of his theoretical principles that still need to be addressed by Voegelin or someone else working within the "paradigm" he has established. Leaving aside the omnipresent questions of internal consistency, I find three problems that seem to require further exploration or further explanation from Voegelin or from some person who may have a clearer reading of him than I have. These are: (1) the possibility that the introspective methods of apprehending noesis in the fullest sense may result in something that is very near solipsism, (2) the opaqueness of the relations between the differentiation of the experience of order and the effective symbolization of that experience as the representation of the meaning of the concrete society's existence in history, and (3) the problem of the relation between philosophy and Christianity as sources for the symbols of order by which Western civilization has represented its truth of existence in history.

As Voegelin moves his theoretical inquest from symbols to experience as expressed through a philosophy of consciousness it seems to me that the inquiry from within becomes so nearly totally subjective that it virtually defies expression, let alone expression in clear enough symbols to permit the noetic order of the philosopher to exert sufficient pull on the noetic potential in nonphilosophers to be effective in bringing order to society. This point is not raised because I find Voegelin's exegesis of the experience of reason in the classical philosophers inadequate. Indeed it is a *tour de force*, although the penetration to the divine ground through noetic consciousness is described in terms which are reminiscent of the ineffableness of mysticism. All of us are aware of the inadequacies of language and other symbols for expressing our deepest experiences in an evocative way, even if we have not had the temerity to inform our instructors in creative writing (as one student is reported to have done) that we had lived a poem so intensely that we could not write it. What really bothers me is that in his latest work Voegelin seems to find so many possibilities for distortions of the symbols through which the experiences of order in the noetic consciousness are expressed that the prospects for societal order on anything other than the most precarious basis are very dim indeed.

The second problem, which should be capable of clarification by empirical study of the emergence or restoration of social order in concrete societies, is closely related to the first one. That is, if the order of society is non-noetic, but dependent on the noetic order of man for its realization, what is the relation between the noetic experience of order and the symbolizations which express the order of the society? If the self-interpretations which constitute society are not noetic, yet *episteme politike* is properly based on a noetic interpretation of man and society, political science should still be able to tell us how the non-noetic interpretations represent an order that is at least a doctrinalized or dogmatized version of noetic order. In particular, are religious symbols invariably involved in the symbolic self-interpretations of any society as the non-noetic expression of the society's relation to the divine ground?

Posing the question in this way leads immediately to the third sample issue. In the earlier works Voegelin regularly stressed that the main constructive symbols in the order of Western civilization were Christianity and classical philosophy. Even in parts of *The Ecumenic Age* he seems to treat the differentiation of consciousness through the noetic and pneumatic experiences as being on essentially the same level. But some of his closest readers have been puzzled by the way in which the concentration on the philosophy of consciousness has been accompanied by an apparent shift of emphasis to philosophical symbolization as the unique form for expressing the order of reality.[28] The criticism also contains some rather disturbing comments that suggest that doctrinal and dogmatic concerns have dominated the pneumatic symbolizations from their beginnings, and even Saint Thomas Aquinas was given a few sharp raps as a non-noetic propositional metaphysician. Has noesis through its experience of the divine ground superseded the pneumatic experience of Christianity entirely? In this instance, at least, one might wish that Voegelin had pursued his originally expressed intention of examining the Christian centuries as part of his study of order and history. The study "The Pauline Vision of the Resurrected" in *The Ecumenic Age* is hardly a theoretical counterpart of the philosophical analysis of consciousness in *Anamnesis* and the essay on reason in classical philosophy. Most of the shifts in the focus of Voegelin's theoretical interests over time can be explained in the total context of his work; as yet this one does not seem to me to be accounted for.

Despite these and other questions which remain about various parts of Voegelin's multifaceted exploration of political reality, it seems clear that he has opened questions that have been neglected or even precluded from examination in recent political science, and that the questions are critical for the development of an adequate theoretical basis for political science. Whether this foundation will be built upon by enough political scientists to make an impact on the orientation of the discipline is, to say the least, problematic.

28. Voegelin, *The Ecumenic Age*, esp. 327. See, for example, Gerhart Niemeyer, "Eric Voegelin's Philosophy and the Drama of Mankind," *Modern Age*, XX (1976), 28–39. The problem has been addressed as a matter of intellectual control in Bruce Douglass, "The Gospel and Political Order: Eric Voegelin on the Political Role of Christianity," *Journal of Politics*, XXXVIII (February, 1976), 25–45.

VIII Michael Oakeshott
Skeptical Idealist

A few years before his retirement in 1969 from the University Chair in Political Science at the London School of Economics, it became publicly manifest that Michael Oakeshott deserved much greater recognition for his achievements as a political philosopher than he had received up to that time. Not that Oakeshott had been an obscure figure in academic circles earlier; his entire career as a scholar and teacher followed a pattern that marked him as successful, even if some of his critics tended to question the solidity of the foundation on which his success rested. Born in 1901, he completed his degree in history at Cambridge in 1923; was made a fellow of his college, Gonville and Caius, in 1925; published his precociously brilliant philosophic treatise, *Experience and Its Modes*, in 1933; compiled a widely used text, *The Social and Political Doctrines of Contemporary Europe* (1939); returned to Cambridge after five years' service in the army during World War II; founded and edited the short-lived *Cambridge Journal* (1947–1953), which served as an outlet for some of his most striking political and educational theories; spent a short time at Nuffield College, Oxford; and, in 1951, was appointed to the chair at London, following the death of the incumbent, Harold Laski.

But throughout a good portion of this steady academic advancement Oakeshott remained something of an anomaly. In part this was due to his personality. Even among those English scholars who take great pride in playing the role of the leisurely amateur in their professional capacities, Oakeshott stands out as one whose casual eccentricity bears something of the mark of the dilettante. Undeniably urbane in conversation, with a keen analytical mind that he uses more often in refutation than in affirmation, he tends in his personal style toward mannerism. His writing style has often been characterized as graceful, even beautiful; but some say he does not

write enough, or that the subjects he chooses are so diffuse and circumstantial as to be unsystematic at best, and destructively negative at worst. The English tolerance for eccentricity may even have
been strained by the fact that, in 1936, Oakeshott was co-author of
a monograph entitled *A Guide to the Classics*, more accurately subtitled *How to Pick the Derby Winner*. In 1947 some restitution was
made for this act of whimsy; a new version of the book appeared
under the more forthright, if less elegant, title *A New Guide to the
Derby: How to Pick the Winner*. Finally, Oakeshott has been an
avowed conservative and traditionalist during a period in which
the prevailing ideology among intellectuals has been democratic
socialism, and the predominant mood in almost all fields of endeavor has been more favorable to innovation than preservation.

The publication in 1962 of a collection of Oakeshott's essays under the title *Rationalism in Politics, and Other Essays* signaled the
beginnings of a widespread reappraisal of the corpus of his work.
Prior to this time recognition had been sporadic and critical conclusions uncertain. R. G. Collingwood had lavished praise on *Experience and Its Modes*, but the book received little attention otherwise. His introduction to the Blackwell edition of Hobbes's
Leviathan was widely acknowledged to be a substantial and original essay, but it certainly did not supplant the standard commentaries on the subject. His writings in the *Cambridge Journal* and his
inaugural address at London on political education were richly
metaphorical, but were so puzzling to many readers in their form
and content that they seemed arcane. But with the appearance of
Rationalism in Politics a quality in Oakeshott's writing on politics
that hitherto had been largely ignored became clear: Throughout
his entire career he had been remarkably consistent and coherent
in the development of his philosophical position and in the implications that he drew from philosophy for the study and practice of
politics. As he puts it in his brief preface, "although they [the es-
says] do not compose a settled doctrine, they disclose a consistent
style or disposition of thought."[1]

1. R. G. Collingwood, *The Idea of History* (Oxford: Clarendon Press, 1946), 151,
159, noted that Oakeshott "dealt at length and in a masterly way with the philosophical problem of history," and he further asserted that *Experience and Its Modes*

The reviews were mixed, as might have been expected, but many of them did indicate that Oakeshott's style, originality of perception, and consistency made the book something of a landmark in restoring the credibility of political philosophy. Perhaps of more importance than what the reviews said were the places in which they appeared; in addition to comprehensive coverage among the professional journals in political science, the leading intellectual magazines and journals of opinion carried extensive reviews. A review of *Rationalism in Politics* occupied the front page of the *Times Literary Supplement* on September 28, 1962; and reviews or review articles appeared in the *New Statesmen, Spectator*, and, most notably, because of its caustic indictment by a former student of Oakeshott's, in *Encounter*.[2]

As political philosophy revived in the late 1960s, and even began to assert its counterclaims against the inadequacies of the positivistic behaviorial orientation that dominated scholarship in the social sciences after World War II, Oakeshott's general visibility increased considerably, and his professional reputation waxed. In 1966 the Cambridge University Press reissued *Experience and Its Modes*; and in the same year W. H. Greenleaf published a concise, intelligible monograph on Oakeshott's work. The editor of the series in which the latter volume was published made an unequivocal claim on a major place for Oakeshott among political philosophers when he said, "It will scarcely be denied, I think (even by those who most dislike what they take to be the practical implications of his work), that Oakeshott is the most profound and original political thinker that England has produced in the twentieth century." As a token of his general influence as a teacher, critic, and stimulator of philosophical discourse on the perennial questions of politics, a festschrift of unusual quality was published in honor of Oakeshott on the occasion of his retirement. The appearance of this book is worth stressing, not only because of the general excellence of its contents and its revelations about the im-

---

"represents the high-water mark of English thought upon history." Michael Oakeshott, *Rationalism in Politics, and Other Essays* (New York: Basic Books, 1962), vii.

2. Bernard Crick, "The World of Michael Oakeshott, or the Lonely Nihilist," *Encounter*, XX (June, 1963), 65–74.

portance of the central concerns of Oakeshott's philosophical activity, but also because a festschrift is a much rarer occurrence in Britain than it is on the Continent, or even in the United States.[3]

What is the background out of which Oakeshott's political philosophy developed? And what are the achievements as a political thinker that have brought him in his own lifetime the status indicated in the preceding comments?

The intellectual foundations of Oakeshott's political philosophy have never been called seriously into question; by his own acknowledgment, as well as by the character of his work, he belongs within the tradition of philosophical idealism. It may seem incongruous that anyone so profoundly skeptical about the ultimate meaning of existence (I have heard him toss off the casual remark that "life has no meaning"), and about the capacity to know anything in a definitive sense, should be associated with a philosophical development that had its origins in Hegel, whose claims to the apprehension of reality are so absolute. But philosophical idealism, except perhaps for pure Hegelianism, has never been so much a doctrine or a set of doctrines as it has been a critical way of looking at things, or an effort to overcome the limited perceptions of other philosophical traditions, which belie their claims to exhaustiveness by attempting to subsume the whole of reality into one of its parts.

English philosophical idealism, though acknowledging its debt to Hegel, has always been less extravagant in its language and in the scope of the problems with which it deals than German ide-

---

3. An augury of the revival is Dante Germino's *Beyond Ideology: The Revival of Political Theory* (New York: Harper and Row, 1967). In this book Germino includes Oakeshott, along with Hannah Arendt, Bertrand de Jouvenel, Leo Strauss, and Eric Voegelin, as the principal contemporary figures responsible for this development. W. H. Greenleaf, *Oakeshott's Philosophical Politics* (New York: Barnes and Noble, 1966), and the comment of the series editor, J. W. Grove, appears in the Editor's Preface; Preston King and B. C. Parekh (eds.), *Politics and Experience* (Cambridge: University Press, 1968). George Feaver has written an extended review article on the Oakeshott festschrift: "Michael Oakeshott and 'Political Education,'" *Studies in Comparative Communism*, II (April, 1969), 156–75. As background for his appraisal of the book, Feaver provides some interesting views on the ambience of the London School of Economics during Oakeshott's tenure there, as well as some insights into Oakeshott's emergence as a major figure in political philosophy and the main problems with which he has been concerned.

alism. It has also been affected as much or more by the practicalities of common sense as by the implacable logic of a system, and has been more concerned with the implication of historical tradition than with an apocalyptic alteration of pragmatic existence. The major figures, associated with the origins of English philosophical idealism were F. H. Bradley, T. H. Green, and Bernard Bosanquet; some of the most prominent recent figures—aside from Oakeshott—include J. H. Muirhead, G. R. G. Mure, and, above all, R. G. Collingwood.

The complexities of philosophical idealism are so great in their details, and the variations among its exponents so extensive, that only a few major points can be touched on in this context. A summary review of any philosophical position is obviously subject to the dangers of gross distortion, and this danger is all the more acute with respect to philosophical idealism because of its emphasis on the treatment of experience as a whole rather than as a sum of its analytic parts. Nonetheless, a brief prefatory note on the earlier phases of philosophical idealism seems to be in order before broaching Oakeshott's version.

Hegel's point of departure was his concern with the effects that "analytic" thinking, under the impact of science, had had on the Western tradition. Essentially, the development of science had tended to abstract certain types of experience from the totality of man's consciousness and to build that abstraction into the sole basis of knowledge. A pronounced tendency among analytic philosophers has been to insist on the apprehension of sense-data as the single foundation for verifiable knowledge, to reduce reason to the instrumental function associated with deductive logic, and to relegate problems that cannot be subsumed by scientific analysis to the realm of unreality. Hegel could not accept Kant's dualism of the pure (or theoretical) and the practical reason, in which one accepted as objective knowledge the empirically verifiable propositions of science on the one hand, and the more subjective and intuitive concept of the categorical imperative as the basis for resolving the problems that arise in practical life (essentially ethics and politics) on the other. Even less could he accept the totally contingent epistemology of Hume, with its absolute separation of reason, fact, and value, and the concomitant dissociation of all

three of these distinct forms of experience from apprehendable
reality. In the face of these types of reductionism, it was Hegel's
purpose to restore the essential unity of the various functions ascribed to rational activity. In order to do so, he had to demonstrate
that knowledge could not be complete until the separation between the knowing subject and the object of knowledge was
bridged. This, in turn, required knowing what the object was for
itself, the manner in which a particular abstracted object of
knowledge fit into the hierarchy of existent things, and the way in
which substance persisted through change in appearance. In restoring the unity of subject and object, matter and form, and being
and becoming, Hegel aspired to a knowledge that transcended its
ordinary human limitations to become in some sense a knowing
with God, and thus transform the ineffable awareness of transcendence into an immanence in which the rational becomes the
fully real, and the real fully rational.

English philosophical idealists have been far less architectonic
than Hegel. They have tended to focus on the idea of the "concrete
universal," which was derived from Hegel but subtly adapted by
Green, Bradley, and Bosanquet to the more practical concerns of
the British philosophic tradition.[4] We can state the matter in an
oversimplified way: The term *concrete universal* expresses the concept that every specific experience must be understood, if it is to
have full meaning, in the context of the general realm of experience. Anything less is an abstraction from the reality disclosed by
reason. If, for example, one asserts a claim to freedom from certain
restraints, and the basis of that claim is restricted to the mere satisfaction of some condition of the individual ego, a concrete experience is present, but it is abstracted in its restrictiveness from
the universal concept of freedom, in the absence of which we cannot really make good on the promise of freedom for the affected
individual. When, however, one perceives the universal content of
the experience of freedom, which would make any application to
the individual a rational extension of the universal quality of the

4. For a clear and succinct treatment of the philosophical idealists (including
an extension to the United States through the treatment of Josiah Royce), see A. J.
M. Milne, *The Social Philosophy of English Idealism* (London: George Allen and Un-
win, 1962).

idea of freedom, one can make good the full potential of the claim to individual freedom. Only by universalizing the idea of freedom insofar as it is applicable to any individual case can we assure that we can maintain an appropriate measure of freedom for the specific or concrete individual. Conceived otherwise, the notion of freedom becomes an unreconciled contradiction or, at the very least, a contingent concept of freedom. Thus in every specific experience there lies the potential for a grasp of the universal content of that particular, or concrete, experience.

The English philosophical idealists were much more concerned with the more "practical" applications of such concepts as the concrete universal than they were with the general metaphysics and epistemology implicit in the tenets of philosophical idealism. The concerns of the nineteenth-century English philosophical idealists were mainly ethical and political, although both their ethics and their politics adhered closely to the philosophical implications arising from the effort to make good on the promise of a unity of the rational activity and reality resulting from the treatment of experience as a whole rather than analyzing it into its empirically manifested, isolated, and abstract parts.

Beyond these purely philosophical considerations, the historical context in which the nineteeth-century English philosophical idealists carried out what they conceived to be their philosophical function was one that furnished them a solid pragmatic basis from which to launch their attack on the effects of an empirically analytical way of looking at things. For the English philosophical idealists followed close on the time when the English utilitarians— Jeremy Bentham, James Mill, and John Stuart Mill—were dominant influences in both the general intellectual environment and in the parliamentary and other arenas in which public policy was thrashed out. The writings of the English utilitarians exerted a strong, direct influence on British intellectual history for roughly a century (*ca.* 1776–1873); and from the 1820s until approximately the 1880s, political reform and public economic policy in England were, for the most part, based on practical applications of utilitarian doctrine.

The utilitarians, especially Bentham and James Mill, were virtual prototypes of the analytic school of philosophy whose effects were deplored by Hegel. The point of departure for the utilitarians was the sensationalist psychology that had exercised a growing influence since it had been advanced by Hobbes. Under this concept, all ideas are imprints on the mind by external stimuli. When the stimulus is painful, we are repelled by it; when it is pleasurable, we are attracted to it. The dichotomy of pleasure and pain is the motivating factor in all human behavior. Since man's behavior is solely the result of his basic motivation to seek pleasure and to avoid pain, it follows that any conception of ethics, and ultimately of politics, that might be ascribed to such a "system" of thought has to be predicated on the notion of examining any action from the standpoint of its effect in maximizing pleasure and minimizing pain among the individuals who compose the society. Indeed, the only function of reason in the utilitarian conception of morals and politics is instrumental. That is, on the basis of past experience and the association of ideas involved in the accumulation of discrete experience, reason is able to provide some advance information on the likelihood that a given course of action will produce, for the individual concerned or, in the case of a political decision, at least a majority of individuals, an excess of pleasure over pain. In ethics, as in politics, reason therefore simply furnishes guidance on the likely outcome of a given course of action; it provides no compelling motivation, since that is furnished solely by the stimuli of pleasure and pain.

As sketchy as the foregoing remarks may be, they indicate that utilitarianism represented an attempt to apply the analytical methods of science to human behavior. Its proponents made the effort to break experience down into its elemental components for purposes of analysis, and then, by a logical synthesis of these parts, to arrive at a general theory of behavior. Utilitarianism thus tended to be materialistic in its assumptions about the nature of existence, radically empirical in methodology, and prone to treat the conscious mind as a passive recipient of stimuli, incapable of doing anything other than collecting and associating in a pattern or patterns the impressions made on it by the impact of matter external to, and independent of, it.

The doctrines of the utilitarians in the practical areas of ethics and politics followed relentlessly on these conceptions of the foundation of behavior. Since man is a psychological egoistic hedonist, any notion of the "good" conceived in terms other than that which brings more pleasure than pain to the individual is untenable. Reason is powerless to produce any objective concept of right action that constitutes a binding obligation on one who faces a moral decision. Nor can there be any collective "good" which supersedes the self-interest of the individuals who constitute the collectivity.

The consequence for public policy is that each individual should be left as free as possible to maximize his own happiness; and a naturalistic reconciliation of the isolated interests of the individuals who compose society is assumed, provided such individuals are educated sufficiently to be able to discern by instrumental reason the means by which long-range pleasure or happiness might best be promoted, as contrasted with the short-range pleasures which result from the mere fulfillment of immediate desire. In brief, the utilitarians represented the culmination of the ideology of classical individualistic liberalism, an ideology which was the dominant influence on public policy during the middle years of the nineteenth century. Under its doctrines, the autonomous egoistic individual is the elemental unit in politics, the government functions most effectively as a referee in maintaining an open field for free competition among individuals, and no romantic conception of the "general interest" can effect a reconciliation of individual interests more effectively than the naturalistic reconciliation that arises from each individual's pursuit of his own interest within a general legal constraint on interference with every other man's equally free pursuit of his interest. These elementary doctrines constituted the most important ideological bases of public policy in England from the beginnings of the liberal reform movement in Parliament in the 1820s until the impact of collectivistic ideas on government action began to be felt in the 1870s.

Although the English philosophical idealists never achieved the dominant intellectual position occupied for a time by the utilitarians, and never were able to translate their ideas into so immense an influence on public affairs as that exercised by the utilitarians, they were certainly very much a part of the late-nineteenth-century reaction against both the ideas and the political and economic effects of the particular English version of positivism represented by utilitarianism. Philosophically, the idealists were concerned, as Hegel had been before them, with the essential restoration of the unity between mind and so-called external phenomena. The idealists, in fact, objected precisely to the analytical reduction of perception to the passive reception of external stimuli. To the idealist, nothing is "real" unless it is perceived and interpreted as a whole by the active power of the rational intellect. Experience is not broken down into an infinite series of discrete impressions conjoined only by associations in memory of similarities and dissimilarities among the received imprints on the mind. Ideas themselves are central to the apprehension of reality, and the function of philosophy is to achieve the highest degree of generality possible with respect to any particular experience. Again following Hegel, the idealists tended to arrange the forms of experience into a hierarchical structure in which the experience in the "practical" realms of morals and politics ranks in the order of existence above the experience of the objective realm of natural phenomena. And it is the rational activity itself, in the form of esthetics, religion, and philosophy, which reaches the very highest levels of consciousness, and in doing so supersedes and gives full meaning to experiences associated with the practical life. In this respect, however, the English philosophical idealists, while tending, like Hegel, to reach out for the absolute, demonstrated a typical English philosophical propensity by concerning themselves more with the experience of the practical life than with ultimate or absolute reality.

In the latter sense, the English idealists wished to restore the independent foundations of morals that the utilitarians had reduced to a naturalistically based behaviorist psychology, and to extend the experience of such fundamental concepts as obligation to the interpretation of politics. Man's political life was not conceived solely as an extension of his individual interests. On the contrary, the capacity for self-fulfillment itself depended on an awareness of the common experience of society, because political association reached beyond the convenience of social relations arising out of mutual self-interest. In consequence, although the English idealists were to remain within the mainstream of liberal democracy, they were not bound to the atomistic individualism of classical liberalism, in which the state is an artificial construction designed to serve naturalistically determined interests.

In a metaphor that is now somewhat archaic, one might suggest that the utilitarians were essentially mechanistic and the idealists essentially organic in their respective views of the nature of political association. The liberal democracy of the idealists is founded on a concept of equality which grew out of the common substance of mankind and human experience; theirs was not extrapolated from an observed objective similarity among the phenomenological response mechanisms exhibited by each discrete individual of which society is composed. Nor is freedom an instrumental means for maximizing pleasure and minimizing pain; rather it is a general condition for the fulfillment of moral responsibility. And political association is not limited to devising institutions designed to assure that each man will be free from the interference of other men in the pursuit of his own interests, for man does not fulfill the potential of his own nature except through moral and political relationships with other men. The liberalism of the English idealists was inclined, therefore, to be a reforming liberalism with strong pluralistic overtones, and without the negative commitments of laissez-faire policy orientations. The liberal state was conceived instead as a creative association for making good on moral and political realities that are merely prefigured in purely egoistic moral and political activities.

But it was less from the social philosophy of the philosophical idealists than from their concept of philosophy in general that Oakeshott took his point of departure.

In *Experience and Its Modes*, Oakeshott sets forth his fundamental conception of philosophy. He acknowledges that he had learned most from Hegel and Bradley,[5] and this early philosophical treatise clearly comes out of the tradition of philosophical idealism, but it equally clearly bears the mark of originality. *Experience and Its Modes* is a difficult book to characterize or to categorize. It is at once a work that emphasizes the necessity for concreteness, but to many readers it leaves the impression of being highly abstract; al-

5. Michael Oakeshott, *Experience and Its Modes* (Cambridge: University Press, 1933), 6.

though it is discursive in the apparently leisurely way it treats its broad topic, it also impresses by virtue of its tight logic; and despite the fact that it repeatedly drives home its main points, it is subtle in the manner in which each apparent repetition adds a new dimension to the argument. The book is poetic in diction and simultaneously rigorous in analysis. Inasmuch as the treatise was written some time after the decline in influence of philosophical idealism (*ca.* World War I), the author was well aware that the book would not be warmly received in intellectual circles dominated by the scientific mode of thought, yet he approaches his thesis boldly and with a confident sense of its continuing relevance.

Oakeshott holds that philosophic experience is experience without presupposition, reservation, arrest, or modification. Since experience is inextricably involved with judgment, it is literally a world of ideas. And that world is satisfactory only when it meets the tests of coherence, unity, and completeness. A division of experience is not tenable, because this involves a reservation, arrest, or modification that results in a failure to meet the criterion of wholeness. What Oakeshott refers to as "modes" of experience are abstractions from the unity or wholeness of experience of parts that are treated as the whole, thus leading to the fallacy of *ignoratio elenchi*. The term most strikingly used to characterize this phenomenon is *arrest*. Although Oakeshott indicates that the modes (or arrests) of experience may be many, possibly even infinite, he confines his analysis to three: (1) historical experience, (2) scientific experience, and (3) practical experience. And reading him gives one pause to consider whether these may not be the most generalized examples that one can examine as claiming completeness, yet examples that exhibit the defect of falling short of that criterion. It is the responsibility of philosophic experience to analyze these abstractions, arrests, modifications, or reservations of experience in order to discover how they fall short of experience as a whole, as well as to discern the way in which each mode of experience intrudes upon, or attempts to absorb, other modes of experience which themselves constitute abstractions from, or arrests in, the totality of experience.

In examining historical experience philosophically, Oakeshott finds that it is a presupposition of history that every event is related, and history's claim to coherence arises from the full account it gives of change. All events of history are related to all other events, and the claim of eventual comprehensiveness rests on the capacity continually to fill in the details of events. As an independent manner of thinking, history is characterized by its capacity to see the past as something to be examined in its own terms, rather than in terms of some other abstraction or experience that imposes meaning on it. But despite its appearance of providing coherence, Oakeshott still holds that historical experience is an arrest or modification of experience because, while the data with which it deals appear to be in the past, the experience *itself* (in effect, the judgment of the events of the past) is always present. By imputing present experience to experience of the past, historical thought produces an unresolved contradiction that indicates its particular modification of—or arrest in, or abstraction from—experience. And perhaps because it falls short of wholeness, historical experience has sometimes demonstrated a tendency to be absorbed by other modes of experience. In the main, the intrusions have been from the world of practice and the world of science. In the former instance, some historians have attempted to adduce from the study of the past solutions to problems of the practical life of the present; in the latter instance, the effect of positivist orientations in historical thought has been to try to produce generalizations or causal explanations of the course of history after the mode of scientific thought.

Scientific experience, on the other hand, attempts to assemble a world of ideas by locating uniformities and stabilities in "objective" phenomena which lead to generalities that may be understood and communicated in apparent completeness of explanation. It is a world of ideas that purports to be complete in itself because of its capability of quantification. But its defect lies precisely in its limitation to the category of quantity; all characteristics which do not submit themselves to the coherence that comes from quantification are excluded from its purview, and it therefore falls short of achieving the full quality of experience. It does often assert itself as the whole of experience, and in this claim it seeks to absorb both the world of practice and all other apparently coherent modes of experience. But in doing so it engages in the naturalistic fallacy by presuming that the world of experience not presently comprehensible in a quantitative manner can, through scientific "objectivity," be brought within its purview.

The third world of ideas that makes the claim to completeness and coherence is practical experience. By contrast with the objective world of ideas involved in scientific experience, the world of practice is a world seen from the subjective perspective. It is a world of desires and purposes, and is therefore a world of interests and of will. But because both the environment and the presence of other individuals and their own interests in the world obviously constitute limits on the fulfillment of individual desires by an act of will, the practical world involves the individual with rules of conduct or morality by which he adjusts to living under conditions external to the self and pertinent to the interests of the individual. The defectiveness of the world of practice is revealed by the fact that it is an experience of constant flux, because we are always seeking to bring the world of ought into the world of is. It is therefore the constant seeking after change in the practical world that indicates the incompleteness of this mode of experience. And in seeking constantly to realize a "better" state of things, we sometimes seek to overcome the limits of practical experience by projecting onto it a teleological principle drawn from the world of historical experience or from the world of scientific experience, or the two in combination. Obviously the problems of practical experience are particularly pertinent to the problems of political philosophy in ways that will appear in the context of the discussion of Oakeshott's specifically political ideas.

Some twenty-five years after the appearance of *Experience and Its Modes*, Oakeshott extended his philosophical inquiry to one additional determinate mode of experience—the esthetic mode. In *The Voice of Poetry in the Conversation of Mankind*, Oakeshott repudiated a statement that he had made in *Experience and Its Modes* to the effect that esthetics belongs to the world of practical experience. But in his later reflections, he holds, or seems to hold, poetry (and for "poetry" read art as a whole) to be a determinate mode of experience having its own characteristics and presuppositions quite apart from those of the realm of practice. The world of poetry is a world of images, of uninhibited imagination. The purpose of poetry is not to explain reality in the objective or scientific sense, as some have held, nor is it to serve the practical purposes of instruction in moral or political or other practical values. It is a transient and intermittent thing which does not partake of the full life of contemplation, but is something by way of being a dream-world in which one indulges freely and without the intrusiveness of other considerations.[6]

Unlike Hegel and virtually all of the philosophical idealists who succeeded him, at least through Collingwood, Oakeshott does not offer a hierarchic or generic explanation of experience in which "lower" forms of experience unfold by a dialectical process into perceptibly higher forms. Although philsophical experience has as its appropriate function the apprehension of experience as a whole, I can discern no completion of this function in Oakeshott's writings. Instead, philosophy performs through him the more limited function of identifying the particular ways in which the presumptively comprehensive (but still incomplete) modes of experience exert their claims to completeness, and the particular defects by which they fail to apprehend the totality of experience. Oakeshott's philosophical usage, therefore, is critical rather than synthesizing, and leaves serious questions about the possibility of making good on its own function of perceiving experience as a whole. I can discern no evidence in him of the propensity common in philosophical idealism to make the idea of perfected reason immanent. Nor does he provide any explanation as to why the arrests occur in face of the philosophical demand that experience be coherent and complete. It is precisely such problems that have led to the supposition that, while Oakeshott accepts the critical manner of thought of philosophical idealism, he remains basically an epistemological skeptic.

As the title of W. H. Greenleaf's monograph on him indicates, Oakeshott's study of politics aims at fulfilling the objective of philosophy with respect to the understanding of politics; that is, an

---

6. Michael Oakeshott, *The Voice of Poetry in the Conversation of Mankind* (London: Bowes and Bowes, 1959). Oakeshott, however, had second thoughts about his view of esthetic activity much earlier than the appearance of this book. Greenleaf, *Oakeshott's Philosophical Politics*, 30.

effort is made to comprehend politics from the perspective of experience as a whole, rather than from that of one or more of the limited modes of experience. As an activity, politics clearly belongs to the practical world, but on the criteria of philosophy the world of practice is not to be perceived solely from the standpoint of practical experience. Given Oakeshott's skepticism, it is certain from the outset that understanding can never be complete; but this doubt cannot excuse the fallacy of looking at politics in the arrested state of experience of practice only; the critical standards of philosophy must apply, even if the function of philosophy cannot be fully realized.

The first instance in which Oakeshott expresses his view of how political philosophy maintains consistency with philosophy in general is in his introduction to the *Leviathan*. After pointing out that reflection about political life may take place at a variety of levels, including both means and ends, he goes on to note that

> Political philosophy may be understood to be what occurs when this movement of reflection takes a certain direction and achieves a certain level, its characteristic being the relation of political life, and the values and purposes pertaining to it, to the entire conception of the world that belongs to a civilization. That is to say, at all other levels of reflection on political life, we have before us the single world of political activity, and what we are interested in is the internal coherence of that world; but in political philosophy we have in our minds that world and another world, and our endeavor is to explore the coherence of the two worlds together. The reflective intelligence is apt to find itself at this level without the consciousness of any great conversion and without any sense of entering upon a new project, but merely submitting itself to the impetus of reflection, by spreading its sails to the argument. For, any man who holds in his mind the conceptions of the natural world, of God, of human activity and human destiny which belong to his civilization, will scarcely be able to prevent an endeavor to assimilate these to the ideas that distinguish the political order in which he lives, and failing to do so he will become a philosopher (of a simple sort) unawares.[7]

In the context of Oakeshott's work as a whole, that seems to me to be an important statement. It clearly imposes a philosophic

7. Thomas Hobbes, *Leviathan*, edited, with an introduction, by Michael Oakeshott (Oxford: Basil Blackwell, [1946]), ix.

burden on the student of politics, and Oakeshott assumes that burden in his subsequent writings on politics. Or at least he assumes
what I take to be the burden of the critical function of philosophy.
And by the critical function, I mean that he tells us how certain
perspectives of politics fall short of the tests for experience of coherence, unity, and completeness, even if he is unable to give us a
positive view of political experience that completely satisfies these
criteria.

A most stringent criticism of the current perception of politics
(and of the way this perception affects practice) appeared in a series of articles in the *Cambridge Journal* in the late 1940s.[8] In a two-
part article, "Rationalism in Politics," Oakeshott set the tone for
most of what he was later to say about politics and political education. He holds that in the whole of post-Renaissance Europe politics has tended to be "rationalist." In Oakeshott's view the rationalist is one who has great faith in the power of unhindered
reason to solve the problems of the world. The rationalist is, therefore, strongly opposed to any authority except the authority of reason, and he is especially opposed to tradition, habit, and other
concrete ways of knowing that result from living within the context of a civilization. The rationalist does not go at all knowledge
a priori; he accepts experience, but only when it is his own experience rather than the accumulated experience of a tradition or an
institutional arrangement. "With an almost poetic fancy, he strives
to live each day as if it were his first, and he believes that to form
a habit is to fail." As an "open-minded" person, the rationalist must
bring every custom, tradition, and habit under the test of reason,
and he always finds it easier to destroy and create anew than to
carry out what Oakeshott frequently refers to as the politics of
"repair."[9]

After carrying out his work of critical destruction, the rational-

8. These include "Rationalism in Politics," *Cambridge Journal*, I (1947–1948),
81–98, 145–57; "Scientific Politics," 347–58; "Contemporary British Politics," 474–
90; "The Political Economy of Freedom," *Cambridge Journal*, II (1948–1949), 212–
29; and several others of a related nature. The main themes pursued in these pieces
are to be found in those selections from the series reprinted (along with some later
essays) in Oakeshott, *Rationalism in Politics*. Further citations of these and subsequent essays are from that volume.
9. Oakeshott, "Rationalism in Politics," 3.

ist fills with ideology the place of the tradition he has destroyed. For Oakeshott ideology is "the formalized abridgment of the supposed substratum of rational truth contained in the tradition." And not only do ideologies demonstrate a philosophically inadequate quality of abstractness in having been distilled from the total experience in which they were set, they also provide a perfectionist view of politics, and are, therefore, the grounds for imposing uniformity on society in the effort to realize the perfected state which is held out as a promise in the ideology. Oakeshott cites numerous examples of the "imposition of a uniform condition of perfection upon human conduct," including Robert Owens' world convention to solve all manner of social problems, the effort to found a society upon the declaration of the rights of man, the reunion of the Christian churches, open diplomacy, the single tax, the Beveridge report, federalism, women's suffrage, etc., etc.[10]

One of the worst features of the modern rationalist tendency is its effect on education. In particular, it leads to the substitution of technique for traditional knowledge. Today, everything must be done by means of the "book" or the "crib." Education for the rationalist is not the "initiation into the moral and intellectual habits and achievements of his society, and entry into the partnership between the present and past, or sharing of concrete knowledge. . . . It is a training in technique, a training, that is, in the half of knowledge which can be learnt from books when they are used as cribs."[11] Mere technique, taken apart from the totality of experience from which it was abstracted, is at best virtually useless, and at worst highly destructive. One of Oakeshott's favorite analogies involves the art of cookery: It is not sufficient to go by the cookbook, one needs more than a list of ingredients and a step-by-step procedure to make a decent cake. The experience with the concrete activity itself is as essential to the realm of practice in morals and politics as it is to becoming a good cook.

Oakeshott goes on to extend his broad analysis of the defects of rationalism in modern politics to the question of moral behavior ("A Tower of Babel" and "Rational Conduct") and to contempo-

10. *Ibid.*, 4, 6.
11. *Ibid.*, 32–33.

rary British politics. In all the areas of practical experience, he finds that the pursuit of abstract ideals, the development of rigorous rules of conduct, the setting of predetermined ends, and the application of scientific technique lead to the same result—a loss of coherence, unity, and wholeness of knowledge about the appropriate ways of attending to our social and political life.

But what, if anything, does Oakeshott have to contribute positively to our understanding of the practical life as viewed from the perspective of philosophy? The answer is not easy, mainly because Oakeshott combines an acute critical perception of the deficiencies of modern life as it has developed under the influence of the scientific mode of experience with a pronounced skepticism about anything that smacks of completeness of knowledge. In one of his own favorite terms, however, Oakeshott does give us "intimations" of the ways in which the practical activity of politics might come closer to satisfying the criteria of philosophy than has been the case under the influence of the rationalist's attempts at resolving the problems of the world. Most of these positive hints or suggestions are contained in Oakeshott's writings on education, and it is interesting to note that he is one of the few recent political philosophers who has had something to say about the relation between politics and education.

Fairly early in his inaugural lecture at the London School of Economics, Oakeshott indicates that he takes politics "to be the activity of attending to the general arrangements of a set of people whom chance or choice have brought together." Although all types of societies have their politics, "the communities in which this manner of activity is pre-eminent are the hereditary co-operative groups, many of them of ancient lineage, all of them aware of a past, a present and a future, which we call 'states.'" Although political activity is not the prime activity for most people in a society, it is one for which every normal adult has some responsibility, and it is therefore a universal activity. It is not, however, an activity which is open to infinite possibilities, and it is not a set of arrangements that will ever achieve a state of perfection.[12]

12. The text of Oakeshott's lecture was published by Bowes and Bowes in 1951. Oakeshott, "Political Education," 112–13.

In order to decide what sort of education one should have in order to practice politics, or to attend to the general arrangements
of a set of people, we need a definition of politics from which to de-
duce the character of political education. Again, we are reminded
that "to understand an activity is to know it as a concrete whole;
it is to recognize the activity as having the source of its movement
within itself." But politics can never be purely empirical—it must
have a starting point of some sort—nor can it take its point of departure from simple ideology, because the political ideology itself
is a mere abstraction from an existing activity, and not a premed-
itated guide to that activity.[13]

It is obvious, then, that one cannot simply initiate political activity; one can practice politics only where a common tradition of
behavior already exists. "To suppose a collection of people without recognized traditions of behavior, or one which enjoyed arrangements which intimated no direction for change and needed
no attention, is to suppose a people incapable of politics. This activity, then, springs neither from instant desires, nor from general
principles, but from the existing traditions of behavior themselves." At this point, Oakeshott's skepticism about the connection between knowledge and practice becomes exceedingly clear.
There appears to be no way in which a society can self-consciously
develop the practice of politics; the origins of the practice of politics seem to be virtually lost in the prehistory of the political activity itself. As others have pointed out, Oakeshott gives us no guide
as to how people without an experience of political activity constitute themselves a political community. Furthermore, even when
political activity is established in the form of a going political tradition, the only form that political activity can properly take "is
the amendment of existing arrangements by exploring and pursuing what is intimated in them." Even the going society can have
no certainty about its directions or its future destination, because
in political activity "men sail a boundless and bottomless sea; there
is neither harbor nor shelter nor floor for anchorage, neither starting place nor appointed destination. The enterprise is to keep afloat
on an even keel; the sea is both friend and enemy; and the sea-

13. Oakeshott, "Political Education," 113.

manship consists in using the resources of a traditional manner of behavior in order to make a friend of every hostile occasion."[14]

So the real problem of maintaining a political society is to get to know a tradition that will appear to be essentially unintelligible, and to adopt as principle the necessity for continuity. And although the study of politics is an appropriate academic study, it must be understood as a concrete manner of behavior, and not as an abstraction from experience.

Although Oakeshott has many subtle things to say about the way in which the effort to achieve such an understanding of politics should be carried out, he also has an overall concern for the general problem of education in a community. Education begins in the nursery, and it starts with helping a child to become at home in the natural-artificial world into which it was born.[15] As one moves into formal schooling, education should be rigorous and general, rather than specialized and adapted to the particular talents and aptitudes of the individual.

Beyond school, education branches into two directions, one being vocational, and the other university education. And university education is not knowledge simply about what has been authoritatively said, but is "a familiarity with the manner of thinking which has generated what has been said." Inasmuch as a university is "an association of persons, locally situated, engaged in caring for and attending to the whole intellectual capital which composes a civilization," a university education is concerned with the "languages" in which the type of thinking characteristic of this activity expresses itself. Since the language of politics "is the language of desire and aversion, of preference and choice, of approval and disapproval, of praise and blame, of persuasion, injunction, accusation and treat [*sic*]," it is necessary to understand how this practical language is generated and what it means. And in order to do this effectively, one must also understand the language of history and philosophy. "The appropriate engagement of an undergraduate student of 'politics' at a university will be to be taught and to learn something about the modes of thought and manners

14. *Ibid.*, 123, 127.
15. Michael Oakeshott, "The Study of 'Politics' in a University." 304.

of speaking of an historian and a philosopher, and to do this in connection with politics"[16]

A merely vocational education can never do more than acquaint its recipient with technique; it cannot provide him with the knowledge he needs to be able to use the language of politics as a part of the general conversation engaged in by civilization. Nor can it provide the basis of understanding that will enable one to perceive the intimations of a particular political tradition that must, in turn, be grasped in order to permit us to attend to our general political arrangements by way of a politics of conservation and repair.

Thus it is that Oakeshott's skepticism, in combination with an epistemology grounded in philosophical idealism, debouches into a deep-seated conservatism with respect to the possibilities of a coherent understanding of society and politics. And as befits one who is concerned with the gradual filling in of the details of experience, Oakeshott has written an essay on what it means to be a conservative. In that essay he documents specifically his love for a wide variety of behavior, institutions, and modes of perception that are identified with what it means to be an Englishman within the broader framework of Western civilization. One runs against Oakeshott's own injunctions when one attempts to abstract from the totality of his writing some particular point, because his writing, like experience itself, needs to be considered as a whole in order to appreciate his use of a language appropriate to political conversation. But one quotation, perhaps even at the risk of being excessively abstract, does seem to sum up his conservative predisposition:

> To be conservative, then, is to prefer the familiar to the unknown, to prefer the tried to the untried, fact to mystery, the actual to the possible, the limited to the unbounded, the near to the distant, the sufficient to the super-abundant, the convenient to the perfect, present laughter to utopian bliss. Familiar relationships and loyalties will be preferred to the allure of more profitable attachments; to acquire and to enlarge will be less important than to keep, to cultivate and to enjoy; the grief of loss will be more acute than the excitement of novelty or promise. It is to be equal to one's own fortune, to live at the level of one's own means,

16. *Ibid.*, 309, 310, 321, 328.

to be content with the want of greater perfection which belongs alike to one's self and one's circumstances.[17]

Oakeshott displays one other tendency that runs strongly through the whole tradition of philosophical idealism, although it is not always recognized by critics as a prominent characteristic of that tradition. I refer to the tendency toward a preference for a pluralistic, as opposed to a monolithic, society. This is a point worth emphasizing, because some persons have taken the stress of philosophical idealism on completeness and coherence to imply an affinity with an authoritarian-based uniformity. A reading of Oakeshott's essay "The Political Economy of Freedom" will soon disabuse one of such notions. The emphasis is on an interlocking series of personal and group liberties that grow out of a wide variety of sources (including the rule of law, private property, and thousands of other devices and arrangements) which are mutually supporting, and each of which signifies and represents "the absence from our society of overwhelming concentrations of power."[18] The emphasis on the freedom of individual and group interests, in fact, is so great, and the stress on the primacy of mutual accomodations is so strong, that one might accuse Oakeshott, in this instance, of relying on naturalistic reconciliation to such an extent that he finds himself in the camp of classical liberalism or utilitarianism. But his opposition to collectivism is based more on the desire to avoid any type of arbitrary "reconstruction of society" than to prevent, in the name of individual freedom, action appropriate to the preservation of the traditional way of attending to the affairs of a society.

From time to time the stability and self-sufficiency of the English tradition both appalls and consternates a Continental or an American. A question that frequently engages one while reading Oakeshott is, How is it possible for three English philosophers as widely divergent in fundamentals as Hume, Burke, and Oakeshott to come so close together on the practical aspects of their treatment of politics? Philosophically, Burke is stringently opposed to systemiza-

17. Michael Oakeshott, "On Being Conservative," 169.
18. Oakeshott, "The Political Economy of Freedom," 40.

tion of any sort, Hume is analytical to a fault, and Oakeshott insists on the pursuit of the philosophical absolutes of completeness and coherence. Burke is a transcendentalist, Hume a skeptic with utilitarian leanings, and Oakeshott a skeptical idealist. Yet all three men are traditionalists in politics, preferring a reliance on habit and custom to any effort to order society on the basis of abstract principles. The three of them also share a predisposition toward the concrete and the personal, as well as a patriotism that clearly reflects a love of the societal arrangements, the governmental institutions, and the general style of British life and thought.[19]

A part of the answer, I believe, lies in the special qualities of the British political tradition. The continuity and stability of British politics are unparalleled in the modern, or perhaps any other, era. The ability to change, and yet to conserve both the form and substance of political practice has produced a great measure of self-confidence in the capacity of British society to meet any tests imposed on it collectively. I have heard Oakeshott say, for example, that any issue which is *really* an issue will not fail to manifest itself in the context of British politics. The practice of what was once called British "historical empiricism" has produced a reluctance to attempt to reduce civilization to a set of formalized principles, or to abandon the concrete rules of common sense for more plausible, but less workable, generalities.[20] It is this characteristic, I believe, that generates in otherwise divergent philosophers a strong sense of patriotism and a basically conservative disposition. Such a society may well merit the envy of less fortunate peoples, who are constrained to try to invent a system they did not have the good fortune to inherit.

19. Oakeshott's language is often the language of Hume and Burke, and especially the latter. *Habit, custom*, and the frequent use of *prejudice* in its nonpejorative meaning are cases in point. And what could be more Burkean than the following aphorism: "A scheme which does not recognize circumstances can have no place for variety"? Oakeshott, "Rationalism in Politics," 6.

20. Since *common sense* has been used several times in this essay, one is tempted to digress into the subtle effect that has been worked on the whole of British thought by Thomas Reid and his "commonsense" philosophy. While Continental philosophers of the eighteenth century were engaging in every conceivable abstract mode of philosophical speculation, Reid was engaged in a quiet restoration of unimpassioned reflection. A revival of interest in Reid is indicated by the recent publication of two volumes of his work: *Essays on the Active Powers of the Human Mind* and *Essays on the Intellectual Powers of Man* (Cambridge: MIT Press, 1969).

IX The Politics of *I'll Take My Stand*

The publication history of *I'll Take My Stand* may, in symbolic ways, yield more immediate understanding of the book's deeper meaning and the abiding interest it has generated as part of the southern and American political self-image than any story told thus far about its prepublication origins and initial appearance. Measured against the standards of human biological chronology, the book, soon to have been in print for fifty years, is a ripe middle age; and in terms of the usual twenty-year span, it is now in the midst of making its impact felt on a third generation of readers.

When the book appeared under the Harper imprint in 1930, the era of the American industrial revolution, spawned by financial and corporate capitalism, had barely entered the stage of its great crisis. The South, permanently depressed since the Civil War, had been touched only limitedly, and mostly indirectly, by industrialization and urbanization. By a combination of internal choice and externally imposed alienation, it remained in an economically "underdeveloped" condition and in a semi-isolated political position vis-à-vis the remainder of the country. The southern literary renaissance had barely begun and was as yet unrecognized either in or outside the region. Reaction to the book tended to be more negative than positive except for those who wanted to annex it to the romantic ethos of the Lost Cause, so it was not reprinted for many years, although it continued to be read and discussed as the literary fame of several of its contributors spread nationally and internationally.

When the book was reissued in the prestigious Torchbook paperback series in 1962, the country had passed through the Great Depression, emerged from World War II as the major power center of the Western world, continued to expand its industrial might to hitherto undreamed-of proportions, and centralized its politics

to the point at which big government paralleled corporate giant-
ism either as a challenger to that power or as its partner. The nation was soon to be caught up in a complicated new crisis that can
now be categorically referred to as the social turbulence of the
1960s. Meanwhile, the South had gone through a major portion of
the civil rights revolution, industrialized and urbanized at a great
pace, and produced a literary revival with which only the flower-
ing of New England in the later nineteenth century could bear
comparison in the annals of American artistic achievement.

In 1977, fifteen years after the Torchbook edition, *I'll Take My
Stand* was entered in the lists of the immortals, figuratively speaking, when it reappeared as a volume in the Louisiana State University Press's Library of Southern Civilization. One hardly need
belabor the point to recall the crisis of public order confronting the
nation then. A few words and phrases will suffice: defeat in war,
Watergate, governmental overload, segmented society, inflation,
multinational corporate power, the urban mess, environmental
pollution and deterioration, bloated bureaucracy, the arms race,
single-issue political movements, depletion of energy sources, loss
of confidence in institutions, lack of leadership, etc. The South, by
contrast, appeared to be less beset by contemporary troubles than
the rest of the country, despite its increasing internal diversity and
apparent capitulation to the urges of industrialization and urbanization. Some questions are raised by this altered basis for comparison and contrast between the South and America at large. Do
some of the moral and social characteristics that define the region's differences from the rest of the country have something to
offer by way of solution to the economic, social, and political problems by which the nation has been perturbed in recent times? Could
the geographic section that is historically closer than any other part
of the United States to its preindustrial social conformation have
a previously scorned legacy to bequeath the nation—a legacy that
might assist in making the transition to a decent postindustrial society? The course of public events in this decade intimates the possibility of positive answers to such questions. And it may not be
extravagant to note that a substantial theoretical part of that legacy may be embodied in the volume of essays, subtitled *The South
and the Agrarian Tradition*, written by a dozen then rather obscure

southern men of letters and published half a century ago. If so, *I'll Take My Stand* is more than a relic that recalls a mythic past; it continues to provide a social critique and some moral and political principles that may enhance our understanding of the current predicament and provide some sense of direction for the future. A surer grasp of the way in which these principles were realized through experience, were expressed in the particular form in which the Agrarians cast them, and have continued to evoke individual moral, social, and political responses over a considerable expanse of time and changing external circumstances may also tell us a little something more than we already know about what that elusive book itself is.

The dimensions of time provided by the larger historical context complicate the problems of longitudinal comparison. The American experience as an independent political entity, or possibly a congeries of political entities, is barely two hundred years old, and the active survival of *I'll Take My Stand* stretches over the last quarter of that period. If the Agrarian collection was as deeply rooted in the mythical nationhood of the antebellum South as those who have regarded it simply as a romantic anachronism from its conception insist, the continuity of its intellectual harvest challenges the imagination anew. We are now almost as far removed in time from initial publication as that 1930 date was from the end of the era of Southern nationalism at Appomattox. And if the beginning of Southern separatist consciousness dates, at the earliest, from the 1820s or even the 1830s the influence of this articulated set of Agrarian principles from the 1920s and 1930s covers a longer span of time than that in which the pragmatic representation of what Robert Penn Warren called the "City of the Soul" developed, tried to establish its separate identity in history as the Confederacy, and was absorbed by conquest.

On the other hand, if the counterinterpretation of this compellingly complex and persistingly controversial book has persuasive validity, as I am convinced it has, these minor dimensions of time bear no more than a contingent relation to the text. By counterinterpretation I mean that exegesis most fully attempted by Louis D. Rubin, Jr., and given evidential support in other works, especially of Donald Davidson, John Crowe Ransom, Allen Tate, and

Robert Penn Warren, as well as in such dialogues as those appearing in *Fugitives' Reunion*, exchanges of letters, and "conversations" between Warren and Cleanth Brooks in *The Possibilities of Order*. At the close of his introduction to the 1962 Torchbook edition, Rubin notes that this "prophetic" book should be read as neither a treatise on economics and politics nor a "guide to regional social structuring, but as a commentary on the nature of man—man as Southerner, as American, as human being." And in the conclusion of his long chapter on *I'll Take My Stand* in *The Wary Fugitives*, after reinforcing the prophetic nature of the Agrarian symposium, Rubin states that the day had long passed since the participants needed to apologize for or explain away their participation because the book "speaks to the problems of today and tomorrow in a way that few documents of its time have done." As a reaffirmation of the humane tradition in relation to a particular time and circumstance, the message of the Agrarians is thus seen as timeless.[1]

I would, at this point, enter one or two caveats with respect to Rubin's interpretation, despite a wholehearted admiration for his comprehensive thesis and the felicity of style with which he presents it. First, in using the term *prophetic* as a general characterizing concept he may have given the essays more of an Old Testament apocalyptic and transformational meaning than the text should be called on to bear. The timelessness of the book's content does not depend on historicism, either in the sense of the discernment of historical determinism out of experience of the past or in the projection of a futuristic teleology within the frame of history. Prophecy connotes foretelling, whereas the more restrained meaning of *prescient*—itself only a relatively more satisfactory term than *prophetic*—denotes foreseeing or foreknowledge that is less than the omniscience with which both prophecy and prescience are sometimes equated. The foresight of the Agrarians is certainly based on their historical perception of certain constants in human experience, but the future is open for them because, as the evi-

1. Twelve Southerners, *I'll Take My Stand: The South and the Agrarian Tradition*, Introduction by Louis D. Rubin, Jr., (New York: Harper Torchbooks, 1962), xviii; Louis D. Rubin, Jr., *The Wary Fugitives: Four Poets and the South* (Baton Rouge: Louisiana State University Press, 1978), 250.

dence of the past suggests, man participates in the formation of history through the freedom to influence the course of human events within the constraints of nature and the limits of his knowledge. The Agrarians, like all those who seriously confront the problems of seeing human experience as a whole in the variety of its manifestations, which include the social and the political, look both to the past and to the future from the perspective of the present. But to place absolute confidence in one's historical foresight or foretelling is to take the participant-observer outside history and thus outside man's experience of time itself.

This is not to imply that the Agrarians, or even a substantial number of them, deliberately ignored the human capacity for religious experience as awareness of divine presence in its infinity and the relation of that experience to the social and political realities with which *I'll Take My Stand* was immediately concerned. Indeed one of the things they were trying to establish was the conditions under which man's religious experience might not only flourish in itself but also exert its influence on the shaping of both individual and social life. Tate's expressed desire for calling the work a defense of "religious humanism" speaks directly to the point. But they were also well aware that the finiteness of man and society meant that the possibilities of history were limited to man's experience in time, with all of the contingencies implied in that perception of reality. The timelessness of *I'll Take My Stand* is thus dependent on its recognition that history itself is a humanly created symbol of man's time-boundness. The foresight discernible in the book is a tentative projection of future possibilities drawn from the experience of its contributors with the social and political conditions of their times as those times were related to what historical experience could tell them about the conditions of the good life manifested through historical continuity and change. If these limits had not been observed, the Agrarians might well have been guilty either of the escape from the harshness of the present into a reified Edenic past that never was, as many of their superficial critics charged, or of the ideological projection of a perfected man and society that was merely a different version of the dreamworld of the progressivist utopias against which the Agrarian critique of modernity was directed.

One can say with some confidence that the retrospective scope of the contributors extends far beyond the view of their immediate relation to the southern tradition, although that relation is certainly the starting point of the endeavor and is a ubiquitous feature of the symposium. But as Tate indicated, the real concerns were with the values of Western civilization rather than with more proximate matters. In addition, the associations of the southern tradition with Europe as opposed to America in general were emphasized; and in ways that will be enlarged upon later, the classical influences are, when not overt, discernible beneath the surface of both the critical and the constructive arguments of virtually all the essays included in the volume.

A related issue arises from Rubin's stricture against reading the book as a treatise on economics and politics. As a warning against repeating the reductionist error of interpreting the substance of the book as a political tract and then excoriating the Agrarians for failing to present a practical program for implementing the good life in the context of a well-ordered polity, the argument has great merit. And one is bound to acknowledge that the larger purpose of the group was to examine the nature of man and to articulate its meaning. Indeed, such a purpose is pervasive in the variety of work of virtually every one of the participants, whether expressed in formal literature, criticism, or economic, social, and political commentary. But one can be misled by ascribing to these men of letters, even by negative implication, a calling so high that they would disdain to engage directly so mundane a topic as politics or political economy. To do so is to belittle, in the name of artistic purity, the importance of the political experience in relation to an understanding of the nature of man as a whole being and to suggest that the corpus of political philosophy from the ancient Greeks onward has not made a worthy contribution to ontology. In point of fact, the great works of political philosophy have always aimed at understanding man in his wholeness of being in much the same terms assayed by the Agrarians. So the calling of the literary artist is not derogated by suggesting that he may also have been engaged with political philosophy, any more than the status of a poet or novelist is automatically increased by denying to a political philosopher the appellation "man of letters." The quality of the created work is the ultimate test of a treatise on political philosophy as it is of a piece of imaginative literature. Only an inability to distinguish Plato's *Republic* or Aristotle's *Politics* from *Mein Kampf*, and *Hamlet* from *Love Story*, would qualify one to establish an absolute order of merit between political philosophy as a whole and poetry, drama, and fiction as a whole, particularly if the determination of quality is assessed in terms of the capacity to apprehend and express the reality of human nature in its wholeness. For the perception of wholeness requires an understanding of the "right relations of man-to-man," which is the proper foundation of political theory, just as "religion and the arts are founded on right relations of man-to-nature," as Ransom stipulated.[2] One is reminded in this context of the final triad in Hegel's hierarchy of rational human activities—Art, Revealed Religion, and Philosophy.

Whatever else it may be, then, *I'll Take My Stand* was a special effort on the part of a community of scholars and writers to come to grips with the political aspects of man's existence. That its main subject was politics need not mean that the participants intended to abstract politics from other modes of experience (to use Michael Oakeshott's language) as though the practical life of morals and politics would subsume the whole of experience. To have done so would have violated the objective of making sense of man's existence as a whole. The book attempted to relate political experience to other modes of experience in a symbiotic way, which is why it may qualify as political philosophy rather than an amateurish social tract for the times by literary romantics who refused to admit they were romantics.

But this does not mean that the book's purpose is not complicated by the fact that the treatise consists of a collection of essays written by individuals engaged in a variety of academic disciplines and other pursuits—poets, novelists, critics, philosophers, historians, a political scientist, and a psychologist—who addressed a diversity of topics through several modes of discourse. The only control was in the common subscription to a statement of principles that indicated the extent to which an unrestrained industrial system had become the organizing force of American

2. *I'll Take My Stand*, xxv.

society, affecting all human relations, and that suggested that the agrarian tradition of the South might embody the principles of a better-ordered social life. The introduction, in which these points of agreement seem to be rather modestly set forth by Ransom, went through much debate and revision after the essays were all in and waiting to go to the printer. Beyond that, it was, as Ransom noted, "through the good fortune of some deeper agreement that the book was expected to achieve its unity."[3] The Agrarians had no intention of presenting a closed "system" of politics, or of setting forth a comprehensive metaphysical "position." But they were intent on reaching beyond the circumstances in which they found themselves to the "principles" in which a good society was grounded. They were, in consequence, engaged in a theoretical quest that necessarily involved them in political philosophy, with all that such a quest meant by way of examining concrete experience in order to extract knowledge from opinion and distinguish between appearance and reality in the effort to apprehend such ends as human good and justice, not as analytical abstractions but as they were manifested in the course of human existence in its natural and social setting. It is as political theory, then, rather than as praxis that the politics of *I'll Take My Stand* has to be assessed, although the connections between theory as an activity and the practice of politics as a form of human action cannot be ignored in that assessment, as both the critics of the Agrarians and the subsequent courses taken by the participants forcibly remind us.

Since politics and morals are practical modes of experience, students of political philosophy tend to agree that efforts to comprehend politics theoretically originate in an awareness on the part of the potential theorist of living in a crisis of social order that affects the capacity of the individual to order his own life satisfactorily. The initial stage of the activity is usually a critical appraisal that seeks to determine the cause of the disorder, followed or accompanied by the effort to understand the principles according to which right order might be restored. The effort can, of course, be misdirected in the critical or the constructive stage, or both, and thus fail in its attempt to apprehend the truth of the matter. To re-

3. *Ibid.*, xix.

sort to the metaphor favored by the Greeks, the diagnosis may be superficial or misconceived, and the therapy may be at the level of symptomatic relief or so heroic that the patient dies. And there is always the case—more common perhaps in political than biological disorders—that the patient refuses to accept the treatment or turns to a quack in search of a cure, which again evokes the question of the relation between theory and praxis. Potential complications and contingencies attend every stage of the examination.

The theoretical inquiry of the Agrarians began, appropriately enough, with their apprehension of a lack of order in society that they perceived as affecting the possibilities of ordering their own lives to the best ends they might be capable of realizing. The three individuals who planned the symposium and attended to the arrangements to carry it through to publication—Davidson, Ransom, and Tate—had earlier been members of the Vanderbilt Fugitives, a small group of poets who launched a minor literary movement. Several among them, of course, later became major forces in shaping the directions of literature and literary criticism over succeeding decades. The magazine that resulted from the group's regular meetings, at which they read and criticized each other's poetry, was given its title, *The Fugitive*, in a somewhat off-hand way. But the designating term symbolized (in its "secret" meaning and in the intention of its contributors to publish anonymously) a partly submerged, partly conscious need to withdraw or flee from the disorienting effects that the group felt the larger society had on the poetic vocation. In light of some of the criticism of the Agrarians for their presumed support of the romantic myth of the southern landed aristocracy, it is ironic that Ransom noted that what the Fugitives fled from fastest was "the high-caste Brahmins of the Old South." By retreating into the relative privacy of a small literary community, they could develop an art that no longer occupied the public place or performed the public function it might have had in a more fully formed society.

It is well authenticated that Allen Tate was responsible for introducing the group to the so-called modern poets, particularly T. S. Eliot and Ezra Pound, as well as the French symbolists. The use of the term *modern* in this case paradoxically confuses the issue because, while the modern poets or literary modernists were, in language and form, breaking out of romanticism and Victorian sentimentality, they were among the most vociferous critics of the intellectual and social consequences of *historical* modernity and the "dissociation of sensibility" that had resulted from the Enlightenment, the rise of progressivism, and the decay of earlier traditions rooted in classicism and Christianity. Eliot's critical attitude toward the dominant culture, expressed in a language appropriate to the experience of a fragmented individual and social identity, had a profound effect on the Fugitives—one that clearly influenced the attitudes of the Agrarian core when, following the dispersion of the Fugitives in the mid-1920s, they began to consider going public with a prose statement that culminated in *I'll Take My Stand*. Their criticism of the dehumanizing consequences of modern materialism, scientism, progressivism, and secularism, as well as their search for the possibility of a healing wholeness in the interrelations among nature, man, and society, owes much to this contact with the larger community of intellect in Europe, including the post–World War I American literary exiles.

The more immediate impetus to do something about a broader expression of these shared attitudes came with the shock of recognition produced by the 1925 Scopes "monkey trial" in Dayton, Tennessee, over the validity of a Tennessee law forbidding any teacher in the state's publicly supported educational institutions "to teach any theory that denies the story of the Divine Creation of man as taught in the Bible, and to teach instead that man has descended from a lower order of animals." Davidson, who in his correspondence and conversation frequently recalled the effect of the trial on the Fugitive-to-Agrarian transition, provided an extended account of the commonplace circumstances out of which the law and the trial emerged and how the latter was turned into a *cause célèbre* in which "painful indignities" were heaped on the people of the Tennessee Valley. The full story is told in the chapter "Trials by Jury and Otherwise" in the second volume of Davidson's eloquent book *The Tennessee* (1948) in the Rivers of America series. The case was tried in what one reporter described as a "half-circus, half-revival" atmosphere, with the deeper issues—scientific materialism versus religion, and the reopening of old sectional hostilities by means of a deliberately contrived cultural invasion in the name of science and liberalism (with some complicity on the part of local adherents to the New South creed)—being sublimated by a sensationalist national and international press coverage. The inadequacies of the defense of the local position from a bedrock fundamentalist platform, occupied mainly by William Jennings Bryan, whose vulnerability is not spared by Davidson, opened the people of Tennessee to worldwide ridicule as a barbaric society of ignorant bigots.

If *I'll Take My Stand* was ultimately a defense of traditional values of Western civilization (characterized as "religious humanism") against the ideological consequences of the triumph of modern science and technology, the particularity of the defense was almost bound, after Scopes, to emphasize local experience with the imperious manner in which that ideology was used to try to conquer and absorb a local culture that still embodied at least the remnants of the older cultural foundation. The local emphasis naturally had a mixed effect on the audience, or more precisely the *audiences*, to whom the book was directed, as well as on the Agrarians themselves. Those responding from the perspective of the dominant culture saw in it a literal defense of everything that stereotypical criticism of the South had erected into the prevailing negative image of the region, from sentimental falsification of the plantation slavocracy to the perpetuation of poverty, race and class oppression, ill health, the Bible Belt mentality, poor education, the Ku Klux Klan, and an undifferentiated economy, all in the interest of maintaining political, economic, and social control in the hands of a small rural autocracy and its county-seat financial and professional allies. In its simplest form such criticism treats the book and its authors (and, by internal implication, the critics' own position) as though the dialectical engagement was taking place solely at the level of a pragmatic power struggle, with all of the complex questions of good and evil, truth and falsehood, image and reality, and opinion and knowledge already settled and beyond the reach of rational discourse. And a number of southerners, as well as a few putative defenders of the South from the outside, made use of the southern agrarian motif in its most egregious form as rhetorical support for furthering their own crude ambitions for political or social influence.

The line between a closed ideology and the openness of philosophical dialogue becomes thinner as the debate is moved from the philosophical circle to the public forum. In this respect the vulnerability of parts of *I'll Take My Stand* as philosophical discourse that was intended to be relatively free from contradiction and ambiguity reveals itself in the extent of the compromise necessitated by the eclectic character of the book. The diffusion of the choice of topics and the individual variations in perspective among the contributors make a reading of the book as a cohesive and comprehensive treatise, other than in the broadest terms, most difficult. And when one adds to this diversity even a sketchy view of the post-Agrarian directions taken by the participants, the attribution of overall unity of meaning may be tested by critical interpretation at many points.

The selection of a title was a point of some contention; the title was agreed to only reluctantly because Tate and Warren thought that the overidentification with the South parochialized the effort too much, with the result that its aim would be perceived as too limited. Furthermore, the use of *Agrarian* as a general term for characterizing the good life and good society in opposition to the constricting influence of industrialism and urbanism was, in Ransom's cautious words, "as much as" agreed to by all the participants as the best representation of the distinction. On these points Rubin's defense of the choice of language is well taken. He does not think it was possible or desirable for the Agrarians to dissociate *I'll Take My Stand* from the South, even though "a more abstractly conceived book might have been less topically identified with one region's particular economic and social problems and therefore less immediately limited." But that would have deprived the contents of the dramatic power provided by the "tangible image of the South that gives the book so much of its compelling quality, its visible, palpable reality." He further notes in several places that the use of *Agrarian* should be seen as metaphorical.[4] To enlarge on Rubin, one might say that the metaphor symbolizes a broad conception of the proper relation of man to nature (especially to the land), a sound grasp of the organic unity of work, family, and community, and a

4. *Ibid.*, xvii.

desirable spatial and personal relation of man to man. To that extent the image is at one with the pastoral tradition that runs throughout Western thought and literature from its origins in ancient Greece onward. Even so, one may see how the dramatization of the image lends credence to the charges that the Agrarians idealized the rural life—in both its plain folk and landed gentry varieties—to the point of romantically eliding the harsh realities of both antebellum and postbellum rural life in the South.

The Agrarians were certainly divided over the practical implications of *I'll Take My Stand*, both at planning stages of their venture into social and political criticism and in later interpretations and courses of action relative to its result. Tate and Warren were less interested in the practical commitments than was Ransom, while Davidson remained convinced that obligations to pragmatic action were heavily involved. Although the idea of advancing a program or policy by which the South might resist the worst influences of the dominant culture and move toward the practical implementation of principles embodied in the agrarian metaphor is repudiated by various statements in the essays, the variations in attitudes on this question are evident throughout the book. And critics were quick to penetrate the gaps, especially when these were seen to involve deliberate omission.

Davidson's response was to adopt the defense of the South as his personal cause, to urge it on the other participants closest to him, to express the meaning of southern agrarianism through his art, to seek modes of action designed to expound the programmatic implications of the book as he saw them, and to attain a wider distribution for the message in *I'll Take My Stand*. In the long run he sought by all means at his disposal to try to stay completely the inexorable hand of change.

Another of the participants, John Donald Wade, returned to his native Georgia to live out the kind of responsible, bucolic, community-oriented life he had set out in his biographical model, "The Life and Death of Cousin Lucius." Others returned fairly soon to their usual occupations, with only sporadic later expressions of their Agrarian ties.

H. C. Nixon, whose essay "Whither Southern Economy?" came closest to providing a practical analysis of the causes of the weakness of the southern agricultural economy and the advancement of a program for revitalizing it, remained politically active, but in a different context. He was a prominent figure in the Southern Conference on Human Welfare and in other organized efforts to improve the lot of the poor farmer, black as well as white, through the development of public programs along New Deal lines. Although widely respected among his professional peers for his work as a political scientist as well as for his personal integrity, he came under criticism from intransigent political forces in the South and may have paid a heavier price, in terms of career advancement, for his practical actions than any of the other Agrarians.

For a time Ransom took on the unusual role of using the public platform to convince others of the virtues of the Agrarian persuasion, and he embarked seriously on the study of economics in the search for practical ways of providing an agricultural and small-scale commercial and manufacturing economy that would support an agrarian society adequately. He published numerous articles along these lines in the *American Review* and started to write a book on economics, but he abandoned the effort as unsatisfactory, as he had earlier dropped plans for the acquisition of a country newspaper for the propagation of Agrarian doctrine. Ransom modified his attitudes on the practical question in a way that disturbed Davidson by admitting the need for a balanced agricultural and manufacturing economy and by accepting the implications of governmental support along New Deal lines. But he continued to maintain that social responsibility should center primarily on the individual in relation to his own welfare, that of his family, and that of his immediate neighbors. Ransom began to chafe under the counterpulls of his commitment to public affairs and the desire to return to poetry. In 1937 he made a clear break with Vanderbilt and with his ventures in public affairs to resume his literary career at Kenyon College, a smaller and less demanding place than the university, located in a small town in the Midwest. He turned not to writing poetry, however, but to the service of literature through criticism that centered on the metaphysics of poetry. It is not an arbitrary connection to suggest that philosophy was the linchpin that always held his literary and social concerns together despite changing emphases over time.

Warren, always somewhat more removed from the center of Agrarian activity than his closest individual associates in the group (he was in England as *I'll Take My Stand* was developed), remained most aloof from the later practical explorations in order to return to literature as an activity complete in itself. His essay "The Briar Patch" was the most controversial one in the book, both within the inner circle among the Agrarians and outside. And this was not simply because his contribution addressed the most persistent problem in southern history—the place of the black man in southern and American society—but because Warren's way of treating the topic was unusual for the times and apparently even for Warren himself. Davidson went so far as to say he was "almost inclined to doubt whether RED ACTUALLY WROTE THIS ESSAY!"[5] Warren indicated, for reasons quite different from those prompting Davidson's comment, that he could not have written it later, and acknowledged that it was a defense of segregation. Perhaps it did assume an indefinite extension of racial separatism, which some of the Agrarians obviously thought the essay should have done in a clearer way, and some critics thought he did clearly enough, although some of the latter may have read the essay with selective perception or even used the whole book as a foil without bothering to read it, as Davidson said some opponents did. But a careful reading today does not disclose such an intention on Warren's part, at least beyond a recognition of the intractability of the arrangements as of 1930, when few American commentators, even those opposed in principle to southern racial practices, could have argued successfully to the contrary. In his insistence on the need for the white man to attend to the task of finding a place for the black man in an Agrarian society and in the stress he places on the ways in which blacks might establish their identity as members of a black community on the way to establishing identity as human beings, Warren does not sound as much like Booker T. Washington (whom he quotes) as he does a more philosophical Martin Luther King or Jesse Jackson. The intimation that whites and blacks might eventually find a common identity in the mutual recognition of

5. Donald Davidson to Allen Tate, July 21, 1930, in Rubin, *The Wary Fugitives*, 217.

their humanity is hardly veiled either, and that is what neither white nor black revolutionary separatism is ever likely to achieve, as Warren carefully points out. Warren, of course, became more specific on such matters in later works. His vocation as a man of letters, however, was so complete that his digression into direct social commentary was brief. But as Rubin cogently argues, the themes of Warren's novels and poetry center on man's individual moral development in its social setting and the complex ways in which both individual and social responsibilities are assumed and discharged. Following the Agrarian experience Warren, the poet and novelist, deliberately chose to assume and discharge these responsibilities in the pursuit of his art rather than through the development of social doctrine or engagement in political action. The New York critic Alfred Kazin observed some years ago that what bothered him about Warren's novels was that they were too philosophical. But is it not true that literature and philosophy are closely related modes of apprehending and expressing as much of reality as possible out of the diffuse array of appearances that human experience presents to us?

Though a bit more engaged for a time with applications than was Warren, Tate was always less attached to the literal aspects of southern Agrarianism than either Davidson or Ransom. In keeping with his growing place in the larger republic of letters, he did join Herbert Agar in editing *Who Owns America?* (1936), which brought together a diverse group of English Distributists, Agrarians (eight of whom contributed essays to the volume), and others to speak to the national problems out of concerns that were similar to those that led to *I'll Take My Stand*. Even so, his own attitude toward the Agrarian experience probably expresses the deeper meaning that held the earlier book together (despite so many differences) and gave it lasting importance. He wrote Davidson that the Agrarian effort was a "reaffirmation to the humane tradition . . . which was . . . an end in itself." The particularities and tentative explorations of programs and policies were of no great consequence, so Tate said that he had no expectations that the book would have any political influence. Nonetheless, he asserted that "it was and *is* a very great success."[6]

6. Allen Tate to Donald Davidson, 1942, in Louis D. Rubin, Jr., Introduction to *I'll Take My Stand* (Baton Rouge: Louisiana State University Press, 1977), xxii.

The critique of industrialism as a mode of production and of the major preconditions, as well as the structural consequences, of industrial development is the most strikingly apparent element of continuity running through *I'll Take My Stand.* It is also the feature of the book that has most clearly maintained its cogency and established the strongest claim to prescience on the part of its contributors. One hears echoes even of its language, which has a strong flavor of the contemporary about it, in prominent social critics covering a broad spectrum of current ideological commitments and ranging in their interests from economics and ecology to the arts, religion, and counterculture. What the Agrarians foresaw imaginatively, because the full developments were in many ways still incipient in 1930, can now be encountered in concrete description in any daily newspaper. Running through all of the critical analyses by the Agrarians of the way industry operated in purely economic terms—the production, exchange, and consumption of goods, including the use of natural resources, capital equipment, and labor as its instruments—was a perception of immediate and long-range depredations that the "system" worked on the uniquely human attributes of mind and spirit that distinguish man from other physical or material "objects" of nature. This central concern of the Agrarians has seldom been as well expressed as it is in *I'll Take My Stand*, and it is missing altogether from the economic and social analyses of most social scientists and many ostensible humanists in their efforts to get at measurable social indicators through scientific and technological means with the eventual aim of "improving" society.

If the "Agrarian" side of the contrapuntal formulation "Agrarian *versus* Industrial" is a metaphor for the proper way to structure the social conditions on which a good life depends, the obverse term *industrial* is, in its negative implications, a metaphorical expression for a conception of society that makes a good life difficult, if not impossible. But the acute exposure of the defects of industrialism makes the substance of the industrial metaphor easier to grasp than the intangibles that inform the agrarian one.

When Ransom noted in his introduction that "industrialism is the economic organization of the collective American society,"[7] he

7. "Introduction: A Statement of Principles," *I'll Take My Stand* (1962), xxi.

was saying in the most compact way possible that industrialism was more than the organization of the instrumental means by which economic goods were produced in the United States. He was declaring that the production of economic goods in the industrial mode was the highest good, or end in itself, for a society organized according to the demands of industrialization, and that all human activities, as well as the relations of man to nature and man to man, were shaped by social forces to the service of this end. The consequences cannot be pursued in detail here, so illustrative examples will have to suffice. In the matter of his relations with nature, industrial man becomes an exploiter of the world around him in order to feed the productive machinery's demands; in Ransom's terms, industrial society fosters the strange idea that the destiny of man is to wage unrelenting war on nature rather than to secure peace with it. Man's control of his own activities, and thus of his self-identification, is constricted, if not completely lost, in industrial society. Work, the activity that of necessity engages man more than any other, is translated in industrial society into labor undertaken solely to enable one to secure the means to acquire as many of the products of the system as possible. The idea that the worker has any choice as to what he will produce or how much time and effort he will put into production of the goods he deems necessary to support him in the style of life he feels appropriate to the satisfaction of his general needs is foreign to the industrial way of ordering man's activities. Also missing from the industrial scheme of things is the concept of organizing work in such a way that human satisfaction (or happiness) might become an integral part of the process itself. In order to reduce the imbalance between an enormous productive capacity and the rate of natural consumption, the public must be coerced and wheedled by advertising into buying more and more goods without regard to the satisfactions provided. The primary effects of industrialism on the relations of man to man include depersonalized life in the city, economic insecurity and restless mobility, threats to the household economy and thus to the family, and a loss of community.

Despite what the harsher critics have said, the Agrarians were not advocates of a return to the cave, and they were hardly Luddites. They really did not offer the vision of a rural utopia of the past as a substitute for the illusion of progress that they punctured pretty effectively in their criticism of the industrial order. They were too realistic not to recognize that both the planter and the yeoman, not to speak of the hardscrabble hill farmer or the share-cropper, had serpents in their gardens. The Agrarians also acknowledged that technology could provide machinery that might ease the pain of labor and open possibilities of greater leisure. No evidence that I have come across suggests that any one of the twelve scorned material comforts. But they also understood that industrialism was "of almost miraculous cunning but no intelligence" and therefore required control to assure that it remained a "menial" in man's service rather than his master.[8]

The attributes of the South that are commonly recognized as distinguishing the region from the rest of the country are obvious influences on the conception of the good society discernible in *I'll Take My Stand*, as they are in the literary works of the contributors. I refer, of course, to the broad religious underpinning, attachment to place and to the extended family, a sense of history, personalism, the code of honor, and the preference for the concrete over the abstract. But the coherence of the diffuse comments that relate to the social or political conditions of the good life and the way that the good life is ordered in the individual and then written large in the good polity comes ultimately from the classics, and especially from Aristotle. At this point the connections with the classics (and through historical continuity with the older, or premodern, European culture) must of necessity of sketched in lightly.

The personal, or biographical, aspects are pertinent. At their reunion in 1956, the Fugitives acknowledged that a southern education in their school and university days was grounded in the classics, and Ransom had read the classics and philosophy at Oxford as a Rhodes scholar. Suffice it to say that any serious treatment of politics (or "quasi-politics," as Ransom referred to the Agrarian symposium) was bound to reflect this classical background. More specifically, it reflected Ransom's preference for the concreteness of Aristotle (the "Athenian Gentleman") over what he regarded as the abstractness of Plato.

The most obvious relation is between the scale of goods, or, more crudely, the hierarchy of values, assumed or declared in most of

8. John Crowe Ransom, "Reconstructed But Unregenerate," in *I'll Take My Stand* (1962), 15.

the Agrarian's essays and the scale of goods clearly set forth in Book VII of Aristotle's *Politics*. In both cases the "external" or economic goods, while necessary to the good life, are at the bottom of the scale and are supportive of, but subordinate to, the higher goods, especially the goods of the soul, as Aristotle puts it, or those of the mind and spirit, as the Agrarians have it. If the hierarchy is inverted by men or in the organizing principles of the polity, the individual will not be able to realize his full potential and society will be in a state of real or incipient disorder.

Many other comparisons can be drawn, some of which may be noted in passing. The formation of the society or polity, for example, is around the family as a household economy, and others beyond the family are drawn in to provide, out of necessity, some cooperative relationships based on variations in occupation. What starts in mutual need at the most elementary level ends, however, with the more intangible, but no less real, benefits that come only through free association in a community. In such matters as the geographic and population scale best suited to the realization of the economic and other social goods of the individual and the society, the establishment of proper grounds for social differentiation among individuals, and the purposes of education, the "principles" set out or implied in *I'll Take My Stand* are classical. And this tends to confirm the view that the breadth of the historical dimensions and the conception of the good life and the good society in *I'll Take My Stand* make it possible to offer a reading of this book as a mode of discourse appropriate to a work in political philosophy, whatever else it may be.

Lewis P. Simpson has recently reminded me that he regards the Fugitive-Agrarian phenomenon as a literary rather than a political movement, although he obviously recognizes that politics was involved in it. At the Fugitives' reunion in 1956 the connection between the Fugitives and Agrarians and the relation of poetry to politics were discussed in some detail, and in ways that clarify some of the issues.

The Fugitives, it was indicated, had stayed with poetry and had not moved directly into the question of the relation of the poet to the general society. At the same time they were aware that their poetry was self-consciously breaking with the "false tradition" represented by the poetic culture of the nineteenth and early twentieth century. They were also attentive to the fact that philosophy and poetry were closely related in that each sought through experience to apprehend and express the meaning of reality to the extent that it was open to human understanding. In Ransom's view philosophy depended on poetry for its mode of generalizing the understanding of reality because the poetic mode was creative in its precise imagistic expression of universal truth perceived in a concrete moment of experience (the influence of philosophical idealism, especially in its English form, is one of the constants in the discussions). Philosophy could broaden the understanding of reality only after poetry had captured its specific substance through the creative act.

The move from the discussion of poetry in a philosophical context to the awareness that the social and political experience was a necessary extension of the poetic concern was directed by Cleanth Brooks, as discussion moderator, when he noted that one of the important topics still to be discussed was "the situation of the poet in relation to culture, in relation to the South, in relation to the whole concept of community, those . . . things about which all of the Fugitives have written or acted and continue to write and act." The statement obviously assumes the connection between the Fugitives and the Agrarians, and Andrew Lytle was quick to note that it was "a false distinction to say that one thing ended and another began, when actually it was a kind of continuation." Merrill Moore, psychiatrist and Fugitive poet, took exception to Lytle's formulation on the grounds that there were two distinct movements (the literary one and the "quasi-political" one) "even though one grew into another"; and he wanted to correct the general misconception that the words *Fugitive* and *Agrarian* can be equated. Moore then went on to try to reaffirm the connection between the poet and the philosopher, while keeping both distinct from the politician (after referring to Yeats as an example of the poet who was not able to bring the poet-philosopher and political functions together). In Moore's words, "I think the poet is much more akin to the philosopher than the politician; and I believe that poets make poor politicians, generally speaking."[9]

9. Rob Roy Purdy (ed.), *Fugitives' Reunion: Conversations at Vanderbilt, May 3–5, 1956* (Nashville: Vanderbilt University Press, 1959), 177, 178, 179.

As Lytle and other Agrarians present showed in their responses to this formulation, the Fugitive-Agrarians understood in ways that Moore did not the difference between political action or a political "movement" that found complete expression in philosophy (or even in poetry as akin to philosophy) and the pragmatic (and always incomplete) action of the practicing politician. Moore seemed to want to purge the poetic act of all political implications, whereas Lytle indicated that *every* act contained political implications. Thus in the act of trying to apprehend and express reality as a whole— the end that ultimately united poetry and philosophy as modes of action—one could not completely separate the "literary movement" from the "political movement" because both were indissolubly connected with man's public or community life, which is an integral part of human experience.

In the end one returns to the classical interpretation for the unifying explanation. The political objective of Plato and Aristotle (who created philosophy as a critical and constructive symbolic form for expressing the reality derived from experience in opposition to doctrinal ideology) was to develop a polity in which it was possible to live the contemplative life of the philosopher, with all that such a possibility implied about the proper ordering of the life of the individual and the reflection of his internal order in the social order in which the philosopher participated. The Fugitive-Agrarian movement was directed, in its political dimension, toward the realization of a community in which it was possible to live the creative life of the poet, whose place and functions in a good society are very close to those envisaged for the philosopher in the classical conception.

The literary movement and the political movement are ultimately inseparable. The perception of human reality expressed in the poetry and criticism of the Fugitives and Agrarians is no more negated by an examination of the practical state of the literary arts in contemporary America than the perception of the truth about man and society expressed in *I'll Take My Stand* is vitiated by the lack of success in bringing a fully formed "Agrarian" community into pragmatic existence.

X Political Education: Who Gets What, When, How, and Why

Occasions such as this seem to me to confront both the speaker and the audience with a dilemma that goes beyond the simple identification of the functional contribution a presidential address makes to the organized activities of what must be considered—apart from the intensity of individual and social identities that sustain any human community—a minor social institution. The Southern Political Science Association cannot assert a claim to substantial public influence either by reason of the number of members or by the measurable influence it exerts directly on the nature and content of the discipline, on the political education of citizens and rulers, and, more remotely, on the practice of politics. In this case, unlike the practical contradiction that followed Lincoln's modest projection in the Gettysburg Address, we can assert with great confidence that the world will little note nor long remember what we say here. But what Webster said of Dartmouth College might well be paraphrased with reference to the SPSA: Though it is a small association, there are those who love it. And if a commitment to common purposes, sustained by bonds of personal affection, unites a sufficient portion of the formal membership into a substantive corporate body, the presidential address seems justified solely as ritual.

If the purposes of the association enable us to articulate a creed of sorts, the liturgy is exceedingly loose, and the clerical hierarchy is vested by the priestly congregation with an authority that is of extremely short duration and virtually without definition. The form and content of the presidential homily I take to be unprescribed. This latitude is either a tribute to the confidence imposed

Presidential address delivered at the annual meeting of the Southern Political Science Association held in Gatlinburg, Tenn., November 2, 1979.

in the selection of presidents or an abiding commitment to ritual for its own sake, since each of these *ex cathedra* pronouncements is allowed to appear in the *Journal of Politics* without prior examination for doctrinal purity at the hands of the far-flung agents of the editorial Grand Inquisitor, whose procedure in the trial of profane texts by critical ordeal is innocuously labeled the "referee system."

Many, perhaps most, presidential addresses use exemplification as the basis for formally affirming that part of the statement of purpose (or creed) of the association pertaining to the promotion of research, now often less modestly referred to as the "advancement of knowledge." That is to say, many presidents use the opportunity offered by these occasions to present the results of their own research. Others take a more critical and/or hortatory line with respect to the sins of omission or commission in the association's attempts to fulfill its purposes, or they make similar efforts to appraise and reconstruct the "state of the art" in the discipline or in some relatively self-contained part of it. In other words, they examine the organized activities of the profession or the cumulative results of the search for an understanding of political phenomena as objects of knowledge, with a view to improving one or the other or both. An occasional presidential address, such as Jasper Shannon's in 1950, defies classification in terms of the more pedestrian categories that we tend to fall into, since it is a work of literary art in the satirical vein that manages to evoke a compelling image of the human side of our common vocation.

Now that it is my turn, I would like to use the indulgence permitted me here to attempt something that varies from either of the two main homiletic types just mentioned, although it is obviously more closely related to the critical/hortatory form than to the exemplary one. My aim is to look behind the propositional statement of the creed itself to the experiences that produced the symbolic expression of purpose contained in it, and to raise certain questions about the extended meanings implicit in the brief enunciation of principles to which the organization originally subscribed as the reason for its existence: "To improve teaching, to promote interest and research in theoretical and practical political problems, to establish closer relations between [*sic*] teachers, administrators, and civic leaders, and to stimulate sound training in citizenship."[1] For this purpose I want to enlarge the "improvement of teaching" clause to the more comprehensive "political education." Political education should include the broadest possible meaning of what we are about when we attempt to realize any of the ends implied in the specifics of teaching, research, communication with public officeholders, and our inevitable engagement in the practice of politics as citizens in a constitutional democracy.

To talk about political education implies a consideration of learning, and that in turn suggests not only that there is something about our experience with politics that can be apprehended rationally and judged by appropriate canons of inquiry to be true but that the pursuit of the meaning of politics is somehow worthwhile—*i.e.*, it has an end or purpose that is a good in itself or is a means to some other good. Furthermore, to speak of political education implies that what we have learned about our subject can be effectively communicated to others, or taught. This second implication further suggests that there are appropriate means of conveying the knowledge we are able to acquire, and that this act of teaching also has a purpose or end that is somehow congruent with the impetus to inquiry into the subject in the first place. Teaching, like the learning from which it depends, is an act that is thought to contribute to the realization of some human good, and the dissemination of knowledge about politics realizes its own good to the extent that it contributes somehow to the apprehension of the goods attainable through politics as a necessary form of human action.

Our discipline may lay a plausible historical claim to having been present at the creation, since it was a subject integral to the "course of study" pursued in that Athenian Academy from which our conception of the university as a place for pursuing universal knowledge derives. Indeed, Aristotle regarded politics as the architectonic science.

Plato and Aristotle fully understood that politics is a ubiquitous human activity; that it contributes something essential to the sat-

---

1. Adopted by the association at its 1929 meeting.

isfaction of the natural needs of man; and that knowledge about politics—or the political experience—is necessary to the realization of the activity in its fullest dimensions. They also understood, in a way that is perhaps lost to us today, that knowledge of politics is not separable from man's knowledge about himself, knowledge of the natural world that man perceives to be somehow external to him even as he is aware of being a part of it, and knowledge, or at least an opaque intimation, of that transcendent source of being with which man is consubstantial through the attribute of rational consciousness.

In the hermeneutic tradition that developed out of Greek philosophy, analysis of the part was always conducted in the context of the whole, and that context includes the relation between the object of knowledge and the knowing subject. Plato and Aristotle were well aware that ethics and politics are concerned with the relation of men, as knowing subjects, to each other. They also understood, as Eric Voegelin puts it, that man is a participant in the structure of reality of which he is a part. If man were not at least partly self-determining, *i.e.*, by nature free within limits, there would be no need to try to understand his relation to the world in which he exists, including the social world he shares with other men.[2]

If that world is structured in some way that is totally external to man, then all human action is shaped by forces beyond men's understanding and without respect to individual or collective purposes. Human actions or behavior under such deterministic conditions would be unintelligible and therefore beyond the possibility of human control, and any "society" constituted as part of that world would consist of relations established beyond the reach of any possible influence by human volition. Indeed, the very conception of such a world is so patently contrary to experience as to be absurd.

In general it might be said that the existential condition of man is such that he is constrained to try to make coherent a world that,

2. For a full explication of the theory of consciousness on which this understanding is based, see Eric Voegelin, *Anamnesis*, trans. and ed. Gerhart Niemeyer (Notre Dame and London: University of Notre Dame Press, 1978), esp. Chap. 1, "Remembrance of Things Past," 3–13, and Chap. 6, "Reason: The Classic Experience," 89–115.

in its manifestation through human experience, is complex, in some aspects impenetrable, and in matters pertaining to the practical arts of morals and politics, incomplete and open to human choice in shaping its specific configurations.

Political education in the classical sense has as its proximate end the cultivation of those capacities of mind that enable one to make judgments about the nature of society and the proper means to the fullest realization of its possibilities. Implied in such a purpose, of course, is the end of education in general, which is knowledge about the nature and condition of man, organized in a way that leads to the development of the Aristotelian *spoudaios*, or fully formed man, who attains the highest level of human potential. The overall end of education, then, is good men; the end of political education is a good society—and the two are inseparable.

One is tempted to trace the way the various parts of classical education (from which the Western idea of liberal education is drawn) are integrated into the whole. But what is essential in this context is the role of the Platonic dialectic in distinguishing *doxa* from *episteme*—opinion from knowledge—in the search for an understanding of the good and how it may be attained. Training in dialectics is the apex of the overall classical education (it occupied the last five years in Aristotle's chronology), and its methods and uses are dramatically exemplified in the Socratic dialogues. Robert Hutchins, a towering figure among American educational theorists, who based his views of liberal education on classical concepts, may have oversimplified the dialectical process in the following summary, but it would be difficult to present it better in so compressed a form: "Socrates collected opinions, asked questions, clarified terms and ideas, and indicated commitments. That is all he did. All that was required of those who took part with him was that they should try to think and understand one another. They did not have to agree among themselves. If they came to conviction, they did so by their own free will. The only constraint upon them was the law of contradiction. They could not answer Yes and No to the same question at the same time."[3]

The Greek philosophers were thus engaged with their students

3. Robert M. Hutchins, *The Conflict in Education in a Democratic Society* (Westport, Conn.: Greenwood Press, 1976), 96.

in the uses of reason as a way of arriving at truth about the fundamental questions of morals and politics. And as Eric Voegelin has said, it was the ancient philosophers who discovered reason in all its capacities, and "they were fully aware of the educational, diagnostic, and therapeutic functions of their discoveries."[4] It is worth noting in passing that Plato, who knew full well that philosophy, as the way of symbolizing the experience of reason, was replacing the classic myth as the means of apprehending the truths by which our lives (and our politics) are to be conducted, used his own mythopoetic artistry in the dialogues as a way of presenting philosophic truth. And he did it that way not only for the purpose of communicating a new mode of experience in a familiar form but also in the interest of not abruptly disrupting a traditional, if no longer effective, way of ordering private and public life.

I make one final didactic point before reluctantly moving out of the classical mode into the problems of our own times. If we abstract *political* education from the context in which Plato and Aristotle place it, we might say that it is the form of education that is appropriate for those who will become rulers, although in the larger sense it is part of the education of the potential philosopher, or lover of wisdom for its own sake. But as Hutchins reminds us, in a democracy we are all rulers, and a liberal education whose end is knowledge directed to the proper conduct of our lives and our politics is appropriate for all. For Hutchins, liberal education is the only education worthy of the name, because it is the only way of evoking the standards by which we evaluate and unify what Michael Oakeshott calls the various "modes" of experience.[5]

Until the late nineteenth century (and in individual cases, beyond that era) the American college offered, largely for the benefit of elites, a liberal education with a curriculum grounded in the classical tradition of British universities as developed in the course of the Renaissance. The humane ends that provided the integrating principles of classical liberal education gradually broke down under the pressures of social change shaped in whole or in part by ideas that emerged from the Enlightenment. Again, time constric-

---

4. Voegelin, "Reason: The Classic Experience," 112.
5. Hutchins, *The Conflict in Education in a Democratic Society*, 84.

tions permit only the sketchiest outline of the massive complexity of these ideas and events. Perhaps it is as well to proceed chronologically.

The cultural tendencies of what we now call modernity reached their intellectual apogee in the eighteenth century. Critical attacks on the values and traditions of social and political behavior rooted in Christian faith and classical reason were launched by the intellectuals—especially French intellectuals from Voltaire onward—who were self-consciously engaged in the transformation of the standards by which knowledge was evaluated.

In Enlightenment thinking, the success of the analytical method of the natural sciences in explaining the structure of the external, or material, world provided a model by which all knowledge claiming the status of truth should be judged. The validity of scientific knowledge was further authenticated by the growth of technology, which applied scientific explanation to the problems of subjugating nature to man's use. These intellectual trends culminated in the French *Encyclopedia*, with its declared intention of synthesizing all *useful* knowledge in a single comprehensive work.[6]

The standards of utility of knowledge were no longer those set forth in the classics; they were now the ways in which nature could be controlled to satisfy natural desires, or appetites. Aristotle's hierarchy of goods either was inverted or the higher goods of the body and the soul were simply deleted from the structure of values, leaving the pursuit of external goods as the sole end of human ac-

6. One colleague who heard this address suggested that I might want to amend my remarks on the Enlightenment to indicate that, while one fork led to positivism, another (perhaps the main one) led away from the theological foundations in biblical natural law to the [deistic?] concept of a "natural moral sense." My point is not that positivism was an Enlightenment doctrine (although it was a nineteenth-century outgrowth of Enlightenment ideas) or that positivism as such is a moral philosophy (although its epistemological propositions seem to me to preclude rational means of apprehending moral and political "goods"). Thus the natural moral sense of the Scottish school (and Jefferson *et al.*), as well as Hume's "moral sentiments," seem to me to have been traditional responses to a problem that went back at least as far as the Cartesian "mind-body" dichotomy, continued with Kant's separation of knowledge into the pure and the practical reason, and reached a cultural polarization in the late eighteenth and nineteenth centuries through the historical movements of the Enlightenment and Romanticism. I was conscious throughout the preparation of these comments of the need to compress into allusions many points on which I wanted to expatiate, thus the attenuated reference to a complex social problem.

tion. Since natural science provides no guide to action in the realm
of morals and politics, and since the traditional constraints on the
passions were no longer rationally tenable, the choices related to
moral and political action became radically subjective. The ethics
of *ressentiment* emerged as the motive force of political action.

This intellectual process involved the shattering of man's understanding of the way the confusing and contradictory world of
experience had been made whole by the rational apprehension of
humane values. T. S. Eliot designated this process as the "dissociation of sensibility," and intellectuals have, with little success,
sought in a multitude of ways to reunite moral sensibility and
knowledge ever since the effects of the dissociation began to be
recognized.

The notion of knowledge as the equivalent of power also sur-
faced during this period. One of the most striking features of Bron-
owski's film series, *The Ascent of Man*, is the way the culture of the
Enlightenment linked the scientific and technological harnessing
of the physical power of nature for man's use to the growth of political power through the exploitation of techniques of social control, mainly in the form of manipulative ideology. Throughout the
nineteenth century, ideologies proliferated and, though each purported to be derived from complete (usually scientific) knowledge,
they were almost without exception variations on the general
theme of progress. The doctrine of progress, in most of its versions,
was directly related to the positivist dogma in which scientific
method would eventually advance knowledge to the point of enabling man to transform nature, himself, and society into a final,
perfected, and presumably unchanging form. The Faustian dream
had come back to haunt us.

Regardless of the amount of revolutionary chaos produced by
such ideology without any sign of transforming man and society,
except possibly for the worse, the growth of science and technology (which are morally and politically mindless) did result in the
establishment of an industrial society in which the capacity to
convert the materials of nature into consumable goods constitutes
a veritable miracle of production. American industrialization,
coupled with an abiding faith in education as the route to economic success and social mobility, obviously had a major impact

on the growth and restructuring of higher education in this country. This massive social change provided a social milieu in which the ethos of the Enlightenment could eventually work its full effect. The Morrill Act, establishing land-grant colleges for instruction in agriculture and the mechanic arts, opened the doors to vocational training as the central focus of the new version of higher education. The importation of German university arrangements for graduate education, with what that entailed in the way of specialization, concentration on research as the key element in academic preferment, and the exaltation of the doctoral degree, contributed to the further diffusion of the idea of the university. And when Harvard led the way in establishing a free elective system at the turn of the century, and was followed in that lead by a host of lesser institutions, the door was wide open to the proliferation of courses and multiplication by fission of new departments either to satisfy student demand or to cater to the entrepreneurial ambitions of faculty and administration.

The one remaining step required to liberate us from the discipline of liberal education—conceived as a way of integrating knowledge— was the complete popularization of higher education that began after World War II and moved with blinding speed from the late 1950s through the 1960s. The ultimate result was the multiversity celebrated by Chancellor Kerr of the University of California—a place in which practically anything any organized group in the society asked for would be offered, with virtually no questions asked about its relation to teaching and learning at the highest level. Liberal education continued to be extended the courtesy of a lower lip-service in most places, and in a few colleges and universities it continued to be practiced.

The most penetrating appraisals of higher education in the 1970s constantly rehearse the theme that the real needs of individuals and society have not been properly served by this massive, ramshackle structure of the "new" university. And the most frequently expressed plea for correction is for a recovery of some ordering principle based on the purposes that informed traditional liberal education.[7]

7. I cite only one example among many, and this one is chosen primarily because it comes from what I regard as a remarkable source: Ernest L. Boyer and

In the case of political science considered as one of the disciplines that is a constituent of liberal education, it might be said that ontogeny has recapitulated phylogeny. For our subject, too, has evolved into a congeries of discrete studies so specialized that one is hard put to see what, if any, integrative principle or purpose informs the knowledge about politics we are busy acquiring and disseminating. As Brooks Adams noted early in the century, modern civilization has no need of more specialists, but we do have an unprecedented need of the generalizing mind.[8]

Perhaps the most revealing aspect of this development is the gulf that seems to have developed between what we teach—at least to undergraduates—and what we do in our research. Much of the inquiry that is carried on today involves the analysis of the relations in such conceptually constricted sets of data, abstracted from politics experienced as a human activity and directed toward the realization of human purposes, that even when the results confirm with great precision the "truth" postulated in our hypotheses, that truth is useless as a guide to any specific political decision that confronts us. It is sad to note how often the "products" of such research plainly convey the sense that the inquiry has been conducted solely for the purpose of satisfying institutional demands for publication as a condition of retention or career advancement. In such cases both the motivation of intellectual curiosity and the cognitive differentiation between real and contrived problems are subordinated to the compulsion to pursue one's occupational interest by the use of the handiest means available. Habits thus developed are subsequently hard to break. In addition to its ephemeral and circumstantial nature, much of this research does not even contribute to the realization of the positivist assumption of a cumulative extension of theory, because the relations hold only in the unique framework of the immediate context out of which they were

---

Martin Kaplan, *Educating for Survival* (New Rochelle, N.Y.: Change Magazine Press, 1977), 79. In view of what I perceive as having gone on in publicly supported higher education, it is as well to have the assurance (on the back of the title page) that the authors wrote this perceptive monograph in their private capacities, and "no official support or endorsement by the U.S. Office of Education is intended or should be inferred."

8. Brooks Adams, *The Theory of Social Revolutions* (New York: Macmillan, 1913), Chap. VI, esp. p. 216.

abstracted, and/or are captured at a fixed point of time even though the whole of politics is in active historical flux.

Except for its use in training our epigone in the methodological techniques involved, most of this research contributes no more to political education than it does to the resolution of the problems of politics, mainly because it has little if anything to do with political reality. What it does have to do with is open to question; perhaps it is about the customary conjunction of discrete facts set forth in Hume's skeptical epistemology.

If I read the broader tendencies in the profession correctly, our teaching of undergraduates seems to take a more traditional turn than does our self-education through research. Surveys by the American Political Science Association show that well over 40 percent of student enrollments in political science throughout the country are in courses in American politics, and a substantial portion of the students involved take nothing in political science beyond the introductory course in American national government.[9] A random scanning of catalogues and syllabi suggests that some coherent treatment of American political experience is offered in these courses, either by design or as a product of inertia. Most include units on the origins and continuity of the American political tradition, the constitutional arrangements for allocating and limiting political power, the structure and functions of major political institutions, the processes of popular participation, and at least some passing efforts at relating the ideas and instruments of government to public policy.

The proliferation of textbooks in political science does little to assuage one's anxieties about the condition of political education in the contemporary academy. The run-of-the-market textbook is little more than a blending machine, perhaps even a disposal, that stirs together packets of indigestible information and a few samples of the latest remains from the synthetic research smorgasbord. A number of them lay claim to the use of some "approach" (*e.g.*, systems analysis) as a unifying principle, but the claim is rarely sustained in the material that follows. One sometimes en-

9. *APSA Departmental Services Program: 1977–78 Survey of Departments* (Washington, D.C.: American Political Science Association, 1978), p. 4, Table 27.

counters a textbook that displays a measure of cohesion by critically relating the parts of the subject to some overt or thinly dis-
guised propositional ideology, and this at least provides a starting
point for dialectical inquiry. In my frustration with textbooks I
sometimes yearn nostalgically for the old Ogg and Ray, which had
the honest character of a substantial encyclopedia. Although not
really suitable for sustained reading, Ogg and Ray was an aid to
be relied on when one needed a particular piece of information accurately conveyed. Its uncluttered comprehensiveness is best indicated by the fact that it relegated the one pass it made at exegesis through humor to a footnote. Rarer than a fine jewel in a
beautiful mount is the textbook that offers a synthesis in which the
symbols of government are construed for meaning against a background of reflection on the proper conduct of the acts of learning
and teaching. Perhaps the entire problem with textbooks is adequately summed up in a remark made by a former teacher of mine
who was a slightly malevolent version of Mr. Pickwick. With reference to a new work by an eminent member of the profession he
commented, "I remember when we read political *texts*, now we
have text*books*."

When we turn, if we ever do, to the specific question of the purposes served by political education in the context of liberal education, we seem to be caught in that dilemma expressed by the
rather pretentious psychological symbol, "cognitive dissonance."
We are aware that the liberal arts tradition is grounded in the humane notion that education should be directed toward a grasp of
the meaning of experience as a whole; that we should seek knowledge about morals and politics in order to decide how we should
act in our relations with one another; and that the ultimate objective of higher education is the realization of the human potential
for the good life in a good society. At the same time, we remain attached to the notion that knowledge in the social sciences must be
assimilated into the canons abstracted by the neopositivists from
the way they conceive the "pure" reason to be differentiated from
the "practical" reason, including the adoption of nomothetic distinctions between subject and object, fact and value, and quantitative and qualitative relations. The applicability of such reductionist rules to the way in which natural scientists actually work

has long been challenged, but acknowledgment of their validity still seems to be the main source of intellectual security for the general run of social scientists.

It may be that this effort to preserve the epistemological and methodological purity of our discipline, and thus enjoy the residual benefit of being able to identify with the mathematized sciences, is responsible for the apparent embarrassment we sometimes display when it is suggested that one of the principal functions of political education is to prepare young adults for active citizenship. Elsewhere I have called attention to the fact that the clause pertaining to the stimulation of sound training for citizenship in the original statement of purpose of this organization was deleted in later constitutional formulations. Yet most of our college catalogues continue to list among their intentions the preparation of students for active leadership roles in society, and some still refer to citizenship as a proper concern of higher education.

Even Bernard Crick, who some twenty years ago provided a cogent, if then poorly received, criticism in *The American Science of Politics*, was a bit caustic about our tenacity in teaching civics as a surrogate for facing up to persisting major problems of politics. In fairness to Crick it should be said that his objections were not so much to the idea of preparing students for active citizen roles, which is a legitimate objective of political education, as they were to the kinds of indoctrination and political training (as opposed to education) involved in many of our courses in "citizenship."[10] And in these objections we can concur with him. What one needs to know to be a good citizen or a civic leader cannot be taught by the articulation of a set of doctrinal propositions. Some corollary objective of liberal education is pertinent here: to develop the capacity to acquire and evaluate information needed to cope with political experience in a framework of a political tradition that is constantly confronting old and new problems through changing historical circumstances.

Joseph Freeman, one of our number who has been engaged si-

10. Bernard Crick, *The American Science of Politics: Its Origins and Conditions* (Berkeley and Los Angeles: University of California Press, 1959), 35–36.

multaneously in political education and active public life, recently sent me the following prefatory statement about political science from the 1909 *Catalog* of Virginia Christian (now Lynchburg) College:

> The study of Civics and Economics is especially important in a republican government. After the basis of right character the next essential for the perpetuity of our government is knowledge of its principles, its practical workings, and a training to take part in its administration. The people should know their rights and maintain them through law. The aims of all instruction in this department will be to inform and discipline the mind, to develop correct ideas of good citizenship, and bring a sense of individual responsibility for economic weal or woe. Current literature furnishes much valuable material for this department of instruction, and students' attention will be called to such matter.

The period charm of this brief discourse is obvious; its substance is still worth pondering.

In case it may be thought that the foregoing remarks about the current problems of political education reflect the cynicism of a spoiled priest who has lost his faith but lacks the courage to leave the church for another vocation, I now propose to offer a few words of consolation and hope. I am heartened, first of all, by the recent revival of interest in the perennial questions about politics that have been addressed in theoretical terms in the great literature from classical antiquity onward, and in practical ways by statesmen of all ages. One of the ironies of history is that the major works of theory have virtually all been produced as responses to political crises. The pragmatic success of the American political tradition has to some extent insulated the country from the crises of modernity culminating in the wars and revolutions of the twentieth century, even though we have been involved in the events that are symptoms of the crises. But in rapid, overlapping succession the Vietnam War, the disruptions and social segmentation associated with the romantic anarchism of the 1960s, the threatened institutional breakdown subsumed under the rubric "Watergate," and the extended economic and social issues arising out of the exploitation of the natural world have disturbed intellectual complacency, brought to the surface the neglected work of some of the prescient thinkers who had not hitherto been in the "mainstream" of the profession, and stimulated many others to move in new directions. Many of the obvious responses came in the form of intensified ideological identifications and a diffuse array of social movements based on them. But one need only peruse the Book Review Section of recent issues of the *American Political Science Review* to be aware of the extent to which the restoration of the classical tradition of political philosophy is under way.

Research in recent years shows signs of a diminishing commitment to sociological and psychological reductionism, and a turn toward the examination of the independent role of politics as a creative way of reconciling individual and collective interests and providing a traditional mode of attending to the needs of *res publica*. Penetrating monographs frequently appear on Congress, the courts, the presidency, political parties, leadership, and the bureaucracy, and we now have available a collection of material that broadens the grounds for deliberation on the historical origins of the American Republic and its adaptation to social change. A number of these monographs even display a sense of style, which is hardly a common property of literature in the social sciences.

I also find encouraging indications in the general shift in focus throughout the discipline toward public policy as a central concern. The promises here continue to exceed the results, even though the volume of research and curricular adjustments related to this trend are rapidly increasing. Given our penchant for pursuing one fad after another, the long-range effects remain problematic, but the issues of public policy are real, the solutions to them depend on broad bases of contextual knowledge rather than on managerial techniques drawn from handbook sources, and individual, popular, and institutional methods of decision-making are essential elements in the total process of policy formulation, implementation, and accountability. In short, the policy focus demands knowledge of politics as a whole rather than as the simple sum of its unidimensional parts.

Some promising developments are displayed in the reconstitution of communities of scholars both within individual universities and across university lines. For example, the small working conference, organized as a dialectical exchange on a unifying theme, is making inroads against the structured meeting in which individuals display their wares before a largely nonparticipating (and often indifferent) audience. I will personalize this theme by reference to an NEH-sponsored summer seminar (1979) for which George Graham, Jr., and I were responsible. Twenty political scientists, literally spanning the geographical area from Maine to Hawaii, representing the main subfields of the discipline, drawn from the full range of institutional types, and widely varying in age, status, and ideological commitment, met for six weeks to explore the theoretical foundations of the discipline with a view to bringing a more recondite perspective to bear on courses in their areas of specialization. The sessions were collegial rather than tightly structured around formal presentations followed by questions. Centering on the masterworks of political thought from Plato to the twentieth century, and working from there to the applicability of grand theory to specialized concerns, the sessions were intense, prolonged, and broadening. We engaged in an extended conversation, conducted in a civil manner, in which our underlying assumptions were exposed, examined, and reformulated, and integrated into our explanation of the particular areas of the discipline with which we were individually concerned. During the course of this collective effort we observed the formation of bonds of community growing out of those commonalities of intellectual interest that enabled us to appreciate, and in some cases reconcile, the differences in individual interests. The Hobbesian masks that hide our real nature were not dropped entirely (even in the tightest communities there must be some room for privacy), but they were lowered. Within this growing sense of common affiliation, subsets of friendship in the classic sense emerged, and the urge to continue the relationships thus developed proved strong. One came away from the sessions with a renewed sense that our discipline is worth pursuing because the questions that engage us are real ones; that they have ultimately to do with the nature and condition of man and society; and, though they will never be answered definitively or in ways that resolve all contingencies, we have a better chance of addressing them effectively and providing bases of knowledge for action on the problems that gave rise to them if we go at them cooperatively. Even the life of contemplation cannot be lived to its fullest if we are totally removed from a sustaining society.

Teaching is a dangerous vocation. I am intimidated when the chancellor of my university quotes Henry Adams to the effect that a teacher affects eternity and can never tell where his influence stops, although I much prefer having a chancellor who stresses this aspect of the university to one who talks solely about "the *management* of higher education." Most, although by no means all, of us are aware of the pitfalls: the excessive pleasure we take in our roles as performers; the temptation to provide ideological short-cuts as substitutes for the gradual evocation of the love of learning that is the abiding motive for the endless effort to make sense of experience in face of the hazards and uncertainties that beset the quest for knowledge; and the abandonment of hope that sometimes comes from the conviction of how little one really understands about what he needs to know to provide the Pilgrim even the haziest guide through the sloughs and around the barriers on the harsh road to self-education.

In the literal sense we do not teach anyone anything: we are fortunate if we can develop enough of that "negative capability" attributed above all others to Shakespeare to enable us to assist our fellow academic citizens, students and colleagues alike, to pull out of themselves their capacity for learning. And this is a mutual process; unless we are simultaneously learning from those we are trying to help learn, we cannot know what or how to try to teach. In a world of contingencies, our failures, too, are likely to be as great as our successes. I sometimes shudder to think of some of the individuals I have "taught" who have gone on to become public figures—rulers, if you will—up to and including members of Congress. In this matter I find no consolation in reflecting on the experience of Socrates with Alcibiades, except perhaps in pondering the mystery of the inversion of virtue and vice, through which the greatest malformation of character can occur only in those who are potentially the best.

The experience of our students is limited by their youth; yet we are called on to assist them in preparing for the world of experience that is before them, and for a lifetime of learning to enable them to cope with that world and make the best they can of it. In *Back to Methuselah* George Bernard Shaw estimated that man would have to evolve to a life-span upward of three hundred years to accumulate enough wisdom to be able to live well. Since we do not have that much time, we have to provide ourselves and our students with vicarious experience, and we do that through the reading we do in common, as well as by letting others share in our own experience and by trying to "displace" ourselves in such a way that we can understand and communicate with our fellow learners in terms that relate to their experiential concerns. At the same time we have to engage in self-examination to evaluate the impact our preceptorial example is having on students, which may be the most difficult assessment of all.

For liberal education, the atmosphere in which learning takes place is vitally important. The metaphor used by both Michael Oakeshott and Robert Hutchins for the most desirable academic procedure is "conversation." Both refer to education as an exposure to the "conversation of mankind," a conversation in which many voices are heard (sometimes in cacophony) in the attempt to understand themselves and each other. The main voices included are those of science and mathematics, history, philosophy, poetry (synonymous with the general voice of esthetics), and the practical voice of morals and politics. Oakeshott extends the metaphor when he says that university education involves learning to use the language appropriate to a discipline, yet he recognizes the need to be conversant with other disciplines, especially history and philosophy, if we are to learn the discourse appropriate to politics as an object of knowledge in itself, as well as the way it is related to the other things that can be known about our world of experience. Cardinal Newman, of course, joins Hutchins and Oakeshott in wanting a university in which all the intellectual disciplines do not just have a place at the organizational table, but are active participants in a conversation in which all can be heard and understood by each other.[11]

11. As suggested at the outset of these remarks, the question of political education has been an integral part of political theory since its beginning, mainly because the preparation of political leaders is a central problem in the establishment and maintenance of the polity, but latterly also because of the need for an educated citizenry in a constitutional democracy. Among contemporary political theorists, I find Michael Oakeshott's conceptions of education generally, and of the teaching of politics in the university in particular, most cogent. See his essays "Political Education" and "The Study of 'Politics' in a University," in Michael Oakeshott, *Ra-*

The Southern Political Science Association is an organization created to unite across university boundaries those engaged with political science as an academic discipline. It seems to me that the aphoristic statement of purpose to which we loosely subscribe as members of this small community of scholars and teachers commits us to major responsibilities, mutually undertaken, with respect to the advancement of "political education" as a part of general education. After examining the implications of this commitment, I think it is safe to say that our common creed remains valid; the problem is that in the course of the practice it is supposed to guide, we too frequently lose sight of the extended meaning of its content.

---

tionalism in Politics, and Other Essays (New York: Basic Books, 1962), 111–36, 301–333.

Cardinal Newman's *Idea of a University* (Garden City, N.Y.: Doubleday Image Books, 1959) remains, in my view, the best single statement of the ends of higher education and the proper way to integrate knowledge in the various disciplines in order to provide for liberal education in a modern university.

XI   Policy Sciences, the Humanities and Political Coherence

In little more than a decade (dating its early visibility from approximately the mid-1960s) the formal study of public policy moved from a peripheral place in the concerns of American political science to a central position in the discipline. To be sure, political science has always paid attention to what was once referred to as the "functions of government." The emphasis on policy was strengthened in the New Deal period, when American political scientists were reassessing the role of government, especially the central government, in response to, first, the economic crisis and, later, the movement away from isolationism to activism in the face of the international disorders leading to World War II. The New Deal also greatly increased the connection between research in the social sciences and active participation in politics and administration on the part of social scientists. Scores of social scientists enthusiastically went to work in the expansive agencies of the Roosevelt administration, buoyed up by a newfound confidence in the practical applicability of the knowledge generated by social science to the social problems at hand, and an urge to be a part of the Baconian translation of knowledge (especially technical knowledge) into power. But today the effect of the study of public policy on the curricula of political science (and other social science) departments, and perhaps even on the renewed efforts to find some way to reintegrate knowledge within a liberal educational context, far outstrips anything that occurred in any earlier period. Policy studies are surely the growth enterprise not only in the social sciences but in higher education generally today, with an expanded production in courses and areas of concentration as well as in the establishment of research institutes of public policy, the organization of professional associations of policy study "specialists," and the enlistment in the cause of scholars in various sub-fields who want to be on the "cutting edge" of knowledge (being at the "forefront" is apparently passé as old fads give way to new ones).

For purposes of advancing the argument rather than attempting to provide a definitive explanation, it may be suggested that two interconnected developments (each in its respective way the product of a disenchanting or disillusioning tendency) affected the shift of attention to public policy as a (possibly *the*) major object of inquiry in political science (and the other social sciences as well). The first was essentially epistemological: Behavioralism, rooted in positivism and its promise of a cumulative theoretical advancement to a teleological culmination in a "predictive science" of politics, had been the dominant mode of the discipline for the preceding generation. Not only did behavioralism fail to fulfill its progressivist promises but its exponents concentrated so much on political processes and so narrowed the range of problems studied (apparently in the interest of relying on method to subsume the substance of politics) that the very nature of politics as a human activity could hardly be discerned in most of what one read in the professional journals.

The second contributing factor was directly political, and it came in the form of the latest crisis (or series of crises) in American society and government. One need not recite in detail the complex course of events over the past two decades to recall the increasing social disruption and individual anomie, the limited effects of the Great Society programs in meeting even basic physical needs (let alone those of a moral and spiritual nature) of large segments of the society, the adverse effects of the Vietnam venture on both foreign and domestic policy, and the threatened breakdown of the constitutional order posed by Watergate and its aftermath. It became increasingly clear that policy issues could no longer be resolved by the application of social technologies (usually in the form of additives) to isolable issues. Some of the symptoms might be relieved, but the basic problems of social cohesion, adaptation of a traditional order to new challenges to its coherence, and confusion in the meaning of the symbols through which the identity of the society as a polity was expressed seemed to demand reexamination by modes of analysis that went beyond instrumental rationality.

Although some of the new or revitalized policy institutes, centers, and publication outlets for policy-oriented study placed some emphasis on the nature of the values that informed policy decisions rather than treating the questions as issues of process involving the authoritative allocation of goods ("goods" being defined *via negativa* as utilitarian), most of the public policy analysts in political science wanted to transfer their behavioral mode and methods from the "science" of politics (*i.e.*, politics as formal processes) to the "policy sciences." In other words, while the problems confronted defied, or seemed to defy, the ingenuity of instrumental reason, and to demand a rational reexamination of the human needs and purposes served by the public order within the context of the limits and possibilities inherent in the practice of politics as this particular society had experienced it, the epistemic foundations of the social sciences were so deeply grounded in the scientistic faith that the change in focus from formal political processes to policy formation and implementation was made without any alteration in the expectation that steady accumulation of positive results to the point of definitive knowledge would result from the proper application of methods to particular problems perceived by the analyst.[1]

The core of the problem, then, is that the eighteenth-century bifurcation of knowledge into the Kantian pure and practical reason, followed by the appropriation of the grounds of truth by the methods of the mathematized sciences of external phenomena, and the relegation of the classical rational sciences of man and society

---

1. The following statement characterizes the aims of a number of political scientists who seek a "hard" social scientific basis of knowledge for policy studies: "There is a profound need to enlarge the zone of understanding of human behavior and society. Those of us interested in the intersection of social science and policy do not question the need for fundamental research. We see no competition with those engaged in developing stronger bodies of verified knowledge and firmer theories to explain patterned regularities of behavior. On the contrary, we welcome these efforts. As social science knowledge becomes sturdier, and more predictive, one of the fallouts is that it becomes more trustworthy as a basis for policy advice." Carol H. Weiss (ed.), *Using Social Research in Public Policy Making* (Lexington, Mass.: Heath, 1977), 1.

to the realms of relativity, subjectivity, and emotive drives or "sentiments" (as in the ethics of *ressentiment* of the French Encyclopedists, or the natural moral sentiments of Hume) have been slavishly adhered to by the general run of the social sciences in the twentieth century. And this trend continues even as the underpinning secular faith in progress through the mediating grace of science and technology is undermined by the historical disorders of the twentieth century.

The new emphasis on policy studies thus grew out of a latent crisis of confidence in the continuing capacity of our public institutions, through their systemically perceived processes, to formulate, enact, and implement policies that are capable of satisfying both the symbolic and the utilitarian expectations of the society at large. But this shift did not alter the direction of inquiry from the phenomenal to the noetic basis of the processes and issues under examination. As a friendly British critic—Bernard Crick—pointed out more than twenty years ago with specific reference to the theoretical weaknesses of American political science, the historic success of the American political experience resulted in our placing so much faith in the problem-solving capacity of science and technology, on the one hand, and reposing so much confidence in the strength and stability of our democratic institutions, on the other, that we tend to ignore the need to confront those persisting, fundamental issues of politics that have been constants in most political societies.[2]

In many respects the academic problems of the humanities that have also clearly emerged in recent years have their origins in the same set of misplaced confidences. When Baconian methods and Newtonian advancements in the sciences were translated by the Encyclopedists into a division of all knowledge into the useful sciences and the study of arcane subjects, the prestige of the classical disciplines in the humanities began to decline by comparison with the scientific and applied scientific ones, and the place of the former in the understanding of, and influence on, the affective areas of both private and public human concerns also began a long pro-

2. Bernard Crick, *The American Science of Politics: Its Origins and Conditions* (London: Routledge and Kegan Paul, 1959).

cess of erosion and displacement by the latter.[3] Obviously these changes have not been complete—the humanities have not disappeared either from the academies or from the bases of individual ethical and collective political actions of the public. But the universalization and democratization of higher education, with the subsequent focus on vocational objectives aimed at the fulfillment of tabulated manpower and womanpower "needs," placed the very conception of an integrative liberal education, and especially those components drawn from the humanities, on the defensive. It is appropriate, if ironic, that this development coincided in time with the beginning of the recognition of the massive public issues that so obviously required reexamination from historical and philosophical perspectives. One might even go so far as to say that the organization of the National Endowment for the Humanities had as one of its implicit (later explicit) motive forces not only the revival of the status of the humanities in academia but the promotion of an active role for the humanities in the understanding of public problems and the limitations and possibilities in politics as a basic human activity.

Despite its long-range dissociative effect on our understanding of human reason and its reductive consequences for epistemology, the division between the pure and the practical reason has a certain heuristic value. In the application of this dichotomy to the objects of knowledge, politics seems to me clearly to belong to that class of phenomenological experience that has to be dealt with by the practical reason. I am acutely conscious of the fact that some of my colleagues insist on scientific purity as a condition of being recognized as a fellow professional, and I think that some behavioral attributes of humans that we consider political can be quan-

3. In *The Brazen Face of History: Studies in the Literary Consciousness in America* (Baton Rouge: Louisiana State University Press, 1980), Lewis P. Simpson examines the way in which an authoritative "Republic of Letters" emerged out of the development of rationally autonomous, literate man in the eighteenth century and displaced the old authoritative structures of religious and political tradition. This new "estate" was composed originally of men of science, letters, and literature generally, but the advancement of science and its claims to certainty and comprehensiveness of knowledge eventually removed the man of letters and literature from a role in the projected transformation of nature, man, and society, thus leaving the scientists and technologists as the sources of knowledge and power on which this form of "progress" depended.

tified and described in terms of empirically testable propositions or hypotheses. But I also think that, quite apart from its *practice*, the *study* of politics reveals serious reductionist problems if the underlying assumptions of the inquiry are rigidly tied to the epistemology and methods of the natural sciences. Only the more superficial aspects of political activity exhibit the regularity of and conformity to deterministic "laws" of action and reaction supposedly characteristic of the phenomena of the natural, or external, world. And even those quantifiable, structured, and presumably predictive aspects of politics are rarely, if ever, universal; their uniformities are the results of habits or traditions of behavior whose meanings are rooted in a particular societal context or even a civilization that has been formed out of its own historical experience and is open to further alteration through conscious adaptation to changing circumstances. I am not, of course, suggesting that either the ends sought through political action or the means through which a political entity conducts its public life are totally derivative or relative. Politics is a ubiquitous human activity, with its elaborate permutations reflecting choices and adaptations that run the full gamut of human ingenuity in the application of the practical reason. The meaning of politics is discovered in the nature of man writ large, and is thus an activity that exemplified Eric Voegelin's profound observation that man is a participant in the structure of reality of which he is a part.[4]

Perhaps the biggest giveaway on the part of those who hold a firmly positivist view about the study of politics is the way they act when they remove themselves from the detached posture of the scholar and become political participants. Rarely, if ever, do they insist on or apply their own articulated canons of science to their judgments on the practical activities that engage them in the real political world, or even to the discourse by means of which these engagements are pursued collectively. One of the most implacable logical positivists I know as a scholar is also the most opinionated man I have ever encountered in his practical life. He never hesi-

---

4. This condition of man's existence is an integral theme in the Voegelin corpus; its extended meaning is explored in considerable detail in several of the essays in *Anamnesis*, trans. and ed. Gerhart Niemeyer (Notre Dame and London: University of Notre Dame Press, 1978), esp. Part III.

tates to assert the most sweeping categorical moral imperatives, his judgments on the character and fitness of individuals and national states are as unequivocal as his expressions of taste in relation to all forms of art, and he shows little evidence of having reduced either his ego or his considerable mental power to mere objects of analysis. Other than being almost totally devoid of a sense of humor, this man might, in the conduct of his practical life—*i.e.*, in his ethics, politics, and all activities other than purely intellectual pursuits—be taken to represent the very antithesis of what he professes to perceive as objective reality. When one observes such obvious discrepancies between the behavior of an individual as a practitioner of value-free science, on the one hand, and as an active participant in the phenomena he studies, on the other, one can hardly avoid entertaining doubts about the extent to which the positive theory is sufficiently encompassing to describe, let alone explain, political experience.

But even if one presupposes that the study of politics may be cumulatively transformed into a "pure" science, the practice of politics can hardly be said to conform to the specifications of an applied science of humanity in the manner in which technology translates the results of natural science into a utilitarian control over natural phenomena. For the practice of politics is purposive and creative; it is a matter of choice and of interest, one's own or that of others, and is, therefore, more fraught with moral than with technical difficulties, although there are decision-makers who try to turn all problems into questions of technique. The very language of politics is, as Michael Oakeshott tells us, "the language of desire and aversion, of preference and choice, of approval and disapproval, of praise and blame, of persuasion, injunction, accusation and treat [*sic*]. It is the language in which we make promises, ask for support, recommend beliefs and actions, devise and commend administrative expedients and organize the beliefs and opinions of others in such a manner that policy may be effectively and economically executed: In short, it is the language of everyday, practical life."[5]

5. Michael Oakeshott, "The Study of 'Politics' in a University," *Rationalism in Politics, and Other Essays* (New York: Basic Books, 1962), 321.

At this point the general objects of inquiry and methods of the humanities seem to me to come into full congruence with the practice of politics in ways that may inform that practice so it can be enhanced rather than perverted. The humanities are concerned precisely with those aspects of life identified as belonging peculiarly or particularly to human beings, but not to human beings conceived simply as objects, or as the mere cumulative results of discretely analyzable properties. We are speaking of human beings considered as a whole and as having certain unique characteristics, characteristics that both define them and make it possible for them to understand themselves. So far as we are aware, humans are the only creatures who have a self-conscious relation both to themselves as individuals and to things external to them. They are the only creatures who reason both instrumentally and axiomatically; who distinguish between good and evil, abstractly and pragmatically; who attempt to establish standards of truth, beauty, and justice; who discern intimations of transcendence; who have inherited and constantly embellish the elaborate logical and affective structures known as languages; who create myths through which they symbolize the meaning of their existence; and who have enough awareness of the past and sense of identity with membership in a tribe, polis, state, or empire to have generated an intelligible history. Without drawing the obvious connections, I submit that these unique qualities are the most generalized objects that the disciplines in the humanities seek to comprehend in whole or in part. And it is because of these qualities, and by means of their mediation, that man is able to conduct his practical life, with the result that the humanities, if they are true to themselves, cannot avoid or ignore the practical realms of morals and politics.

It is true that there are purists who argue that the humanities have to do solely with an esthetic mode of experience complete in itself, and that its devotees should not grub around in anything so mundane as the practical arts of morals and politics which, by contrast with the absolute ideas of the idealized humanities, are subject to so many contingencies. But I submit that the humanities, if they are not to abstract themselves from the human experience they are seeking to symbolize and explain, must cope with the practical in its own terms, because its terms are so much at one with those of the humanities.

One may, of course, admit that all of this high-blown rhetoric does say something about the connection between the objectives and pursuits of the humanities and those of practical life, and still ask the question, What, if anything, can the scholar in the humanities do specifically that will contribute to a more effective resolution of public issues? The answer is both positive and negative: In a positive sense, the humanities can bring special understanding to bear on political questions in a way that clarifies the grounds on which choices are made and refines the manner in which the advocate of a particular position presents his conclusions and supporting arguments. On the negative side, the student of the humanities can warn and constrain because he knows the limits imposed on any form of human activity by what is so often referred to in a shorthand way as the human condition itself. And in the process the scholar may learn some things about the nature of human experience and the way human beings express their understandings of experience that the literature of his discipline has not sufficiently illustrated.

In the matter of clarifying the grounds on which choices are made, those engaged primarily with the humanities are accustomed to bringing a holistic perspective to bear on human concerns. Certainly analysis of political issues is important, but so is the reintegration of all the specifics disclosed by analysis. Politics does not take place in a vacuum; it is integrally related to nearly all other forms of human activity, and man has a need to explain his actions to himself so that they appear to be internally consistent. The student of literature has a trained awareness of this necessity because it is implicit in the very form of literature, with its ultimate reconciliation, or denouement, of the complex characters and events on which a play or story turns. And it is worth noting that literature is a refinement and extension of the primitive mythic symbols by which man first demonstrated his need to integrate the confusing and conflicting experiences confronting his consciousness.

The historian has a similar unifying point of view to bring to bear on issues. Out of a vast agglomeration of historical facts the historian is constrained to select those events and personalities through which the past becomes a connected or continuing account of human experience right into the present, and even into the as yet unexperienced, but anticipated, future. A political order cannot long survive without an awareness that its very existence is a matter of historical interpretation, and it needs to bring the implications of the experience of its own past way of doing things to bear on the problems of the present. Societies and governments are held together by a set of common beliefs, habits, and traditions. Historians are concerned with the critical elucidation of these socially binding forces as part of their connective account of the past. How are the society's successes and failures related to these agents of cohesion? How have they changed, and how adaptable are they to the threats of social dissolution? Such considerations are as crucial to the intelligent discussion of public issues as they eventually are to the survival of a working political system.

In an address delivered at an early meeting of members of the committees of an NEH program in the humanities and public policy the late Charles Frankel noted that philosophy has been, above all, a discipline that looks into the coherence of our working assumptions. Others have projected more grandiose ends of philosophy by suggesting that it aims at reconciling at the highest level the apparent contradictions or contingencies in the more specialized intellectual pursuits, or even that its function is to come to terms with experience as a whole. If philosophy's function is to seek coherence, to reconcile seemingly conflicting objects of knowledge and to unify the whole range of experience, and if it assimilates both observed phenomena and introspection into its conclusions, it may be said to be the most comprehensive of the humanities in the application to problems of public policy. In this respect all of those engaged with the humanities may be said to be philosophers *manqué* when they turn their attention to the practical life. Philosophy, then, is not one way of attempting to deal with the existential, moral, and esthetic realities of public affairs, it is the ultimate way of dealing with them as a fully developed human being.

In all this discussion of applications of the humanities to public affairs, one should not neglect the implications of language as the medium through which issues are articulated and eventually resolved. And as students of language clearly know, language is not a simple thing in either the structural or the symbolic sense. Since ordinary language is our means of communicating about politics, it behooves us to understand that its uses in this context can be so diversified that only its most astute students can classify its intentions and effects. It can be used analytically or hortatorily, creatively, or destructively, and it can be designed to clarify or confuse, placate, or incite, motivate or inhibit, and it can be an instrument of freedom or of repression. Surely we cannot consider any effort to offer a forum to the public for articulating its views on issues to be a success unless it seeks to exercise some influence on the improvement of the association between reality and its expression through the written or spoken word. Oakeshott wisely reminds us, and not in a derogatory sense, that politics has always been three-quarters talk, and if we do not know how to use the current vocabulary of politics we are seriously hampered in our wish to participate. In a democracy, where it is assumed that everyone may, and should, participate in politics, students of language have a special obligation to provide assistance in the developing of the essential tools of political action.

Perhaps I can illustrate by an example from the real world how some or all of these possible roles of the humanities need to be applied to the discussion of a social issue. For this purpose I choose a homey, localized incident that is universal in its implications. A few years ago a controversy raged in parts of West Virginia, and in some places in southwest Virginia, over the reading materials used in English courses in the public high schools. The dispute was acrimonious, and soon debouched into direct political action in the form of strikes and picketing against use of school buses and school attendance. Individuals were arrested for creating disturbances, property was damaged, and it was even reported that physical harm was inflicted on a few persons. Certainly real or perceived damage was done to the human spirit and to the social harmony of the affected communities.

On the surface the issue may appear simple to the putative man in the street, especially if the adjective "enlightened" can be applied to him. The parents who demanded replacement of the reading series then in use presented their arguments in the form of fundamentalist religious doctrines: The literature was said to be full of obscene expressions; it was designed to tear down belief in God; it was anti-Christian; it was atheistic, Marxist, antipatriotic, amoral or immoral, disruptive of parental and other authority, etc. As one of the presumably enlightened men in the street, my first reaction to the protesting parents and their supporters was extremely negative. As one who thinks that his basic religious and social values may be expressed with some degree of logical and linguistic refinement, I tended to deplore the simplistic views expressed by the antitextbook crowd. As one whose value system is impregnated with the ideals expressed in the First Amendment to the Constitution, I looked on the efforts of the parents and their ministerial spokesman as attempts at censorship in its most blatant form. And as a longtime member of the academic fraternity, I had a conditioned reaction against those who wished to override the judgments of professional educators about what should be taught and how it should be taught.[6]

But as I followed the events reported in the newspapers, I reached a point at which I realized that the issues were far more complex than the overt representations of the disputants made them appear. In fact, they now seem to me to have reached toward certain basic human concerns that may be merely prefigured or inadequately symbolized by the specific texts around which the controversy revolved. Certainly values, interests, and choices were at stake. So were questions of citizenship, social organization, and political power. The parents obviously felt that, as measured by the standards they had adopted or been socialized to, the texts had a corrupting influence on both individuals and society. Patterns of authority were also being called into question. The authority of

6. The discussion of the particular instance in which this recurring (or constant) issue developed and spilled beyond the bounds of orderly political resolution was chosen because of its dramatic illustration of the interrelatedness of the components of the practical experience of morals and politics. It has recently been revived in an even older form with the efforts of the religious fundamentalists to secure parity of treatment of "scientific creationism" in the classroom with evolutionary theory. It is not difficult, by the application of dialectical philosophical argument, to establish the lack of relevance of scientific evolutionary theory to the questions of transcendent existence addressed in theology, and vice versa. But the hardening of ideology on both sides (scientism versus religious fundamentalism) has been a constant in this issue since the nineteenth century.

parents in a family-oriented society seemed to have been threatened by educational institutions whose socialization processes
differed markedly from traditional ones, and the schools appeared
to be part of a monolithic rather than a customary pluralistic governmental system. Perhaps the parents heard echoes of the counterculture of the 1960s whose spokesmen threatened to take over
their children. Considered from the latter perspective the confrontation may be perceived to have been directed against an imper-
sonal, unmalleable, and unresponsive educational bureaucracy
bent on changing man and society without let or hindrance. To
those involved, the replacement of the books under attack was apparently a matter not of censorship, but of removing an absolute
and irresponsible public authority from control over the ends of
education, especially as these related to its moral and social content.

Here, then, was a controversy over a literature that had been selected by public employees and made required reading in a state
school system. It was a literature, furthermore, that was apparently perceived by all parties to the controversy as having historical and philosophic content that in its own way interpreted reality and influenced practical—*i.e.*, moral, social, and political—
existence.

What was most disheartening was the rhetorical and evidential
inadequacy of the debate because one set of protagonists, and perhaps both, lack a sufficiently developed political vocabulary to
carry on the type of discussion that is at the heart of all effective
resolution of issues by ameliorative politics, based on a publicly
oriented, classical dialectical exchange, as opposed to persuasion
by demagoguery and action through physical force. As long as the
concerns over values, power, social stability, tradition, and change
remain inchoate because the means of expressing them in ways that
can be understood by all affected parties is not available to the
participants in a controversy, unrelieved frustrations will drive
some beyond the limits of political endurance and restraint, and
others are likely to respond with resistance in kind. And I am afraid
that this breakdown of normal politics is becoming too ubiquitous
for comfort. I am reminded by the behavior of the more adamant
parties in the textbook confrontation of the statement that was so

often made about erstwhile rebellious college youth: "They are trying to tell us something, and we had better listen." To which I would like to add: We had better find out how we can assist our contesting publics and their ostensible representatives to express their concerns by means of an adequate political vocabulary, and help resolve the issues raised through the application of the perspective of the humanties to their discussions.[7]

I have argued here, in an obviously general way, that the objects of study, methods of analysis and theoretical integration of knowledge constituting the substance of the academic disciplines in the humanities have a unique connection with the modes of human experience—particularly morals and politics—apprehended by the practical reason. And in the course of that argument I have implied that students of the humanities have an obligation to assume an active role in shaping the world of experience embraced by morals and politics. Indeed the connections are so inseparable that even the refusal to consider the problems of politics and public policy as objects of inquiry appropriate to scholarship in the humanities has major practical effects on both the humanities and politics. In the first place, the world of politics constitutes the most important conditioning environment within which students of the humanities pursue their particular activities as scholars and teachers. Freedom of inquiry and the dissemination of its results in all areas of scholarship are dependent on the nature of the political regime and its policies, and the humanities may be more vulnerable to the vagaries and exploitative tendencies of politics than the sciences. In the second place, even if scholarship in the humanities remains "pure" and cloistered, the minds and characters of the students taught in humanities courses will be affected by their exposure to the contents of these disciplines. Ever

7. The decline (to the point of disappearance in many instances) of the place of classical rhetoric in liberal education is an important, if little noted, contribution to the development of the problems discussed here. We have recently addressed the implications of the connections between the uses of rhetoric and the sciences of ethics and politics in Aristotle for contemporary politics in George J. Graham, Jr., and William C. Havard, "The Language of the Statesman: Philosophy and Rhetoric in Contemporary Politics" (Paper delivered at the International Seminar for Political Philosophy and Theory, Montebello, Quebec, Canada, May, 1981). This essay is also in J. M. Porter (ed.), *Sophia and Praxis: The Boundaries of Politics* (Chatham, N.J.: Chatham House Publishers, 1983).

since the emergence of the Academy in ancient Greece, the mission of the university has included as its main purpose the shaping of the Aristotelian *spoudaios*—the fully formed person; and the identification of the *spoudaios* with the good citizen in a properly constituted polity has always been an integral part of the higher educational objective.

The restoration or revival of an appropriate role for the humanities in the public arena naturally involves risks. The cultivation of the classical virtue of prudence has been, and remains, critical to the enterprise. Students of the humanities are as susceptible to ideological traps as other people (including "scientists"), despite their presumed grasp of the subtleties of human nature as explored in their respective literatures. The romantic subjectivism that seems so pervasive in both literature and life today, for instance, seems to be the most frequent answer offered by the humanities to the critical issues of our times. And that response is a final demonstrated capitulation to the instrumentalist's rejection of the essential unity of reason, and thus the abandonment of the quest for a rational foundation for moral, political, and esthetic values. At the other extreme, the centrality of the critical spirit in the makeup of the scholar in the humanities has often led to an excessive cynicism about the existential world, and a retreat into the "Republic of Letters," from which idealized sanctuary the total critique of society can emanate without the need to assume responsibility for what goes on in the workaday world.

The challenge is to find a way between the extremes of activism aimed at complete transformation of a practical world that is less tractable than we would like it to be and the passivity that can render us powerless to effect even the incremental change needed to avert disaster or to arrest decay. The humanities, like it or not, are the main carriers of the symbols by which we express our experience as a civilized society. They are thus the conservators of tradition. But they are also the constant reinterpreters and even modifiers of those symbols as experience unfolds through history. Neither preservation nor change is a given, although paradoxically each may be a necessity for man's continuing participation in the structure of things of which he is a part.

Index